THE
CAMERA
BOOK

THE CAMERA BOOK

Everything you need to know about choosing and using photographic equipment to create better pictures

MITCHELL ARTISTS HOUSE BEAZLEY

Consultants: David Kilpatrick, LIIP;
Michael Langford, FIIP, FRPS, Fellow and Senior
Tutor in Photography, Royal College of Art, London
Series Editor: Alison Louw
Editor: Christopher Angeloglou
Art Editor: Carol Collins
Copy Editors: Louis Jordaan, Philippa Longley,
Tina Rogers
Contributing Editors: Ed Buziak, Gary Ede, Rex
Hayman, David Kilpatrick, Robin Laurance, Gillian
Lythgoe, Kevin MacDonnell, Barry Monk,
Ken Moreman, John Penfold, Tina Rogers,
Peter Scoones, Peter Sutherst

Published in 1980 by
Mitchell Beazley Artists House
Mitchell Beazley London Limited
Artists House, 14-15 Manette Street
London, W1V 5LB

Designed and produced for
Mitchell Beazley Artists House
by Eaglemoss Publications Limited
First published in *You and Your Camera*
Copyright © 1980 by Eaglemoss Publications
Limited
Reprinted 1981, 1982

ISBN 0 86134 022 1

Printed in England by Severn Valley Press Limited

CONTENTS

INTRODUCTION

Creating fine photographs begins in the seeing eye of the photographer. But it is equally important to have the right equipment and to understand how to use it to best advantage. Whether you are choosing your first SLR camera or exploring the subtleties of synchronizing a pair of flash guns you'll want to know how the equipment works, how it compares, and the kind of photographs it will help you create.

The Camera Book sets out to show you everything you need to know about choosing and using photographic equipment—with the emphasis on practical methods. Comparative photographs, diagrams and sectional artwork all explain clearly and simply how to get the best out of your camera and its controls. . . how to choose and use filters. . . how to handle flash. Detailed chapters open up the world of lenses by examining wide angles, telephotos and zooms, and showing how to use each one creatively to produce memorable shots.

Throughout, first class photographers reveal the potential of cameras and lenses, of autowinders and close-up attachments, of studio lighting and different films. If you want to build up a worthwhile system of camera and accessories and use them like a professional, *The Camera Book* will show you how.

Types of camera

There is a vast array of cameras on the market, so what are the main things to remember when choosing a new camera? Cameras range in complexity from easy-to-use elementary models to high precision instruments capable of recording a split second in the flight of a bumble-bee. The sort of camera you buy depends on what you want it to do for you—provide a record of your family or document the habits of an insect. So it is a case of choosing the type that is best for your kind of photography—and within your budget.

Choose wisely

Before you decide on a particular camera, try to do as much preliminary research as possible; ask your friends about their cameras and if possible gain first–hand experience by borrowing a camera from a friend, or the camera dealer may let you run a roll of film through the camera in the shop. Treat lavish advertisements with caution—do not buy a camera just because some famous photographer uses one—your type of photography may call for an altogether different piece of equipment. Make sure that, in practice, you need the specialized technical capabilities of a certain camera.

Ultimately, the quality of your photographs depends on a combination of factors, not just the performance of the camera. It depends on your ability to use the camera correctly, your personal judgement in 'seeing' a good picture and the quality of the film processing.

Counting the cost

When it comes to buying a camera, most photographers are price con-scious—what you might like to buy if you were left a legacy and what you can actually afford are often somewhat different. For a particular type of camera you will often find that there is a broad range of prices, so what might you expect to get for more money?

With any camera, but especially a 110 camera or a rangefinder camera, more money will get you a better lens. There will also be more controls. On simple cameras this may only amount to more shutter speeds but on SLR cameras the body may be designed to accept motor-drive, the lens mounting designed to accept different manufacturers' lenses and the exposure meter may provide both spot and general readings. And you would pay more for a more robust camera. If the camera you like is over your budget, don't dismiss the idea of buying a secondhand one. There are

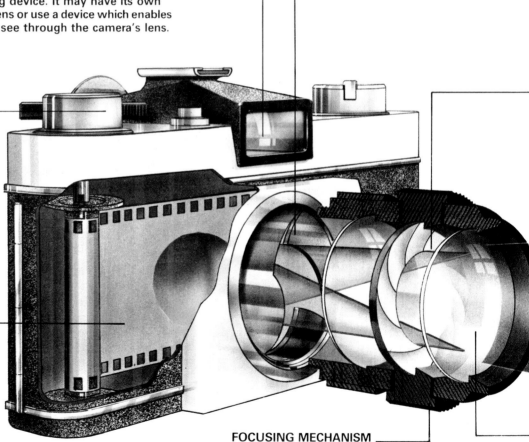

VIEWFINDER
A photographer views the subject through the viewfinder, which is a sighting device. It may have its own small lens or use a device which enables you to see through the camera's lens.

FILM ADVANCE
This device moves the film on by the correct distance after each exposure. In most cases, it is coupled to the shutter so if you forget to wind-on the shutter cannot be released. A frame counter records how many exposures you make.

FILM
The film, held flat inside the back of the camera, records the image. Both black and white and colour films are coated with light–sensitive emulsions which react in proportion to the amount of light that falls on them.

FOCUSING MECHANISM
This control moves the lens in and out to alter the distance between the lens and the film so that a sharp image of the subject falls on the film.

many bargains to be found in this market. A reputable dealer will probably ask more for a camera than a private seller but he should offer a written guarantee which makes it an attractive buy for those who are worried about the true condition of the camera.

The vital questions

To help you choose the right camera here are some of the points to consider. First, what subjects will you be photographing most of the time—moving subjects, such as sports events or children on the move, or portraits, still life and landscapes? Do you want a light, uncomplicated camera or are you prepared to carry a heavier camera with a full range of lenses?

Next, pick the camera up and handle it. Does it feel comfortable and can you hold it steadily? Make sure that you can reach all the controls, and that they are easy to operate. Don't accept that if a part is stiff or jerky it will 'work in'—try another camera.

Can you see the image comfortably in the viewfinder? Do you find it easier to compose well when you can see the exact edges of the picture or are you satisfied with the corner right angles in most 110, 126 and some rangefinder cameras? Think too about the film formats of different cameras: do you prefer square or rectangular pictures? Make sure the camera takes a good range of film types for the work you want to do.

If you intend to do your own processing, there is a wide range of equipment available for 35mm film, much less for 110 film. If you want to make enlargements, the larger the negative size, the better the quality of the print. If you plan to project your colour transparencies, there is a wider range of projectors available for 35mm film.

Do you really need a heavy f1·4 lens which is mainly useful in poor light conditions? Most pictures are taken around f4 to f11 and a good quality f2·8 lens is better value than an indifferent f1·4 lens at the same price. Glamorous advertisements promote shutter speeds of 1/2000 which are only really necessary for scientific work; 1/500 is suitable for most general photography.

If you want to do close–up work or use telephoto lenses, you need a camera with interchangeable lenses. Are you intending to use flash? Then you need to discover the pros and cons of built–in flash and a unit with a battery pack.

— SHUTTER

This keeps light from the film until the instant of exposure. It also controls the length of time light falls on the film. Typically, it remains open for a fraction of a second. So a fast shutter speed and large aperture can allow the same total amount of light through as a slow shutter speed and small aperture.

— APERTURE

The aperture is the circular hole in the middle of the lens through which light enters the camera. Its size can be altered to vary the amount of light entering the camera and falling on the film. Wide open it lets through as much light as possible, as would be necessary, for example, on a dull day. 'Stopped down' in very bright conditions it reduces the amount of light.

How cameras work

Every camera, from the simplest pocket-size model to the most sophisticated SLR, is basically a light-tight box with a piece of film at one end and a hole to let the light in at the other. The light is focused on to the film by a lens, forming an image of what is in front of the camera. The amount of light entering the camera is controlled by the size of the hole and the length of time it remains open. On top of the camera there is a viewing device that allows you to select the area of the subject to be included in the picture. Additions to this basic camera may make it more versatile but they are not essential.

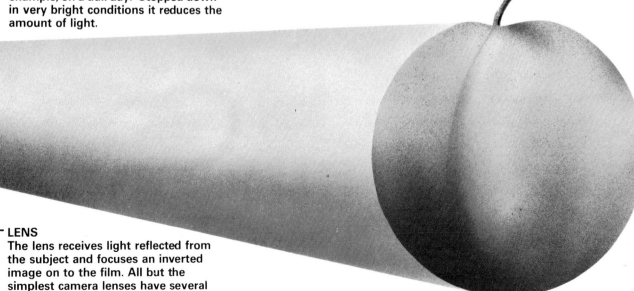

— LENS

The lens receives light reflected from the subject and focuses an inverted image on to the film. All but the simplest camera lenses have several separate elements working as one.

11

Check that it works

Whether you end up buying a new or secondhand camera it is advisable to test it before the guarantee runs out.

● Check all the shutter speeds; they should sound satisfactory and, if you open the back of the camera, you should be able to see the differences between the slower ones when the shutter is released. A specialist camera repairer will be able to test the shutter accurately.

● You can use the guide that comes with the film to cross-check that the exposure meter gives you the same information under the same conditions. But the best test is practical: run a roll of film through the camera.

● Check the sharpness of the lens by running a roll of film through the camera. Include pictures focused at the closest distance, 5m and infinity.

● Make sure that the wind-on and film counter work accurately.

● Test the camera body for light-tightness by orientating it in various positions towards the sun.

● To test the camera's flash synchronization, take the back off the camera and look through the lens to see if the light from the flash coincides with the release of the shutter.

● The next four points are specifically for secondhand buyers:

● On an SLR camera always check the condition of the focal plane blinds. To look for pinholes, remove the back of the camera and the lens, gently push the mirror out of the way and hold the camera against a strong light while you slowly wind the shutter.

● The condition of the lens is also important so look at it obliquely to see if it has any scratches and check that there are no finger marks on it.

● Examine the general condition of the inside of the camera body and check that none of the screws is burred which may indicate that an amateur mechanic has been at work.

● If the camera has battery-powered controls, check that the batteries have not leaked and caused any corrosion.

1 EYE–LEVEL VIEWFINDER CAMERA

These are the simplest cameras, one step removed from the old box camera. You view the subject through a separate, small lens system, so you never see *exactly* the same view as the main camera lens. Framing marks in the viewfinder help to compensate for any parallax errors arising from this slight discrepancy.

For: many of these lightweight cameras are pocket–size. All are easy to use as the controls are minimal and usually keyed to simple symbols.

Against: these simple cameras are not suitable for close–up work or moving subjects and cannot be used in poor light. Lenses are not interchangeable but some models have supplementary lenses. On those models which focus, the distance between camera and subject must be guessed. If the camera has a fixed focus everything from about 2m to infinity is always in focus so you will not be able to have the subject sharp and the background blurred.

Film sizes: 110, 126, 135, 120

2 RANGEFINDER CAMERA

This is a viewfinder camera with more advanced controls which sometimes include a built–in exposure meter. The rangefinder measures the distance the subject is from the camera for accurate focusing. The system of small lenses works in combination with those of the viewfinder so you see either a split or a double image in the viewfinder and turn the focus control until they line up accurately. These cameras give greater flexibility and quality than the simpler viewfinder models.

For: they are fairly easy to use and usually offer a wide range of shutter speeds suitable for most light conditions. Most take 35mm film which provides a wide choice of film type.

Against: only a few models have interchangeable lenses; the rest have fixed lenses, so are not suitable for close–up work. The image in the viewfinder, though bright, is small and sometimes difficult to focus.

Film sizes: 110, 135, 120, 220

3 SINGLE LENS REFLEX, 35mm PENTAPRISM CAMERA

This is the camera most widely used by both professional and serious amateur photographers. The SLR camera offers the most efficient viewing system. A mirror at 45° behind the lens directs the light upwards to a focusing screen. (The pentaprism turns the image right way round and up.) In this way you see the subject through the camera's lens, which eliminates parallax errors.

For: these cameras take a wide range of accessories which gives them great versatility. Focal plane shutters in front of the film allow the lens to be changed safely with a film in the camera. A 35mm SLR is quick and easy to focus. The exposure metering is through the camera lens which is more accurate than a meter placed elsewhere on the camera body.

Against: the image is lost temporarily during exposure. A 35mm SLR cannot be used with electronic flash at fast shutter speeds which rules out 'fill–in flash' or 'synchro-sunlight' work with some films. They are heavier, bulkier and more complex than rangefinder cameras, and usually more expensive.

Film sizes: 135 (there are a few similar cameras that take 110 film)

4 ROLL FILM SLR CAMERA

The roll film SLR is favoured by many professionals. They have waist-level viewfinders but most also accept pentaprism and other viewfinders. Most produce 6 x 6cm negatives, which means the camera does not have to be turned on its side for vertical pictures. The models that produce oblong negatives are difficult to use vertically unless fitted with a pentaprism.

For: the bigger negative gives better quality than a 35mm negative. It is easy to see detail on a large viewing screen. Most models have interchangeable magazines or film-inserts that allow the camera to be reloaded very quickly. Some are fitted with between-lens shutters which are flash-synchronized at all speeds.

Against: extra lenses are heavy, bulky and expensive. When a waist-level viewfinder is used the image is reversed left to right. The basic camera is bulkier than a 35mm SLR.

Film sizes: 120 (6 x 6cm, 6 x 7cm, 4.5 x 6cm), 70mm double perforated

5

6

7

5 VIEW CAMERA
This is a large, specialized camera, which is used mounted on a tripod. It is used mainly by professionals for high quality studio and architectural work. The subject is viewed with the shutter open, the lens forming an image directly on a ground–glass screen. This camera takes sheet film.
For: the large viewing area makes it the easiest camera for composing a picture and allows the sharpness of focus to be checked in detail. It gives brilliantly sharp image quality. The front and back of the camera can be tilted, twisted, and moved up and down to control shape and perspective.
Against: it is an expensive, heavy and bulky instrument. The inverted image must be viewed under a dark cloth.

Film size: 6.5 x 9cm, 9 x 12cm, and others. Adaptors are available for 120 and instant–print film.

6 TWIN LENS REFLEX CAMERA
In effect, the TLR camera is two cameras mounted one above the other. The lenses are identical; the top one, with a fixed mirror at 45°, is used solely for viewing and focusing, and the bottom one takes the picture. A TLR is often used for studio work. It is usually held at waist–level or mounted on a tripod.
For: the large focusing screen makes it easier to compose the picture and, with the help of the magnifier, focus it. It is quiet and free from vibration and the between–lens shutter makes it ideal for flash. Most makes are strong and reliable.
Against: the image is reversed left to right and there is a difference between the close–up image seen on the screen and that on the film. Only a few have interchangeable lenses; most have a limited focusing range.

Film size: 120

7 INSTANT PRINT CAMERA
These cameras produce a print within minutes of taking the picture. They range in complexity from those which are focused by estimating the distance to those with an automatic sonar rangefinder, manually operated controls and a lens of good quality.
For: instant prints enable you to reshoot quickly. They are good for snap-shots or quick reference photographs and give good quality as such.
Against: the size of the print is limited to the size of the film unless special negative/positive material is used that provides a negative for enlargement. The cameras are fairly bulky, and the film is more expensive than other types even though you save yourself the cost of the processing. Many people find it difficult to achieve accurate colour.

Film size: 8.3 x 10.7cm, 8.3 x 8.6cm, and others

Avoiding camera shake

Camera shake ruins more photographs than any other basic mistake. To prevent this happening you must keep the camera steady, hold it comfortably and operate the controls without strain. Supporting the camera underneath helps to prevent movement when the shutter is released.

When taking the photograph don't jerk the shutter release button, press it smoothly—and try holding your breath at the same time.

You will find that you take most of your pictures standing. To help you hold the camera steady, balance your body properly by standing with your feet firmly planted and slightly apart.

With any camera the prime rule is 'always secure the camera strap'. Then if, inadvertently, you let go of the camera it can't fall far. But that is not the sole use of the strap. It can also be used to help steady the camera. On a 35mm camera you can put the strap round your neck and wind the slack round your wrist.

How to hold a 35mm eye-level camera

To hold a 35mm camera horizontally, support the camera on your left hand (cup it slightly) so the thumb and first two fingers are free to work the focusing or aperture controls. The right hand grips the camera firmly at the side, also steadying it. The index finger works the shutter release.

There are two ways to hold the camera vertically. Here the right hand supports the camera and holds it steady from below, while the index finger works the shutter release. Keep the right elbow tucked in. The left hand simply works the focusing or aperture controls.

In the other vertical position, the right hand holds the camera steady from above, while the index finger works the shutter release. The left hand, slightly cupped, supports the camera body below, leaving the thumb and first two fingers free to work the focusing or aperture controls.

How to hold a waist-level reflex camera

To hold the camera at waist–level, slightly cup both hands and support the camera from below as shown. Tuck your elbows in and brace downwards on the camera strap.

To use the magnifier hold the camera at chest level so the eye is close to the viewing screen. Support the camera with both hands and keep your elbows tucked in.

To shoot over the heads of a crowd, use the camera like a periscope. Grip the camera with both hands, holding it upside–down above your head. Brace the camera with the taut neck strap.

Taking sharp pictures

Different types of cameras use different methods to focus their lenses, but with the common aim of providing the photographer with a sharp image on the film.

Focusing is either done by guessing or actually measuring the camera-to-subject distance using a rangefinder. The lens is then set manually to the correct distance, or in some cameras the rangefinder is coupled to the focusing mechanism. In other focusing systems the image is seen through a ground-glass screen and the lens moved until the image is sharp.

Viewfinder cameras

There are two types of eye-level viewfinder. Cartridge loading 110 cameras mostly have fixed focus lenses, although the more sophisticated ones use zone focusing symbols. Some can focus their lenses by zone focusing or a distance scale.

Fixed focus lens: most 110 cameras have fixed focus lenses which cannot be adjusted. Everything in the viewfinder from about 2m away to the furthest horizon will be sharp. With a pre-set lens you cannot move in for close-ups without getting a fuzzy image, although some of these cameras have an additional close-up lens which slides across to solve this problem.

Front cell focusing: some of the eye-level viewfinder cameras have front cell focusing. The lens is permanently focused on infinity, but the front element can be moved forwards to shorten the focal length of the lens. This adjusts it to focus on objects up to about 1·5m from the camera but, because it cannot focus closer without loss of image definition, it has become less popular.

Whole lens focusing: precision viewfinder cameras use a screw-out focusing system which shifts the whole lens away from, or towards, the film.

The control ring for front cell focusing and whole lens focusing is marked in subject distances or symbols.

Calculating distance: on eye-level viewfinder cameras without a rangefinder, the distance from camera to subject must either be guessed or measured. Measuring is accurate but often too slow. Guessing within a reasonable limit, though faster, takes practice. It is easier to learn to estimate a few distances such as 2m, 5m and 10m, and to move your camera to one distance or the other, rather than move the subject.

Zone focusing: some eye-level viewfinder cameras use a system of zone focusing which divides the areas of focus into settings for landscapes, groups, half length, and head-and-shoulders portraits. These are shown pictorially on the lens, and sometimes appear in the viewfinder. They make focusing easy but only give the photographer an approximation of distance.

Rangefinder cameras

Many eye-level viewfinder cameras have a built-in device called a coupled rangefinder with either a double image or a split image centre spot in the viewfinder which merges into the rest of the image when the lens is correctly focused.

The rangefinder system is ideal for a normal lens but less good with a close-up lens (the angle is too great for the mirror movement) or a telephoto lens over 135mm (the angle is too small). As a result, it is used mostly on cameras with fixed lenses, the exception being precision cameras like the Leica for which a series of rangefinder-coupling lens is made.

Double and split image rangefinders: when you look through the viewfinder there are two images. One is the normal viewfinder image, the second is reflected from a movable mirror at the other end of the camera on to a reflective surface in the viewfinder. Moving the mirror, by turning the focusing ring on the lens until the two images coincide exactly, automatically focuses the lens on the subject. More expensive models use prisms instead of mirrors for greater accuracy.

A variation is the split image rangefinder which uses a similar system of mirrors or prisms. This time the centre of the picture in the viewfinder appears split in two until you focus the lens correctly when it becomes lined up.

Parallax error

If your camera is the viewfinder/rangefinder type you may have noticed that the picture you see through the viewfinder is often slightly different from the picture photographed by the lens. This effect is called parallax error and accounts for so many photographs in which a head has accidentally been cut off. It happens because the photographer does not view the subject directly through the lens with a viewfinder camera. The viewfinder and lens are separate and their different positions alter the viewing angle between what the eye sees and what the camera sees. This change in angle is small for distant objects, but increases if the subject is closer. Although some cameras have compensating framing lines in the viewfinder, the best solution when taking close-ups is to leave some extra space above the heads.

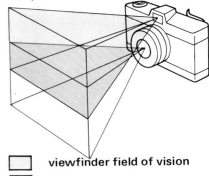

☐ **viewfinder field of vision**

☐ **lens field of vision**

Automatic focusing

Eye-level viewfinder cameras, with automatic focusing, are already available. The photographer simply points the camera at his subject and presses the shutter release. Camera-to-subject distance is measured in a similar manner to the rangefinder using the contrast between two superimposed images. When the two images are merged completely, contrast is at its highest, the lens is sharply focused and a special electric cell allows the shutter to fire.

The difficulty is that the camera does not know which part of the subject is the most important to the photographer and produces a sharp picture of the object at the centre of the viewfinder. Good composition is not always possible, but the camera is easy to use.

Hyperfocal distance

The hyperfocal distance is the point closest to the camera which is still in focus when the lens is focused at infinity—the distant horizon. When you set your lens for this point everything in the viewfinder from half this distance to infinity is in focus. If you are in a hurry, setting the lens at the hyperfocal distance ensures that you get the greatest possible depth of field, covering all but close subjects.

You can find the hyperfocal distance at a given aperture by using the depth of field scale. For example, if you are working at f16, set one of the f16 marks at infinity; the other mark then shows the closest point that will be in focus.

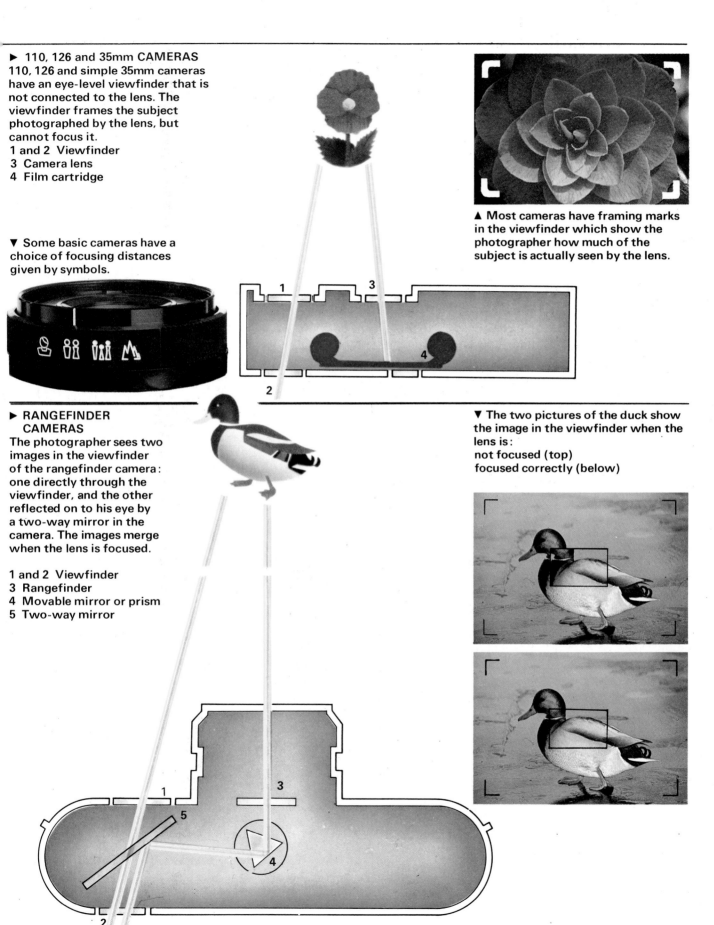

► **110, 126 and 35mm CAMERAS**
110, 126 and simple 35mm cameras have an eye-level viewfinder that is not connected to the lens. The viewfinder frames the subject photographed by the lens, but cannot focus it.
1 and 2 Viewfinder
3 Camera lens
4 Film cartridge

▼ Some basic cameras have a choice of focusing distances given by symbols.

▲ Most cameras have framing marks in the viewfinder which show the photographer how much of the subject is actually seen by the lens.

► **RANGEFINDER CAMERAS**
The photographer sees two images in the viewfinder of the rangefinder camera: one directly through the viewfinder, and the other reflected on to his eye by a two-way mirror in the camera. The images merge when the lens is focused.

1 and 2 Viewfinder
3 Rangefinder
4 Movable mirror or prism
5 Two-way mirror

▼ The two pictures of the duck show the image in the viewfinder when the lens is:
not focused (top)
focused correctly (below)

Reflex cameras

Reflex focusing is quick and easy to use and extremely accurate. With this the photographer sees an actual image of the subject focused on to a viewing screen. A surface silvered mirror, set inside the camera at 45°, reflects the lens image upwards on to a horizontal glass screen which acts as a precise focusing device.

Although the image is reversed from left to right, unless a prism finder is used, it is easy to focus by turning the lens focusing ring. The picture is composed with the aperture wide open to give the brightest image and smallest depth of field. When the shutter release on an SLR is pressed the aperture automatically stops down to the selected f number, the mirror swings up and the shutter operates.

Twin lens reflex cameras: with the reflex system described above there are two drawbacks. Firstly, vibration caused by the mirror movement; and secondly, the image on the viewing screen blacks out at the instant the picture is taken. These problems are solved on a TLR camera by mounting two cameras on top of each other. Both have similar lenses: the upper one is fitted with a static mirror and focuses the image, while the lower camera exposes the film. The two focusing mechanisms are linked and work together. However, because there are two lenses, parallax error occurs with close-ups, and the camera can only be used in a vertical position.

Single lens reflex: the modern SLR camera has done much to eliminate the vibration caused by the mirror movement and has one further modification. A five-sided prism (called a pentaprism) is mounted on top of the horizontal glass screen and turns the image on the viewing screen the right way round. The camera can be used either horizontally or vertically.

Twin lens reflex: this type of camera views the subject and focuses via a fixed 45° mirror set behind the top lens. The focusing mechanism is coupled to the lower lens which takes the picture.

Single lens reflex: the addition of the pentaprism means that this versatile camera can be used in any position and the photographer will still see an image the correct way up on the viewing screen. As the shutter releases the mirror swings up.

TWIN LENS REFLEX
1 Waist-level viewfinder
2 Focusing lens
3 Reflex mirror
4 Taking lens
5 Film

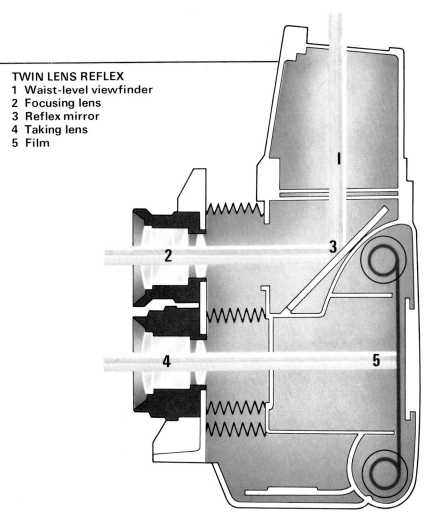

SINGLE LENS REFLEX
1 Lens
2 45° reflex mirror
3 Film
4 Pentaprism
5 Eye-level viewfinder

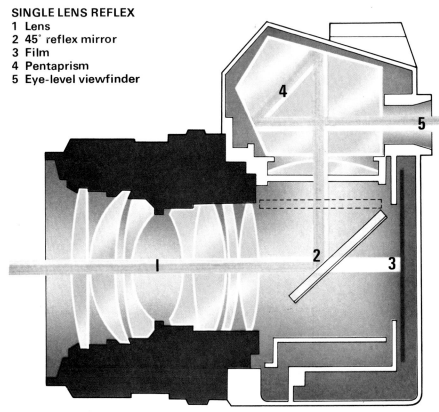

▲ **Twin lens reflex:** the image on the viewing screen is often crossed by a grid to help with composition. The subject is seen reversed from left to right, and focused on the ground-glass screen. Top picture shows image as the eye sees it.

Focusing screens

The standard focusing screen for most SLR cameras is matt glass with a central microprism. This is a series of tiny pyramids embossed on to the screen which gives a jagged view of the image when the lens is not in focus.

Some cameras have interchangeable focusing screens. They can be either matt or clear glass with the microprism or a split image centre-spot. This latter consists of two optical wedges which align the image perfectly when it is in focus. On many models it is used in combination with the microprism. Matt screens are easier to focus for most people and show how much of the picture is sharp, but clear glass focusing screens are often used when a brighter image is required. The split image centre spot is not effective for extreme long focus or wide angle lenses. Focusing for these lenses is done either using a plain matt or clear screen.
Fresnel screen: embossed on many types of focusing screen are tiny concentric ridges which act as a condensing lens and evenly illuminate the image on the screen. Without the addition of these the image would tend to darken towards the edges.

▼ **SLR:** the photographer sees a correctly oriented view of his subject, framed by information giving the exposure settings he has chosen. The microprism and split image centre-spot show the precise point of focus.

▲ The photographer may choose between a sharp foreground image or a focused background unless he uses a wide angle lens. This choice can give two very different results.

If you wear glasses . . .
Using a camera, like an SLR, which is focused according to the image seen on a viewing screen can be tricky for spectacle wearers. Looking at the viewing screen with your glasses on is often uncomfortable, but the alternative is to risk an out of focus result. Soft rubber eyepieces which soften the meeting of glass and camera are easily obtainable and can help, but the real solution is to get a + or − diopter lens which can be screwed into the eyepiece permanently. The top quality manufacturers all make these in various magnifications, and they are stocked by most dealers.

Focusing screens and viewfinders

Most popular SLR cameras have a fixed focusing screen and pentaprism, both of which are more than adequate for day to day situations. Although both of these features make rapid focusing and composition easier, neither can be the perfect answer in every situation. For that reason many photographers choose an SLR with an interchangeable focusing screen, viewfinder, or both. You will find that some of the more expensive cameras have this facility.

Special screens

It may be possible to have your camera's fixed focusing screen changed by the manufacturer or importer if you don't want the expense of changing your camera system. Another choice of screen may be more suitable for your specialist subject when the 'general purpose' screen is a disadvantage. With interchangeable screen cameras you can have a number of alternative screens for different types of photography. Manufacturers like Nikon and Pentax have a range of screens suitable for close-ups and photomicrography, architecture and astrophotography, for example.

Handling focusing screens

Interchangeable screens can usually be inserted above the mirror chamber through the front of the camera (with the lens removed). In the case of cameras with an interchangeable viewfinder, screens are dropped in to position from above the camera top plate with the pentaprism removed. Because the screens are plastic (or thin glass) and are therefore relatively easy to damage, take care not to touch or scratch the surfaces. Handle the screen by its special tag using the tongs provided for front-inserting screens, or by the protective frame if the screen fits via the top of the camera.

Never use a spirit-based lens cleaning fluid because it will crack or melt the plastic and ruin the screen — they are not cheap. A water-based solution, such as Kodak Lens Cleaner, is suit-

A selection of focusing screens

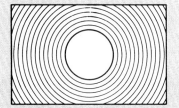

▲ A clear circle in the centre of a fresnel matt screen gives undistracted central viewing while focusing the subject.

▲ When both the central crosshair and the subject look sharp the subject is in focus—used for high magnification photography.

▲ An overall fine matt screen is for close–up or telephotography and gives an unrestricted viewing area to help composition.

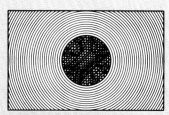

▲ A clear fresnel matt screen with a central microprism circle gives a bright image for accurate focusing in dim light.

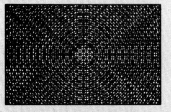

▲ A fresnel screen with microprisms over the whole area eases focusing in dim light and with moving subjects.

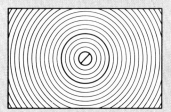

▲ A split–image spot in the centre of a fresnel matt screen is for rapid focusing in general photography.

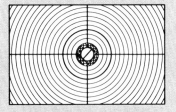

▲ This all–purpose screen has microprism and split–image focusing aids, and vertical and horizontal reference lines.

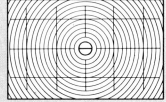

▲ A grid can be used to work out magnification; in architectural photographs it is used to check vertical and horizontal lines.

◀ A notch is provided on focusing screens which are changed through the mirror chamber. Gripped with the tweezer–like tool supplied, the notch eases screen insertion and removal with reduced risk of scratching or marking the delicate screen surface.

▶ Top–inserted screens are usually surrounded by a frame to keep fingers off the surface and to ease screen changing.

Standard focusing screen

A focusing screen provides a flat surface on which an image can be precisely focused and allows the eye to see the whole image at once for framing and composing. It normally comprises a ground glass screen, a fresnel lens and one or more focusing aids.

A ground glass screen scatters light in all directions allowing the whole image to be seen, but the picture you see is brighter in the centre. Coarse etching of the glass reduces this.

A fresnel lens comprises a series of stepped, concentric rings. Each step is a tiny portion of a curved lens (the same curve for each step), and bends light the same degree. Inclusion of a fresnel screen combines maximum brightness with even illumination. A number of stepped concentric rings, moulded in plastic, are in contact with the underside of the focusing screen. The effect is an even image with undisturbed detail sharpness.

Most modern SLR focusing screens include a central split-image rangefinder area and a circle of microprisms in the centre of the screen. These are focusing aids, and are designed to work most efficiently with standard focal length lenses. With other lenses, and with extension tubes, part of these central areas may black out, so use the plain area for focusing.

Microprisms: the criss-cross pattern of the prism circle is clearly visible and shimmers when the image is out of focus. The pattern and shimmer disappear when the image comes sharply into focus. Use this area of the screen for high contrast patterned or textured surfaces.

Split-image spot: the split rangefinder area is two semi-circular wedge-shaped prisms. These make an out-of-focus image appear as two off-set halves which apparently join up when sharply focused. A horizontal split is fine for vertical lines, but a diagonal split works equally well with vertical and horizontal lines. Use the area for bold straight lines, and when focusing in dim lighting.

With focusing aids in the centre of the screen you tend to position the main subject centrally too — which may not be the best place from a compositional point of view. Focus before finalizing composition.

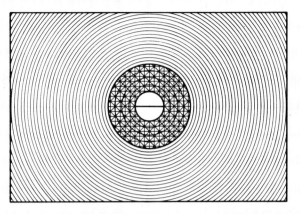

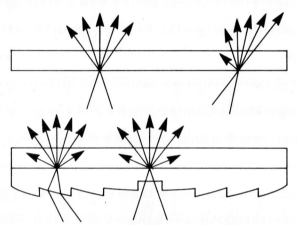

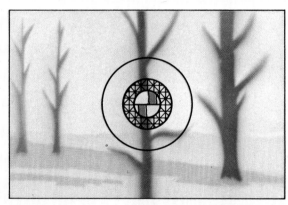

◄ A typical screen may include a split–image spot for rapid focusing on straight lines or in dim light. Microprisms enable fast, accurate focusing especially on textured subjects. Use the plain area of the screen for close–ups, with wide angle and telephoto lenses and for general or fine focusing.

◄ Top: a fine ground glass screen scatters light enabling the entire image area to be seen, but the centre is brighter than the edges. A coarser screen would improve this unevenness but only at the expense of screen brightness. Below: a fresnel lens ensures even image brightness throughout. When combined with a fine ground glass screen an improved focusing screen is produced.

◄ Whether horizontal (as illustrated) or diagonal, a split–image centre spot shows an out–of–focus image as two separate off–set halves. Select a part of the subject which contains a distinct line on which you can focus. You can adjust the composition once you have obtained sharp focus.

◄ If the image is in focus the line which you have selected will appear continuous across the centre spot. A horizontal split is best for a vertical line in a landscape composition; sight a horizontal line in an upright photograph. A diagonal split–image is easy to use for either type of composition.

able. If you have several screens keep them in the individual dust-proof containers provided when you are not using them.

Viewfinders

For the most expensive reflex cameras there is a range of viewfinders as alternatives to the pentaprism. A pentaprism provides an upright, right-way-round image for easy composition, and is usually fitted as standard on 35mm reflex cameras, but special finders may be more appropriate for particular projects.

There are three different pentaprisms in the Nikon range — non-metering, CdS or silicon — as well as three special purpose viewfinders.

A 6x magnifier is used for close-up photography and for copying. It enlarges the image on the central part of the screen six times. Because the magnifier is not a pentaprism the image appears laterally reversed — just like a mirror image. Diopter correction in the eyepiece is included to allow spectacle wearers to focus accurately without the need to wear glasses.

Cameras with fixed pentaprisms can often be fitted with a focusing magnifier which fits on to the eyepiece. They generally magnify the centre of the screen image two times.

The waist-level finder for many larger format cameras (such as twin lens reflex) is popular for rapid framing of a subject with the camera held at low level.

An action finder provides a full view of the focusing screen with the eye away from the eyepiece — behind or to either side. It is used by sports and action photographers, and by people wearing industrial goggles. It is also useful when the camera is in an underwater housing.

An interchangeable viewfinder connects to the camera top plate directly above the focusing screen. When properly aligned it will click and lock easily in to place. It can only be removed by disengaging the locking mechanisms — this can often be a little more tricky than attaching it. When the viewfinder is removed take the opportunity to dust the focusing screen using a blower brush.

Eyepiece accessories

You can fit a right angle finder to the eyepiece on your camera. It allows you to view at 90° to the subject, and this is particularly helpful if the camera is positioned at low level, such as on the floor. Of the two types available, only the more expensive ones produce an image the right way round.

If you wear spectacles and have difficulty in focusing, eyepiece correction lenses can be fitted on to the camera viewfinder enabling you to focus accurately without your glasses. Ask your optician about your lens prescription. Some specialist opticians and camera distributors can supply you with the appropriate correction lens to suit your eyesight.

An interchangeable viewfinder camera allows you a number of options. Four viewfinder pentaprisms are shown:
1 The Action Finder has a large rear screen allowing the whole image area to be seen with the eye a little behind or to one side of the finder (no meter).
2 A standard pentaprism with silicon metering.
3 A similar metering pentaprism with CdS cells.
4 Non–metering pentaprism.

▲ The interchangeable viewfinder slots into the top of the camera and must be correctly aligned to engage properly. Removal involves releasing the retaining levers at the same time lifting the viewfinder upwards.

▲ This focusing finder magnifies the screen image six times. It is used for high–magnification photography. This particular model has diopter correction, variable between –5 and +3 diopters to suit the vision of most photographers.

▲ A waist–level finder enables you to use the camera at low level, viewing the image on the focusing screen from directly above. The hood shields stray light, and an image magnifier can be flipped up for critical focusing.

▲ When not in use the waist–level finder can be folded away to keep dust and grit off the focusing screen. The finder does not have a meter built–in, so separate light readings are taken with a hand–held meter.

Understanding the lens

▶ The lens illustrated is the type usually fitted to an SLR camera. It encompasses more or less the same view you see with one eye closed. The information on the front of the lens gives its focal length (50mm), maximum aperture (f2), maker's name, brand name, and serial number. The side view shows scales for focusing, aperture setting and depth of field.

Modern lenses are made up from several glass elements ground to a precise shape and mounted inside a tube.

▼ The 110 camera usually has a lens with a similar view to the 50mm lens above but the focal length is shorter because of the film's small size.

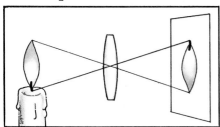

▲ With an object at infinity, such as the sun, light rays become parallel. The distance between a magnifying glass and the paper as it scorches— when the rays are focused—is the focal length of the lens.

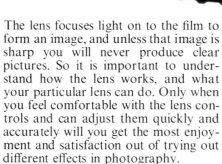

▲ A candle flame is much closer than the sun so its light rays are not yet parallel on reaching the magnifying glass. To focus sharply on the flame the lens must be moved further from the paper.

The lens focuses light on to the film to form an image, and unless that image is sharp you will never produce clear pictures. So it is important to understand how the lens works, and what your particular lens can do. Only when you feel comfortable with the lens controls and can adjust them quickly and accurately will you get the most enjoyment and satisfaction out of trying out different effects in photography.

Focal length

The amount of a scene photographed by any lens is governed by its focal length. On a 35mm camera a normal lens of 40-50mm has roughly the same view as the human eye. To photograph more of the subject, or to pull distant objects closer, you need lenses with different focal lengths. The shorter focal length (under 35mm) of the wide angle lens gives a broad view of the scene, while the much longer focal length of a telephoto lens shows up detail in distant objects.

Focal length is the distance between the lens and the film when the lens is focused at infinity (for a normal lens, that means set for objects more than 30m away). You can set fire to a piece of paper by holding a magnifying glass at exactly the point where a sharp image

of the sun (at infinity) forms on the paper, and a camera lens focuses an image on film in the same way. In each case, the distance between the lens and the image is the focal length.

Now imagine a magnifying glass forming the image of a candle flame on a sheet of paper. The distance between paper and glass before a sharp image is formed is greater than when the sun's rays are used. The closer an object is to the camera, the further the lens must be from the film to focus correctly.

Most simple 110 and 126 cameras have lenses with no focusing adjustment. These have been factory set to keep everything sharp between 2m and infinity. Most 35mm cameras have lenses which must be accurately focused by the photographer. These are set in helical mounts, two telescoping tubes with a screw thread between them. The closest focusing distance is determined by the maximum movement of this mount: for example, the shortest distance a 50mm lens fitted to a 35mm reflex camera focuses at is usually about 30–50cm.

If you have a reflex camera, try this yourself by setting the lens to minimum distance and moving backwards and forwards until an object close by be-

24

focusing ring

scale for focusing
(in metres and feet)

depth of field scale
(colour coded)

aperture settings
(f numbers)

lens mount
(where lens fits into camera body)

DEPTH OF FIELD SCALE
On this lens the depth of field scale is colour coded to correspond with the relevant f number. You can see that f16, for example, is shown in blue and so is the depth of field marking for that aperture setting. Other lenses may use diverging black lines running from each f number to the depth of field scale.

comes sharp in the viewing screen. Then measure the distance in between.

Normal lenses

The standard lens fitted to a camera is referred to as normal because, like the human eye, it takes in a 45–50° section of the scene. The focal length is usually more or less equal to the diagonal of the negative. Negative size varies, so the focal length of a normal lens depends on the film size a camera takes. In a 35mm camera the normal or standard lens is between 40–50mm, but for a small pocket camera taking 110 film it need only be 25mm.

The larger format cameras have correspondingly longer focal-length normal or standard lenses.

Brightness control

The brightness of the light reaching the film is controlled by a hole called the aperture. It works like the pupil of the eye, large in the dark to let in more light and small in bright conditions. The camera lens controls its aperture with a diaphragm (a mechanical iris) which is operated by a ring or lever outside the lens. The dimmer the light the larger the aperture must be to keep the brightness of the light on the film constant.

f numbers

Simple cameras often mark the aperture control with weather symbols, but the more complex cameras use a numerical system called f numbers. The smaller the f number, the larger the aperture; for example, f2·8 lets in more light than f5·6 and much more than f16. (The next chapter describes this more fully.)

Depth of field

Changing the f number also affects the depth of field, or amount of the scene in front of the camera that appears in focus. The depth of field scale on the lens indicates how much of the area in front of and behind the subject is in focus. If you move the aperture ring on the lens through the range of f numbers you can see how this control over sharpness can be used to subdue unwanted background and emphasize the main subject or, at a smaller aperture, to take a picture which is sharp from foreground to infinity.

Caring for your lens

• Never touch the lens surface. Greasy fingermarks are hard to remove.
• Use a soft lens brush to remove dust particles from the lens, or polish lightly with a rolled up, lint-free cloth, moving from rim to centre.
• Never clean your lens with solvent. If absolutely necessary; flood the glass surface with distilled water, invert the lens, and blot dry carefully.
• If you drop the lens in water, sand, or mud, dry it gently and take it to a camera shop for cleaning. Do not dismantle it yourself.
• Always replace the case or lens cap after use. When changing lenses, put the rear cap on and look after your lens mount fitting.
• Never oil the moving parts of your lens.
• A skylight or UV/haze filter kept permanently on the lens is a sensible protection against dust particles.
• Always keep your lenses in a cool, dry place.

Changing the angle of view

The angle of view, or the amount of a scene taken in by the lens, is governed by the focal length of the lens; for example, a short focal length will give a wide angle or view. So you can photograph different parts of the view just by changing lenses—as shown in the three pictures on the right. The girl and the camera stay in the same position for each photograph, showing that subject and background enlarge equally as the angle of view narrows.

1 WIDE ANGLE LENS

The short focal length of a 28mm lens on a 35mm camera means that the angle of view is wide, allowing the whole of the building behind the subject to be photographed. Object size in the viewfinder is small and the foreground prominent.

2 NORMAL LENS

The normal angle of view of a 50mm lens gives a view comparable with your own. Less of the building can be seen as the angle narrows; both the girl and her background have enlarged equally.

3 TELEPHOTO LENS

A 135mm telephoto lens concentrates on the girl. Its long focal length magnifies, but the much narrower angle of view includes less of her surroundings. Compare this picture with the top one: the girl's head is in the same position in relation to the window in the building behind. Both subject and background have grown equally.

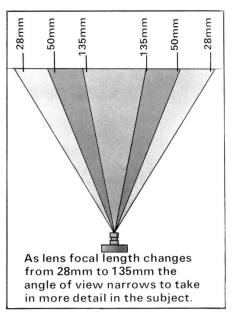

As lens focal length changes from 28mm to 135mm the angle of view narrows to take in more detail in the subject.

1

2

3

4

If, instead of changing the lens, you move the camera to include a different amount of the subject in the viewfinder the angle of view stays the same, but the size of the subject changes in relation to the background. Perspective enlarges objects close to the camera, and is especially noticeable when you photograph a nearby subject with a distant background. If the subject is further away, the effect is less apparent.

The three pictures on the left were all taken using a 50mm lens on an SLR camera. The girl did not move but the camera position was altered. Compare these pictures with the ones opposite; the angle of view has not changed, but the subject gets larger in relation to the background as the camera advances.

4 DISTANCE OF 12m
The building looks tall in relation to the girl; building and subject both appear distant and close together.

5 DISTANCE OF 7·5m
As you move closer to the girl she becomes larger in relation to the background. The feeling of depth in the picture has increased with perspective.

6 DISTANCE OF 2·75m
Here the background is even smaller. The steeper perspective creates the illusion of great distance between the girl and her background. Compare this picture with the one at top to see how the girl's size has altered in relation to hedge, trees and building.

5

6

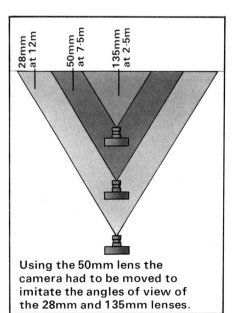

Using the 50mm lens the camera had to be moved to imitate the angles of view of the 28mm and 135mm lenses.

The full range of lenses

There is a wide range of lenses currently available. The photographer has to choose the focal length that he needs for a particular subject. The 28mm, 50mm, and 135mm focal lengths used on cameras which take interchangeable lenses cover most situations. Beyond these there are the ultra-wide angle (below 28mm) and long telephoto (over 200mm) lenses for special effects. These special lenses and the equipment for close-up photography, zoom lenses, and mirror lenses are discussed in the chapter on additional lenses.

The short focal length of a 20mm lens gives great depth of field, which means that most of the picture is sharp and focusing is not critical. Distortion of the subject at the picture edges must be taken into account, although makers' corrections do compensate for this. Lenses as wide as the 8mm fisheye are not corrected and the result is a completely circular view with only the centre of the picture retaining familiar proportions.

Powerful telephoto lenses—such as 1000mm lenses—show detail in distant subjects which, pictured on their own, look normal. If other objects are included in front of or behind the subject, distance appears compressed. As focal length increases through the lens range, the depth of field shortens dramatically and accurate focusing is essential to get a sharp result. These long lenses are large and heavy so a tripod should be used to avoid camera shake.

A change of lens gives the photographer a changed angle of view. If you turn this page on its side you will see, on the left, some of the many different focal length lenses available—from the 8mm fisheye to the 1000mm telephoto. The diagram in the centre shows the angle of view of each lens. The picture opposite each lens shows the angle of view—from the 180 degrees taken in by the fisheye to the minute 2·5 degrees seen by the 1000mm lens. All these pictures were taken from the same camera position.

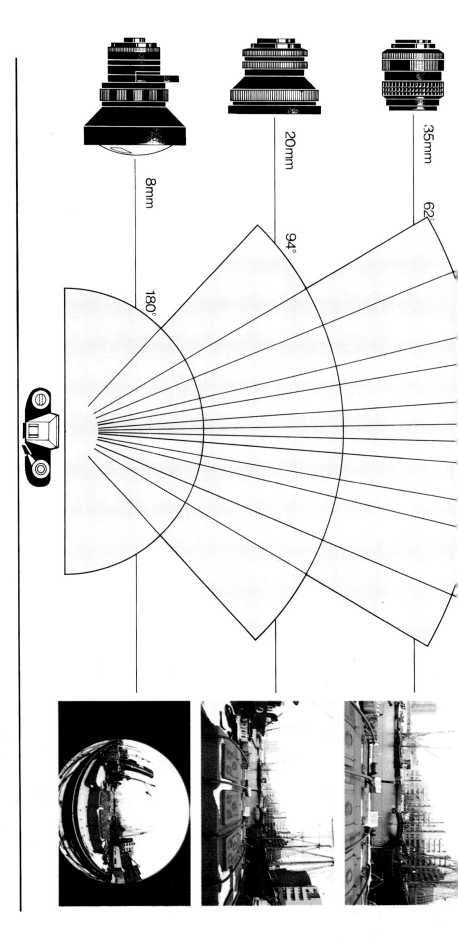

Focal length and angle of view

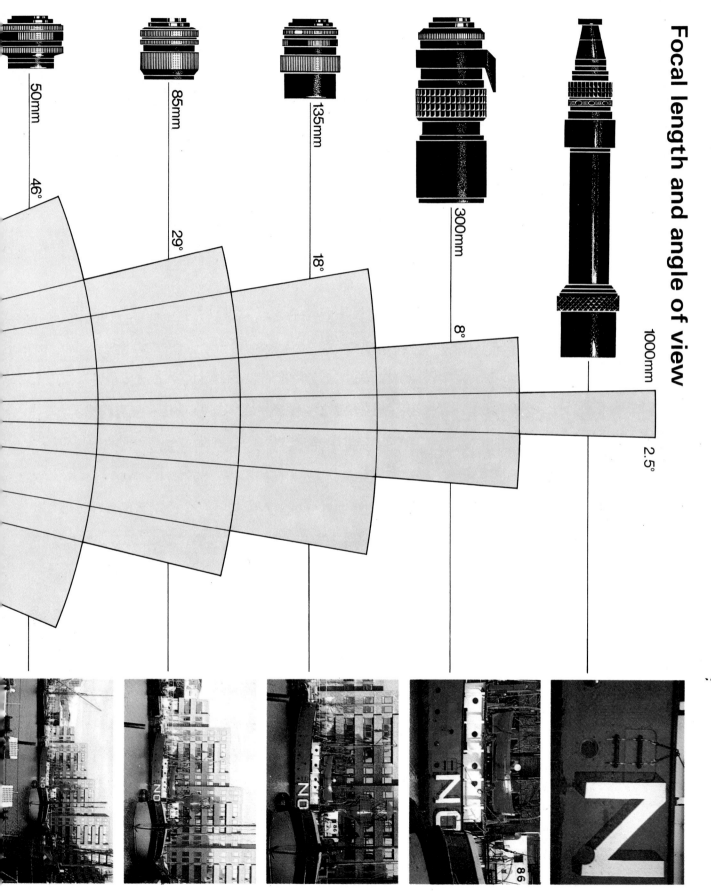

50mm   46°

85mm   29°

135mm   18°

300mm   8°

1000mm   2.5°

The aperture

When you open the back of a camera to change the film, look inside and then press the shutter release. As the shutter opens the aperture can be seen beyond it. This shows more clearly if you look through the front of the lens or, on a camera with interchangeable lenses, take the lens off and look through that. Turn the aperture control and the size of the aperture will alter within the lens as you change the settings.

As the size of the aperture changes, so does the brightness of the light allowed through the lens. Aperture size, and therefore brightness, is controlled by the iris diaphragm, made up of a number of thin, interleaving blades which rotate to make the aperture larger or smaller. Making it smaller (stopping down the lens) reduces the amount of light reaching the film; increasing the size allows more light through.

The f number system

The brightness of the image on the film depends on the combination of the aperture size (the stop) and the focal length of a lens. So a large aperture and long focal length can transmit the same brightness of light as a small aperture and short focal length.

The scale photographers use to relate focal length and aperture size is called the f number system (f stands for the mathematical term, factor) and it is calculated by measuring the diameter of the aperture and dividing it into the focal length. An aperture of 25mm on a 100mm lens represents f4, but the same diameter aperture on a 50mm lens will represent f2. The smaller the f number, the larger the aperture and, therefore, the more light reaches the film.

The f numbers for any lens are calibrated by the maker on the basis that an aperture of f8, say, will always transmit the same brightness of light whatever the focal length. The series as a whole is arranged so that each f number lets in twice as much light as the number on one side of it and half as much as the number on the other. For example, f4 admits eight times more light than f11, but only half as much as f2·8.

You can see this relationship more easily on the chart on the right. Imagine that f16 allows through half a unit of light: as each f number becomes smaller, so the number of light units doubles.

The size of the aperture affects the image definition of a lens. At maximum aperture the sharpness of the image in

▲ The iris diaphragm controls the size of the aperture. The thin metal blades rotate with the ring on the lens to make the aperture larger or smaller.

▼ Large aperture and long focal length can transmit the same amount of light as a small aperture and short focal length.
An aperture of the same diameter— say, 25mm—will give a different f number on two lenses of different focal lengths.

the centre of the picture is nearly always greater than in the corners. Stopping down the lens improves central definition slightly and corner definition much more.

Lens construction differs so much that it is impossible to generalize but a sophisticated, large aperture lens of f1·4 probably performs best two or three stops up from its maximum aperture. At small stops such as f16 there is usually slight fall-off in sharpness caused by diffraction, the scattering of light rays collected in the front of the lens as they pass the edge of the iris

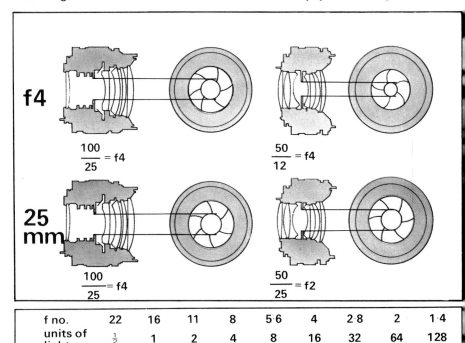

f4

$$\frac{100}{25} = f4 \qquad \frac{50}{12} = f4$$

25 mm

$$\frac{100}{25} = f4 \qquad \frac{50}{25} = f2$$

f no.	22	16	11	8	5·6	4	2·8	2	1·4
units of light		$\frac{1}{2}$	1	2	4	8	16	32	64	128

▲ The iris diaphragm alters the size of the aperture and therefore the brightness of light reaching the film. Small apertures—f22 and f16—cut down brightness and have great depth of field so all of the picture is sharp. Larger apertures—f11 to f5·6—increase image brightness for normal conditions, while f4 and f2 let in even more light on dull days. Larger apertures have short depths of field decreasing until, at f2, only the subject in focus is completely sharp.

diaphragm. Both these points are really only important when a very high degree of definition is required—such as when copying documents. Other factors, such as camera shake, an incorrectly held camera or incorrect focusing, will have a far more noticeable effect on your pictures.

Depth of field

Depth of field describes the extent of the picture in focus at a given f number. The length of the zone on either side of the subject depends on the size of the aperture and the focal length of the lens. In theory, only the subject on which you focus is completely sharp but an area of acceptable sharpness lies in front of and behind it.

As the size of the aperture decreases, the depth of field lengthens, bringing more of the picture on either side of the subject into focus.

Most rangefinder and reflex cameras have depth of field scales on their lenses, which show the limits of the area in focus for any combination of aperture and distance. A study of this scale shows that the subject focused on is not at the centre of this sharp zone, which extends two-thirds beyond the subject, and one-third towards the camera—unless, of course, the subject is very close to you.

On cameras with separate viewfinders the scale on the lens is the only indication of depth of field, so you should check that the aperture size set will give you the depth you want, before pressing the shutter release.

On SLR cameras, which view through the lens, the photographer can immediately see how much of the finished picture will be in focus by using the depth of field preview button mounted on the camera body.

▲ The atmosphere of the dimly lighted fish market is brought out by using a wide aperture and narrow depth of field to show the patterns made by rows of fish.

▼ The entire cobbled street has photographed sharply using a small aperture. The harsh outlines and narrow shadows are indications of the bright conditions.

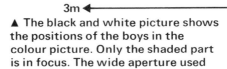

▲ The 50mm lens is focused on 2m with an aperture of f1·4, the widest possible setting. The depth of field scale on the lens tells the photographer how much of his subject is in focus (indicated by the shaded area on the lens).

1·40m

2m

3m

▲ The black and white picture shows the positions of the boys in the colour picture. Only the shaded part is in focus. The wide aperture used for this picture gives very short depth of field, extending from immediately in front of the boy with the kite to only about 40cm behind him.

▲ The much smaller aperture of f16 used for this second picture has altered the depth of field reading on the lens scale (indicated by the wider shaded area) and includes all objects in the viewfinder between 1·5m and 6m.

1·40m
2m
3m

With the boys standing in the same positions, the photographer uses a smaller aperture to photograph all three sharply. Again the shaded area denotes depth of field.

Comparing these two pages you can see that depth of field has grown unequally—two thirds beyond the middle child and one third in front.

▲ **24mm lens:** extensive depth of field is characteristic of wide angle lenses—a result of their short focal length. Unless the subject is very close, accurate focusing is not always critical because a large part of the picture will be within the sharp zone (depth of field) of the lens.

▲ **50mm lens:** the longer focal length of this lens shortens depth of field. The distant trees and near end of the bench are out of focus, only the boy and nearby tree are sharp. To give an exact comparison between these different lenses the same aperture, f3·5, is used for the first three illustrations.

Focal length/depth of field

The focal length of the lens on a camera also affects depth of field, as the pictures on this page show. Using the same f number—f4—each time but progressively extending focal length by changing lenses alters the degree of sharpness surrounding the subject in each photograph. So if the same f number is used throughout, depth of field shortens as focal length becomes longer.

To sum up:

● The focal length of a lens determines the angle of view it takes in—that is, the 'width' of the scene.
● Depth of field describes how much of the scene, from front to back, is in focus.
● Depth of field shortens as focal length becomes longer, or as the aperture becomes larger.

Depth of field table

The chart on the right is a rough guide to depth of field at various apertures for each of four lenses, all focused on a subject four metres away. So, depending on the subject and how much of the scene you want to be in focus, you can use this chart to find the right aperture setting for each lens.

The numbers in the boxes give the distance in centimetres that will be in focus (∞ = infinity). For example, 275–765 means that the nearest point in focus is 275cm away from the camera, while the furthest point in focus is 765cm away. Depth of field therefore extends over almost five metres.

Now take, for example, a normal 50mm lens on an SLR camera. Focus on a subject four metres away and look through the camera. Close the aperture progressively from f2·8 to f22. At f4 everything just over three metres to just over six metres will be sharp. At f11 everything from two metres to infinity will be sharp.

Reading down the columns, note how depth of field increases as the aperture becomes smaller—represented by a larger value f number.

Reading across, depth of field for a given aperture decreases as the lens is exchanged for one of longer focal length.

The colour coded diagonals pick out some of the constant depths of field: this way you can choose the right aperture to maintain the same depth of field with different lenses.

DEPTH OF FIELD EXTENDS FOR . . .

	1 metre
	2 metres
	5 metres
	2m to infinity
	1·3m to infinity

▲ **135mm lens:** though taken from the same position as with the other two lenses, the telephoto picks out a smaller area of the view. Compared with a 24mm lens depth of field is minimal and focusing is therefore critical. Only a very small part of the picture is sharp.

▲ **135mm lens:** to show that depth of field can be increased dramatically with the use of a smaller aperture, this photograph was taken with the same 135mm lens but set at f22. Changing to a small aperture brings the tree and bench into sharp focus.

DEPTH OF FIELD TABLE (IN CENTIMETRES)

f no.		25mm lens	50mm lens	100mm lens	200mm lens
2·8		275—765	325—525	355—455	375—425
4		240—1430	310—610	340—480	360—450
5·6		200—∞	275—765	325—525	355—455
8		170—∞	240—1430	310—610	340—480
11		130—∞	200—∞	275—765	325—525
16		110—∞	170—∞	240—1430	310—610
22		80—∞	130—∞	200—∞	275—765

∞ = infinity

The shutter

Early cameras had no shutters as we know them today. Films were so slow and exposures so long that the photographer simply removed the lens cap, then replaced it at the end of the exposure time. But, as film emulsions became more sensitive, a device was needed to control the length of time the light was allowed to fall on the film. Today's shutter can give accurate exposures as short as 1/1000 of a second.

The range of shutter speeds on a camera are similar to the aperture's f numbers in that each speed either doubles or halves the one next to it. A range, which is calibrated in fractions of a second, will usually read: 1/1000, 1/500, 1/250, 1/125, 1/60, 1/30, 1/15, 1/8 1/4, 1/2, 1, and B. B stands for Brief time and is used for longer, manually timed exposures, because the shutter stays open as long as the release is pressed open. This makes it possible to take night-time photographs and interiors without using additional lighting. All modern cameras, apart from large format types, have a dual-purpose film advance lever, tensioning the shutter at the same time as the film is wound on. This saves time between exposures and prevents the possibility of accidental multiple exposures.

Shutter types

Basically, there are two main types of shutter: those that work inside or just behind the lens, known as between lens shutters, including sector shutters; and focal plane shutters, which are positioned close to the film.

Between lens shutters

The between lens shutter closely resembles the aperture and is positioned between the lens elements, near the aperture blades. It is made up of two or more overlapping metal blades, which spring open for the time of the exposure and then close again. These shutters are very light and compact, and can synchronize with flash at all speeds. But between lens shutters have two drawbacks: few work at speeds of over 1/500, and they are costly to produce for cameras with interchangeable lenses. This is because each lens requires its own integral shutter and a separate means to block light from the film when the lens is removed.

Between lens shutters are used mainly on rangefinder 35mm cameras and roll film cameras.

Sector shutters

The sector shutter is used on many cameras with small diameter lenses, such as the pocket 110 and simple viewfinder cameras. It is mounted just behind the lens, and consists of a spring-loaded metal plate which prevents light reaching the film until the shutter release is pressed. There is usually a choice of two speeds, indicated by weather symbols marked on the outside of the camera. The faster speed is used in bright, sunny conditions and the slower one on cloudy days. Some cameras also have a separate setting for flash attachments.

◄ The section through a 110 camera shows the sector shutter, coloured red, lying just behind the lens.

▼ A typical sector shutter. When the shutter release is pressed the plate springs back momentarily to let the light reach the film.

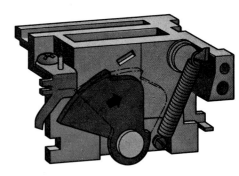

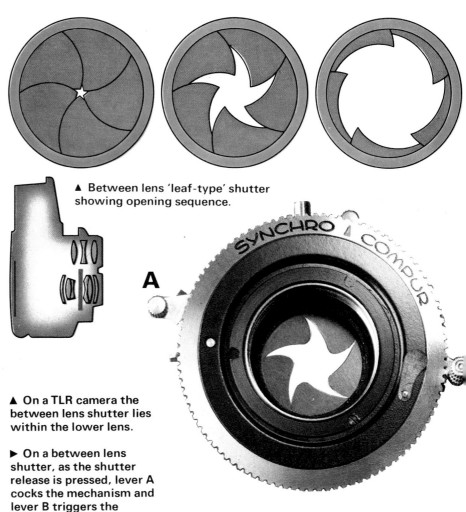

▲ Between lens 'leaf-type' shutter showing opening sequence.

▲ On a TLR camera the between lens shutter lies within the lower lens.

► On a between lens shutter, as the shutter release is pressed, lever A cocks the mechanism and lever B triggers the exposure.

Focal plane shutters

Focal plane shutters are made up of two blinds positioned just in front of the film, with an adjustable gap between them, which follow each other across the film plane. High speeds (up to 1/2000) are obtained by altering the size of the gap between the blinds, and lower speeds (down to 30 seconds) by holding back the second blind after the first has travelled across.

The majority of focal plane shutters are made from rubberized cloth and move horizontally across the film, but they will only permit flash synchronization on speeds up to 1/60. A growing minority use metal bladed shutters which travel vertically, and can synchronize with flash at speeds to 1/125, because of the shorter distance the shutter has to cover in a 35mm camera. As a focal plane shutter is mounted inside the camera body, close to the film, it protects the film from light when the lens is changed. Extra lenses do not need their own built-in shutter.

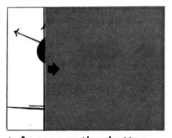

▲ As soon as the shutter release is pressed the first blind starts to move across. Light can reach the first section of film and begin the exposure.

▲ The gap between the blinds passes across the film. The width of the gap depends on the shutter speed, so the second blind may now start to cross.

▲ The second blind continues its passage across the film, completing the exposure on the first part of the frame. The leading blind has almost finished its crossing.

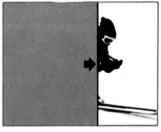

▲ The trailing blind completes the exposure, making sure that the entire frame receives an equal amount of light. When it has crossed, light is again blocked.

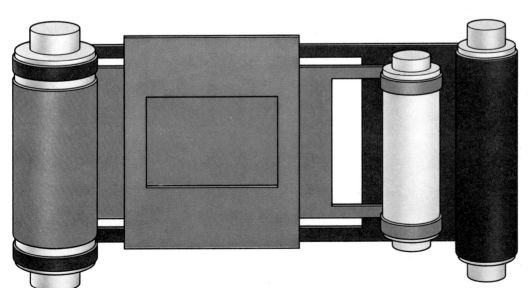

◄ As the film is wound on for the next exposure the shutter blinds are tensioned and light is blocked from the film.

▼ The focal plane shutter is mounted immediately in front of the film.

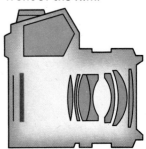

Stopping movement

The shutter can also be used to express movement in different ways. A fast shutter speed will stop or freeze movement and a slow one will register a blurred image of a moving subject.

The very short exposure time of a high shutter speed can freeze movement and give a sharp image of a moving subject. The speed needed to stop this movement depends on three things: the speed of the moving subject, the distance between the camera and the subject, and the angle at which it is travelling towards the camera.

The closer the subject is, the higher the shutter speed must be. But a great deal depends on the direction of the movement—something travelling towards the camera photographs more sharply at a lower speed than something moving across the camera's field of view. As a rough guide, in normal conditions objects moving towards the camera photograph sharply at 1/125; at an oblique angle of, say, 45°, at 1/250; and if they are travelling parallel to the camera, at 1/500.

Expressing movement

But the photographer will not always want to 'stop' the movement of the subject. A racing car, a running child or someone on a bicycle all involve movement—and the camera can be used to express this.

You can convey the feeling of movement by using a slow shutter speed. However, take care to avoid blurring the whole picture, which can happen with too slow a shutter speed, and resulting camera shake. The background needs to stay sharp to keep the feeling of movement. A trial-and-error guide is to estimate the shutter speed necessary to stop the subject completely and then use the speed one setting slower.

▼ In the pictures below and right the shutter speed on the camera has been increased from 1/15 to 1/60 and 1/250. At 1/15 the motorbike travelling towards the camera is slightly blurred, but as it crosses in front of the camera it is almost unrecognizable.
At 1/60 the lower picture is sharp but the bike travelling across is quite blurred.

At 1/250 the much faster speed just stops the motion of the cyclist. It would have been even sharper if a speed of 1/500 had been used.
Picture A, also taken at 1/60, shows the motor-cyclist travelling at an oblique angle to the camera.
Compare the blur in this picture with the two taken at 1/60 to see how blur increases as the angle of the subject changes.

A

SPEEDS TO STOP MOVEMENT			
Camera to subject distances	Movement towards	Movement at 45°	Movement across
slow subjects: 5 metres under 5 mph: 10 metres 20 metres	1/60 1/30 1/15	1/125 1/60 1/30	1/250 1/125 1/60
faster subjects: 10 metres 20 metres 30 metres	1/250 1/125 1/60	1/500 1/250 1/125	1/1000 1/500 1/250

▼ Using a slow shutter speed is often an extremely effective way to express movement in a subject. Enough of the picture must be sharp to tell a story, but the photographer has caught the gay mood of the two Indian girls on a swing by emphasizing the flow of their movement.

Selecting the shutter speed

The speeds most often used by photographers are 1/125 and 1/250, but 1/60 and lower can be used if you avoid camera shake. If the camera moves, even slightly, while the shutter is being released the edges of an otherwise sharp picture will be blurred. Longer focal length lenses accentuate any camera movement so, if you can hold the camera still at 1/60 with a 50mm lens, you should increase this to 1/125 for a 105mm lens. On a 28mm wide angle lens the shutter speed can be as slow as 1/30 without loss of sharpness.

Panning the camera

One of the ways often used to express movement is to pan the camera. This has the effect of keeping the moving subject sharp while blurring the background, giving subject detail plus a strong feeling of speed and motion. To do this the camera follows the path of the subject, keeping pace with its movement. It takes practice and a steady hand.

Stand with your feet apart facing the spot where you intend to take the picture. Without moving your feet, centre the subject in the viewfinder and, as it moves towards you, follow its movement smoothly swinging from the hips. When the subject is directly in front of you, press the shutter but continue to follow through the movement to avoid any possibility of jerking

1 f2·8 1/500

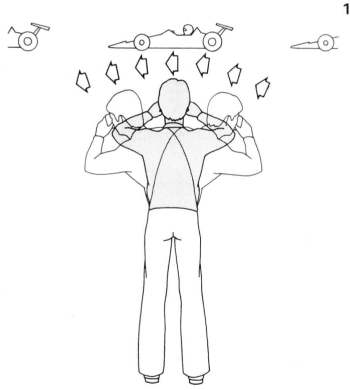

EXAMPLES OF EXPOSURE SPEEDS

The larger the f number the greater the depth of field but the slower the shutter speed for given exposure.

Limited depth of field					Large depth of field	
f2	f2.8	f4	f5.6	f8	f11	f16
1/1000	1/500	1/250	1/125	1/60	1/30	1/15
Movement stopped					Movement recorded blurred	

the camera. Try using 1/60 or even 1/30—once the technique is mastered you can use very slow shutter speeds to increase the degree of background blur.

Obviously, you can achieve varying degrees of sharpness and blur by using a range of shutter speeds and these techniques. These combinations can, for instance, blur the feet and arms of a sprinter but register the agony of exhaustion on his face.

Shutter and aperture

Both shutter and aperture control the amount of light reaching the film, but their effects are quite different. The size of the aperture controls the depth of field—how much of the picture will be sharp—while the shutter speed dictates how sharp a moving subject will be. Correct exposure is a combination of shutter speed and aperture setting, but the photographer can select any combination of these settings that adds up to the correct amount of light. For example, if the correct exposure for the photograph of the child is 1/125 at f5·6, the negative will be correctly exposed at either 1/500 at f2·8, or 1/15 at f16. But both these combinations have certain limitations. The photographer nearly always has to choose between a fast shutter speed to stop a certain movement or a small aperture to give a sharp result from 5m to infinity.

Both combinations can give the correct exposure but produce different pictures. Sometimes it is possible to achieve both a small f stop and high shutter speed in very bright conditions.

▼ These pictures illustrate the shutter/aperture combination.

1 A high shutter speed freezes the girl skipping, but the wide aperture needed for a correct exposure shortens depth of field, putting the trees out of focus.

2 A medium speed cannot stop the faster movement of the girl's hands and feet although her body is sharp. The medium aperture gives greater depth of field, with the background in focus.

3 A slow shutter speed blurs the subject entirely, but the complementary small aperture extends depth of field beyond the evergreen tree in the distance.

f5·6 1/125

3 f16 1/15

Getting the exposure right

Choosing the best exposure for a picture is just as important as getting the image sharp. A beautiful holiday picture on the beach is spoiled if you cannot see details of the people in the photographs—they may be too light or dark.

A correctly exposed negative or slide will have a full range of tones from deep shadows to bright highlights. Under-expose your photograph and the darker parts of the picture will contain little detail; over-expose, and the bright parts will appear all washed out and lacking in detail.

Guessing the exposure (based on the film manufacturer's guide sheet in every film pack) may be successful on a reasonably bright day when there are no deep shadows or patches of very strong sunlight. But the more extreme the lighting conditions become, the more difficult it is to guess accurately.

Types of meter

An exposure meter measures the brightness of the subject and, based on the speed of the film you are using, gives you a guide to the f number and shutter speed to use. Most 35mm cameras, especially SLRs, and even some 110 cameras, now have built-in exposure meters. Some work automatically and set the camera's controls for you, but with others you have to adjust either the shutter speed or the aperture manually. Hand-held exposure meters are still used too, mainly for special situations like low light or night photography, and for incident light readings (see overleaf).

Both hand-held and built-in exposure meters contain a photo-electric cell which measures the amount of light falling on it. There are three types of cell.

Selenium cell: too large for most built-in meters, a selenium cell powers itself. It needs no batteries. Any light which reaches the cell generates a small electric current which is measured by a galvanometer needle along a scale. Used mainly in hand-held meters, this type doesn't respond well in very low light.

The CdS cell: the development of a tiny, sensitive cell using cadmium sulphide made built-in meters possible for the vast majority of 35mm cameras. It can give readings even in moonlight, but takes a little time to settle down if you move quickly from bright sunshine to dark shade.

Silicon cell: the newest meters use a miniature silicon cell. This is very accurate and adjusts quickly to changing light conditions. It can cope with any contrast, from the brightest sun to night-time. Miniaturization has made this cell so small that, even with an amplifier and batteries, it can be fitted into a 110 camera.

Through the lens metering

The majority of SLR cameras have built-in meters which measure the light entering the lens. The meter often has the same angle of view as the lens on the camera so measures light over a wider area for a wide angle lens, and over a narrower area for a telephoto. Some TTL meters take an average reading from the total amount of light entering the lens, not differentiating between bright areas of sky and the darker land. Others, which are more accurate, also measure the light as a central spot (perhaps one-fifth of the total picture area). The best alternative is probably to use a third system— centre-weighted. This gives preference to the light reading at the centre of the picture using one cell, but co-ordinates with a second cell which takes the rest of the frame area into account.

Exposure information collected by the metering system is usually displayed in the viewfinder in one of two ways: either by a needle which moves between two markers or by LEDs (small bright lights) which are colour coded for correct over- or under-exposure. These lights are less easily affected by rough handling than the older, needle systems, but use up battery power much faster.

Automatic metering

An increasing number of SLR and viewfinder cameras with meters are semi or fully automatic. The latter select the correct exposure combination without the photographer's help. But there are two types of semi-automatic cameras; those which select a shutter speed to match the f number chosen by the photographer (aperture priority) and those which select the right aperture to suit a manually set shutter speed (shutter priority).

Aperture priority suits still subjects, landscapes and pictures in which depth of field is important.

HAND-HELD METERS
The Russian Leningrad 4 is a simple and inexpensive selenium cell meter. It is robust and, like the distinctive Weston Euro Master, needs no batteries. The Weston, widely used by amateurs, is unique in that its cell is at the back and not at the top of the meter. The more sophisticated Metrastar and Lunasix meters use a CdS cell which can operate in very low light. They both require batteries and the Metrastar has a viewfinder window just under the scale. The silicon cell Calculight is extremely sensitive. It has no moving parts and has a digital readout. All have domes for incident light readings.

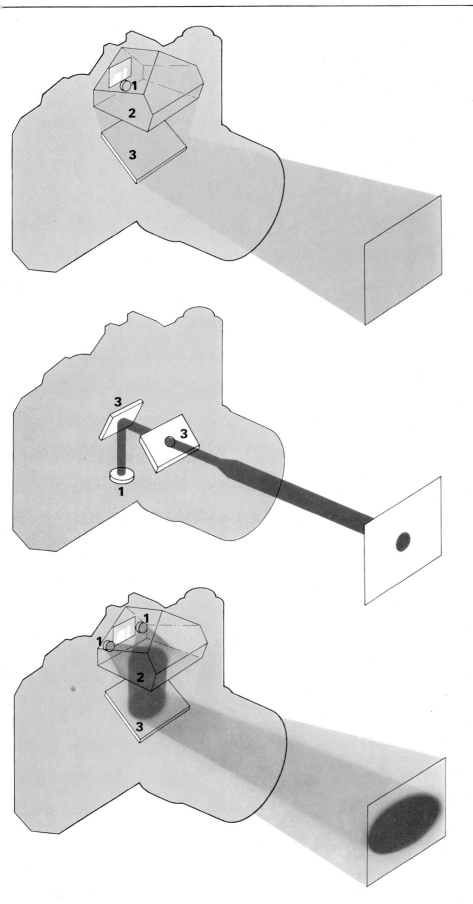

Average reading: two photo-electric cells receive light from the lens via the pentaprism, and average it across its entire area. The result can be misleading unless the subject is fairly evenly lit, but a simple solution is to take the reading close by the subject.

Spot reading: this type of meter is very precise, but harder to use. Only light at the centre of the lens is measured so, for overall views, choose a mid-tone as representative and line it up in the centre of the lens. Alternatively, take several readings and average them.

Centre-weighted reading: this is probably the easiest type of TTL meter to use. The meter takes the whole area viewed by the lens into account but gives more importance to the central area. Be careful if your main point of interest is not, in fact, at the centre of the picture.

Shutter priority has the advantage when photographing moving subjects, because you choose the shutter speed. Stopping movement is more important than depth of field.

A few of the more expensive cameras, like the Canon A-1, have a choice of priorities, including fully automatic exposure control which requires no manual setting of aperture or shutter speed. You can move from one to the other or take full manual control at the flick of a lever.

Integral exposure meters

Some viewfinder cameras also have integral exposure meters. These do not meter through the lens, but use a cell mounted either next to the viewfinder window or surrounding the lens (Olympus Trip 35). They are usually coupled to the aperture/shutter mechanism in the same way as SLR cameras, although most are fully automatic. With other models, you simply align a needle or see a light that indicates the correct exposure.

Taking a reading

You can measure the light either from the camera position or from close to the subject. The reading can be taken in two ways: using the light reflected from the subject or the incident light falling on the subject. Incident light readings can only be taken using a hand-held meter.

A reflected light reading, taken by both built-in and hand-held meters, measures the light bouncing off the subject. It can be measured either from

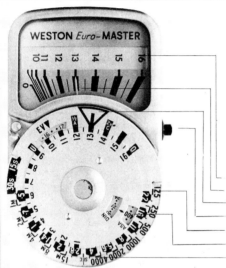

USING A HAND-HELD METER
Hand-held meters usually have two scales, with different numeric values, one for high-intensity, the other for low-intensity light. The photographer transfers the value recorded on the scale to the calculator dial by hand: this sets a full range of aperture/ shutter speed combinations.

LIGHT READING SCALE
GALVONOMETER NEEDLE
CALCULATOR
NEEDLE RELEASE SWITCH
SHUTTER SPEED SCALE
FILM SPEED SETTING
APERTURE SETTING

▲ To take a reflected light reading point the meter's cell at the subject. Do not cover the cell with your hand. It can be taken at either subject or camera position.

1 It is important to set the speed (ASA) of the film in your camera on the meter before taking a reading.

2 Point the cell on the meter where you wish to take a reading, releasing the needle release switch with your thumb.

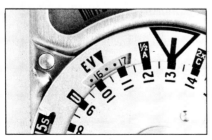

3 Find the value of the reading on the dial and move the aperture setting scale until the pointer lines up with the right number.

4 Several exposure combinations of shutter speed and aperture are now lined up on the dial. Choose one appropriate to your subject.

▲ To take an incident light reading from the subject cover the cell on the meter with its dome and point the cell towards the camera.

the camera position, where you will actually take the photograph, or close to the subject. Taking the reading from the camera position will give an overall impression of the available light, including the background. But, if one part of the picture is more important than the rest, walk up to it and take the reading, or measure the light on a substitute. For example, a hand held close to the meter will represent skin tones in a portrait if similarly lit.

An incident light reading measures the intensity of the light falling on the subject. You need a hand-held meter with a translucent dome or Invercone covering the cell in order to do this. The reading is taken close to the subject with the meter and incident light dome pointing towards the camera. It is a more accurate way to measure the exposure for a subject with a broad range of tones and ensures properly exposed highlights. To use an exposure meter in this way takes a little longer and so works best with a static subject, but the result is a correct exposure in a difficult situation.

TTL meters are quicker to use than a hand-held meter. Simply line up the needle in the viewfinder between its over- and under-exposure markers by altering the aperture or shutter speed. Several combinations of aperture and shutter speed will make the needle line up, or the correct LED shine, and it is up to you to choose the best combination. Avoid shutter speeds less than 1/60 unless using a support.

Estimating the exposure outdoors without a meter is not impossible. The following suggestions will give reasonably accurate results, provided you choose uncomplicated situations with fairly even lighting.

• Match the shutter speed as closely as possible to the speed (ASA) of the film in the camera.

• Presuming that the sun is more or less behind the camera, the correct f number will be:

Bright summer sunlight	f16
Hazy sunlight	f11
Bright, cloudy days	f8
Overcast sky or shade	f5·6

• To avoid over-exposure of a subject which is fairly light in tone and lit by strong, direct sunlight, use f22.

These combinations will be accurate to within half an f stop. But, provided you keep the total exposure constant, there is no reason why you should not change a setting of 1/125 at f16 to one of 1/250 at f11 for a moving subject.

▲ These two pictures represent situations where a general overall reading will give good results. The lighting is fairly even, the small area of deep shadow under the bridge and the highlight on the parapet are both too small to affect the exposure. In the lower picture the area of bright yellow flowers equals the area of dark stalks.

The exposure guide in the film pack and our suggestions for estimating exposure should give similar results with or without a meter.

▼ Bracketing exposures: to be sure of a correct result take two more (identical) pictures using one click stop or shutter speed setting over or under the original setting.

Solving exposure problems

There are certain lighting situations where exposure calculation can be difficult. The lighting may not be constant across the picture area, leaving a crucial part of the subject in deep shadow, or the light may be so dim that a built-in meter cannot give a reading.

Silhouettes: you may want to create the effect of a silhouette outlined against a bright background. This is best done by photographing the subject in front of a bright sky, or even a bright lamp. If you take the light reading from the bright area the subject will be under-exposed and stand out as just a dark shadow. Obviously the brighter the background the stronger the silhouette will be, so you could even photograph against the sun. But watch out for flare, or 'sun spots' on the lens which might spoil the picture. Positioning the subject directly in front of the sun, and blocking it out, will avoid the problem.

High contrast: a scene containing both very bright and very dark elements is difficult to measure accurately. A reading from one part of the picture will not be right for the rest of it. The solution is to take two readings, one from the brightest point and one from the darkest. Average the two for an exposure which will give a full range of tones and the most realistic result.

▶ Above: expose for highlight. Point the meter, either TTL or hand-held, so that the reading is taken from the sky. The brighter the area of sky you use, the darker will be the silhouette. *John Bulmer*

▶ A close-up reading of the bright railings is needed here. A general reading would over-emphasize the shadow area. Detail is good on the caps of the railings and the foliage. *Michael Busselle*

Large background area: photographing a person or a small object set against a very bright or a dark background can be difficult. The exposure meter will take its reading over the total picture area and give a result which may not suit the more important, smaller subject.

For a back-lit subject a large expanse of bright sky behind will influence the meter to under-expose a darker subject in front of it. A large, dark background, like the wall of a house, will suggest an exposure too long for a lighter object in front of it.

To find the correct exposure for the main subject, take a reflected light reading from close to the subject or use a substitute of the same colour and texture. The meter may suggest one or two stops more exposure than for the whole area. If you have a large expanse of sky in a landscape, try tilting the meter down a few degrees to get a reading from the land for a better balanced exposure.

Dimly lit or night exposures: a TTL meter cannot cope as well in very dim light as a quality hand-held meter like the Lunasix. If the conditions seem too dark for the meter in your camera to measure, try taking a substitute reading from a piece of white card held close to the lens. Use the result from the card

to estimate the exposure for your photograph. To do this, either open up the aperture $2\frac{1}{2}$ stops more than the reading indicated by the card, or multiply the length of the exposure by 6. Either compensation should give a reasonable result. In addition, when photographing at night it is always

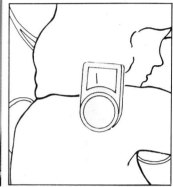

◀ By taking a reading close to the lit side of the girl's face and shoulder the photographer keeps a full range of tones around the edge of the figure, but lets the remainder of the figure and the room interior appear in semi-silhouette. *John Garrett*

sensible to bracket your exposures—photograph the subject several times using different exposures.

▼ At night the meter may not give a reading. Take a reading in a lit doorway, double it, and then bracket exposures. *Tomas Sennett*

Exposure metering systems

Most modern cameras have a light meter built in. This has proved to be very popular among amateurs and professionals alike because of the speed and convenience it offers.

All exposure meters work towards the same end—to give the photographer exposure information—but the ways in which they operate vary widely. There are two basic types however: coupled and uncoupled. Examples of both systems are found in 35mm reflex and non–reflex as well as in smaller and larger format cameras.

Uncoupled meters

Although the light meter is built in to the camera it is not directly linked with the aperture and shutter speed controls. The Zenith EM and Zenith E are two examples of uncoupled meter cameras. Such meter cells are usually of selenium which does not require battery power but takes up a lot of space. The cell responds to light which makes a meter needle move in direct proportion to the amount of light falling on to the cell.

The film speed must first be set before a valid reading can be taken. This moves the settings on the exposure calculator dial for aperture and shutter speed in relation to each other and to the film speed. The meter needle moves along the calculator dial to give a light reading. You can then read off the combination of shutter speed and aperture which will provide a correct exposure, and set the camera controls accordingly.

Because the cell is built in to the external casing of the uncoupled meter cameras the light readings can be unreliable. The cell does not measure the light entering the lens, and can therefore be influenced by a light or dark area near to the subject but not

1 **Zenith TTL:** stop–down TTL meter, CdS cell, manual exposures.
2 **Pentax MX:** full aperture TTL meter, GaAsP cell, manual exposures.
3 **Zenith E:** external uncoupled Se meter, manual exposures.
4 **Ricoh 500GX:** coupled CdS meter, automatic and manual exposures.
5 **Rollei 35 LED:** coupled silicon meter, manual exposures.

6 **Olympus Trip:** coupled external Se meter, automatic exposures.
7 **Rollei 35S:** coupled CdS meter, external scale, manual exposures.
8 **Olympus XA:** coupled CdS meter, automatic exposures only.

▼ The CdS cell in the Vivitar 35EM is close to the lens. A shaped slot moves over the cell as the lens aperture is changed to adjust light reaching the cell corresponding to aperture size.

▼ The cell in the Ricoh 500GX is covered by a wheel with varying size holes, connected to the film speed dial. A fast film provides a large hole, a slow film speed a small hole.

▼ The external meter scale on Zenith E (left) is not coupled to the camera controls. Rollei 35S (right) has an external meter scale too, but it is coupled to the camera settings.

included in the frame. If a filter or different focal length lens is fitted to the camera the meter cannot take this into account. Care must also be taken not to cover the meter cell with a stray finger because this would influence the meter into drastically over–exposing.

Coupled meters

These are far more popular than uncoupled meters because their direct link with aperture, shutter speed and film speed settings makes them more convenient to use. You do not have to waste time reading a set of figures on a calculator dial and transposing them to the camera controls.

Exposure information is generally given directly through the viewfinder, allowing the photographer to make exposure adjustments without taking his eye away from the camera. The other major advantage of a coupled system is that it is quick to use. This is important when light on the subject is rapidly changing—when clouds suddenly obscure the sun, for example.

Non-reflex cameras: some 35mm compact cameras have a single light-sensitive cell built into the camera lens housing. In many cases adjusting the film speed dial changes the diameter of a hole over the cell. This obviously adjusts the amount of light falling on to the cell which in turn provides specific exposure information for different film speeds and lighting conditions.

Although the cell is very close to the lens it can sometimes be influenced by the subject's surroundings. It is also possible accidentally to obscure the cell window with a finger which would influence readings. When filters are fitted however, they also cover the meter cell and automatic exposure compensation (for a neutral density filter, for example) is provided.

SLR cameras: because the light–sensitive cell is built into the camera body the cell must be small—selenium is therefore unsuitable and most cameras use cadmium sulphide or silicon metering cells.

The camera may have one, two or perhaps more meter cells which can be located behind the lens or close to the focusing screen. Therefore when different focal length lenses are fitted, the cell(s) can respond instantly to the resulting variation in angles of view to give accurate exposure information. This is called through the lens (TTL) metering and is by far the most popular system. The meter reading is taken only from the area actually imaged by

the lens, so that dark or light surroundings outside your picture have no influence on readings, unlike external meter cells.

A few sophisticated automatic cameras have a dual metering system, one to provide guidance to the photographer in the form of a viewfinder exposure display, while the other system takes a reading of light reflected from the film plane during exposure. The Olympus OM2n is an example where CdS cells provide viewfinder information while silicon cells control the exposure when the camera is set to automatic.

Stop down metering: many cheaper TTL metering cameras determine exposures at the working aperture. The lens must be stopped down until the viewfinder display indicates that the correct settings have been made. Quite logically, this darkens the viewfinder

image according to the aperture selected. Although it also acts as a depth of field preview it can make accurate focusing difficult. The best alternative is to focus the image first and then take a light reading. This is a fairly slow system and may mean that the subject takes flight before you are ready to take the photograph.

Full aperture metering: with this system the viewfinder image remains bright during focusing and exposure determination whatever aperture you may select to provide a correct exposure. A special linking mechanism on the back of the lens relays information to the meter to show what aperture has been selected. If a depth of field preview feature is important to you and you prefer full aperture metering, choose a model with a depth of field preview to gain the best of both worlds.

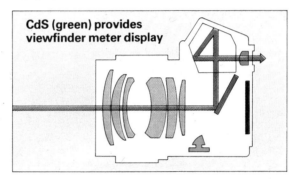

CdS (green) provides viewfinder meter display

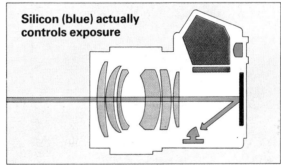

Silicon (blue) actually controls exposure

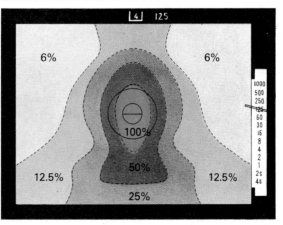

◀ Many TTL metering auto cameras have a light sensitive cell in the pentaprism housing which reads the amount of light entering through the lens. The meter provides an exposure display in the viewfinder which exactly corresponds to the shutter speed and aperture chosen for exposure.

◀ The Olympus OM2n, when in the automatic mode, is unusual in that the light is measured at the film plane during exposure. CdS cells in the pentaprism give a viewfinder display, while silicon cells in the mirror chamber control the exposure. When sufficient light has reached the film the shutter is closed.

◀ Like many SLR cameras the Leica R3 has a bottom centre–weighted meter to emphasize light from central and lower subject areas. The red areas show the sensitivity pattern and percentage reading from three CdS cells. Spot readings can also be taken by moving a switch on the camera. The entire light reading is taken from the central area, shown in blue. Few other cameras can do this.

Meter displays

Although there are several variations on a theme, viewfinder meter displays consist of one of two types: moving (or pointer) needle and light emitting diode (LED). It is impossible to say that one system is superior to the other—everyone has his own preference.

Moving needle types can sometimes be influenced by gravity if the camera is held on either side (or upside down), and can be damaged by rough hand-ling. They may also be difficult to see in low light levels, or when a large part of the subject is dark in tone.

LED displays have rapidly gained popularity with the advance of solid-state electronics enabling smaller, lighter and cheaper construction. They have no moving parts, and should in theory be more robust than moving needles. The light display can be single or multi-coloured, and is easy to see when the surrounding light is dim.

Using the exposure to your own ad-vantage is merely a matter of inter-preting the exposure reading to suit the subject and the effect you want to produce. Don't be afraid to over- or under-expose deliberately if you want to emphasize a particular part of the subject or create a particular mood.

To over-expose deliberately you can choose to use a slower shutter speed or larger aperture than those. which in-dicate a 'correct' exposure, or perhaps

---

SLR moving needle and LED meter displays.

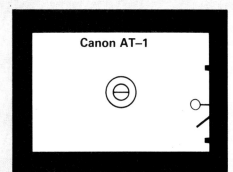

Canon AT-1

▲ The simplest type of moving needle display involves adjustment of aperture and/or shutter speed until the needle intersects the circle. This gives a 'correct' exposure. No other exposure information is provided, making it difficult to keep track of what aperture and shutter speed combination you are using without taking your eye away from the viewfinder.

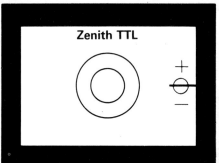

Zenith TTL

▲ Though no shutter speed or aperture information is shown in the viewfinder, you can quickly see whether under (–) or over (+) exposure would result from the settings you have made on the camera. This makes it easier to deliberately give a little more or a little less exposure for a difficult subject, although you cannot determine the degree of exposure compensation.

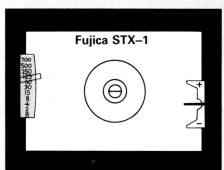

Fujica STX-1

▲ Correct exposure results when the meter needle is centred in the notch by adjustment of the camera exposure controls. Over- and under-exposure zones are shown, as well as a shutter speed scale. This provides far more exposure information with the eye at the viewfinder so that you can change the shutter speed to suit the subject without risk of 'losing' it.

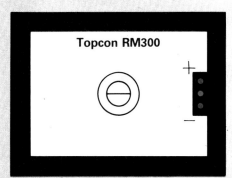

Topcon RM300

▲ The simplest type of LED (light emitting diode) display is often a green light which glows when the correct camera settings have been made for the level of light reflected from the subject. A red LED close to the plus sign indicates that over-exposure would result, whereas the red LED near the minus sign warns of under-exposure. No other exposure information is given, making it hard to interpret if, for example, you wanted to give one stop over-exposure.

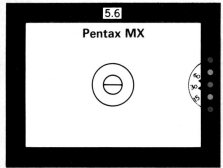

Pentax MX

▲ With a three-colour LED system exposure adjustments are simpler than with single colour lights. The green light indicates a correct exposure. Red and orange lights above indicate one stop and half a stop over-exposure respectively. The two lower lights show the same respective amounts of under-exposure. With this system it is easy to make exposure adjustments, and you can see how much compens-ation you are making without taking your eye from the viewfinder.

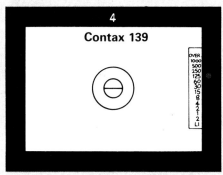

Contax 139

▲ Many SLRs have one red LED for each shutter speed setting. Combined with a flash symbol, long time exposure and a B setting and over- and under-exposure warning lights, the aperture display gives full exposure details. One LED glows opposite the set shutter speed, another shows the correct speed for the selected aperture. (One or other often flashes.) The two lights must be reduced to one constant glow by adjusting aperture or shutter speed.

a combination of the two. Stopping down to a smaller aperture or using a faster shutter speed gives under–exposure. For example, if you decide that you want to give one stop less exposure than the meter readout indicates to create a moody sombre atmosphere or to give more highlight detail you can do one of two things. If the lens is set on f8, say, you should adjust the aperture to f11. If, however, you wish to keep the depth of field

provided by f8 then you should halve the selected shutter speed—for example, if 1/125 second is selected use 1/250 for one stop under–exposure.

Reverse this procedure for deliberate over–exposure. In both cases the degree of over– or under–exposure is entirely at your command.

Some cameras have full exposure information in the viewfinder so that one glance shows aperture and shutter speed already set. A needle or light indicates the correct settings for a 'normal' lighting situation to give an average exposure for mid–grey tones. On other cameras only a 'correct' exposure signal may be provided and it is then up to the photographer to remove his eye from the viewfinder in order to adjust shutter speed or aperture ac-

cording to the effect he wants.

Many 35mm non–reflex cameras have fully automatic exposure control (programmed) over which the photographer has little, if any, control. Often the only exposure information provided is a warning light for under– and over–exposure. Others, however, with a degree of exposure control inform the photographer of the aperture or shutter speed (or both) which will be automatically selected.

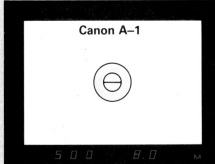

▲ The green pointer indicates the shutter speed you have already set; the moving black needle points to the speed required for a correct exposure. Adjusting the aperture makes the black needle move, while adjusting shutter speed moves the green pointer. When the two coincide exposures are correct. The selected aperture is also shown to give complete information at a glance.

▲ Digital LED viewfinder displays are a recent introduction. The figures on the right indicate the aperture which should be selected for the set shutter speed (on the left). The two sets of figures change as the shutter speed is adjusted. The lens aperture should be made to correspond to that shown in the viewfinder. The alternative is to change the shutter speed until the aperture read–out corresponds to that preset on the lens. 'M' shows that the automatic camera is set to manual.

Types of exposure meter cell

Selenium (Se): this type is too large to fit inside a camera. The Weston is a typical example of a hand–held selenium meter, and the Olympus trip has the cell outside the camera body. Selenium is reliable, and has the advantage of needing no battery power. It does not respond well in extremely low light levels.

Cadmium sulphide (CdS): this cell is found in the Lunasix and in many TTL metering cameras. It responds well in low light. Its major disadvantage is that it retains (or memorises) a light reading for several seconds so that there is a time lag in response when switching rapidly from bright light to shadow. The cell is also over–sensitive to red light which can cause under–exposure of red subjects.

Silicon: these small cells are commonly fitted with a blue filter (then called silicon blue—SBC) because silicon is also sensitive to red light. The cells respond rapidly to changing light and have no memory but they can be unreliable in temperature extremes.

Gallium arsenide phosphide (Ga AsP): this is a compact fast–reacting photo cell. It provides reliable readings in red and blue light, responds well in low light levels, and is not over–sensitive to extreme temperatures. Like silicon the cell responds about 1000 times faster than CdS. It is a recent discovery and only a small number of cameras currently use these cells.

35mm compact meter displays

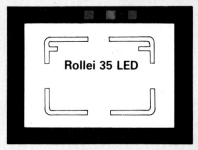

▲ Over– and under–exposure zones and a battery check mark are shown in red. An aperture reading and manual symbol are also provided.

▲ A green LED confirms a correct manual exposure. If the left red LED shows, under–exposure results. The right LED warns of over–exposure.

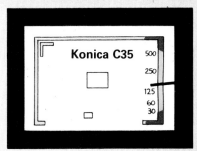

▲ Automatic aperture and shutter speed settings are shown, with under– and over–exposure zones and a flash ready light.

How to solve exposure problems

Exposure meters indicate light intensity and are designed to help you get a correct exposure every time you take a photograph. When a light reading is taken the meter indicates the correct adjustments needed to the camera aperture and shutter speed settings. This sounds simple, as indeed it is, but not all subjects can be treated in a straightforward way. How would you tackle a backlit subject, a snow scene or subjects in deep shadow, for example? In such situations your exposure meter can well mislead you into giving the wrong exposure. 'Correct' exposures are a matter of interpreting meter readings and applying them to the subject in hand.

Hand–held or TTL?

Many photographers use a hand-held light meter because of its accuracy and adaptability. Hand-held meters can also be used to measure incident light (light falling on a subject). A diffuser is clipped over the meter cell and a reading taken from close to the subject pointing at the light source (see page 44). This is particularly suitable when the highlights are the most important tones in which to show detail.

For convenience, however, most people prefer to take reflected readings (light reflected from the subject) which can be taken by pointing a hand–held meter from the camera position, or measuring through the camera lens if the meter is built–in.

Hand-held meters are a little more difficult to use for reflected light. Most have a fixed acceptance angle which cannot take into account whether you have a wide angle or telephoto lens on your camera, both of which have different angles of view as demonstrated earlier in the chapter. Accuracy also depends on the user aiming the meter correctly at the area to be measured. The choice between hand–held and TTL meters is almost always decided by the fact that most modern SLR cameras have built–in meters. Through the lens metering means that you have one less item of equipment to carry, and it is quick and easy to take many of your readings at the position from which you will take the photograph. They automatically take in a wide or narrow angle of view depending on the lens fitted to the camera.

TTL meters can only be used for reflected light readings, however. You also need to know how much of the area shown on the focusing screen your particular TTL meter is designed to

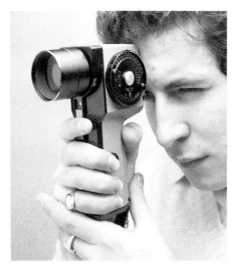

◄ A spot meter is used to take precise exposure readings from a tiny area of the subject. The acceptance angle may be only 1°. The item is fairly expensive.

▼ Most exposure meters give average readings and indicate the exposure needed to reproduce the subject as a middle tone. In a light, bright subject (top) you should give more exposure than that shown to maintain white as white rather than mid–grey. Interpretation of the meter reading is equally important with dark subjects (below). When you want to retain a shadowy, sombre atmosphere give less exposure than that indicated by the meter.

◄ BACKLIGHTING: near silhouettes can be reproduced by taking a general reading from the camera position (far left). This allows a bright background, strong light source, or flare to influence the meter. To show detail in the backlit subject (left) you should allow up to two stops more exposure than the meter shows, depending on the effect you want. The background is then over–exposed but the subject is isolated from a pale backdrop.

▲ SUN: an intense light source, such as the sun in the middle of a centre–weighted meter viewfinder area, results in under–exposure of the rest of the picture, rendering the skyline as a silhouette. If this is the effect you want, follow the meter recommendations.

◄ To show detail in darker parts of the scene over–expose by one or two stops. Alternatively you might move the camera so that the sun is at the frame edge while taking a meter reading. Reposition the camera and expose the frame at those settings.

◀ MONOCHROME: here monochrome does not apply to black and white, but to the true sense of the word—single colour. Soft, even light falling on to a single tone can produce drab and uninteresting photographs unless you increase colour saturation by under–exposing (up to one stop). Remember that with red subjects CdS cells may automatically under–expose, such as with this red door and latch. In such cases no further exposure adjustment will be necessary.

▶ SKIN TONES: dark skins reflect less light than pale complexions. For full detail the exposure given should be ½ to 1½ stops more than the meter indicates. But it is probably more reliable to take a selective reading from close to the subject's face. If the skin tone is identical to your own, take a reading from the back of your own hand. Only use this type of substitute reading if it is lit in precisely the same way as the subject. You can use this system for other subjects too.

▶ FILTERS: when using colour or neutral density filters, more exposure is needed to compensate for the reduction in light reaching the film. The increase in exposure depends on the filter. With deep colours it is best to take a reading through the lens with no filter attached, then adjust exposure according to the figure engraved on the filter (a x4 filter requires two stops more exposure). Pale filters permit TTL readings.

measure. Of course there is no reason why you should not have both types of meter, using one or the other depending on the particular problem.

Meter weighting

The area of the scene measured by a TTL meter depends on the positioning of the meter cell(s). A few measure a small 'spot' area of the composition; some integrate the light over the entire area of the viewfinder and give an average reading; the great majority in SLR cameras are centre–weighted.

A typical example of centre–weighting is where 60% of the reading is taken from the central zone of the viewfinder screen and the remaining 40% from the lower portion of the screen. This is known as bottom centre–weighting, and may give two very different exposure readings when the camera is held first horizontally and then vertically. If you rotate the camera vertically through 180° you may also notice two very different readings. Try this out with your camera so that if necessary you can compensate for the exposure readings given when you take vertical pictures.

▼ SHADOW DETAIL: if a subject is mainly dark, or large parts of it are in shadow, shaded details can only be shown by exposing for the dark areas. Take a reading from close to the darkest area, and give just enough exposure to hold important detail, at the same time ensuring that light areas are not grossly over–exposed. As a rule of thumb take a shadow reading and give one stop more exposure.

▶ HIGHLIGHTS: there is no point in taking a general reading if you want the highlights alone to dominate. This would only provide full detail in the middle tones of the subject. Take the meter reading from the lightest subject areas and expose at the indicated settings. If you cannot get sufficiently close to take a selective reading, then under–expose by about two full stops over a general reading.

Average readings

All meters are calibrated to give correct exposure for the amount of light reflected from a middle tone of the subject. (To be more exact this corresponds to a neutral grey card which reflects 18% of the light falling on to it—and this is considered to be an average tone.)

You will realize where problems arise from this averaging of light to a mid–grey tone when you apply the principle to specific situations. If a scene is predominantly dark the meter computes this to record it as a mid–grey tone by indicating that more exposure is required. To reproduce those dark areas correctly as dark a lot less exposure is actually needed. Conversely, if you are photographing snow the meter responds to the white surface by indicating that little exposure is necessary in order to reproduce the snow as a mid–grey tone. To produce white snow as white on film the exposure must be increased, probably by about two full stops. Learn how to interpret your exposure readings.

Spot readings

Spot or selective readings can be taken with an averaging meter used very close to the separate tonal areas in which you want to show detail. Simply get close to the subject and take a light reading from the important tone or tones only. A separate or TTL spot meter allows you to take selective readings farther away from the subject. A spot meter has a narrow angle of acceptance (perhaps only 1° of the whole scene). A separate spot meter has a viewfinder to allow general framing of the subject and the selective reading area is usually outlined. Because of its selectivity a spot meter can be extremely accurate, but you must understand what you are doing—carelessly aimed at the wrong part of your subject it can give totally wrong exposures.

Brightness range readings

When a meter reading is taken from a subject containing contrasting tones (brilliant white and the darkest black), an average reading will more often than not give incorrect exposure to the most important part of the photograph. It is also possible that the contrast range may be outside the latitude of the film you are using.

Take a selective reading from the darkest and lightest parts of the subject in which you wish to show detail. With many black and white films shadow and highlight areas within seven stops of each other will record accurately. For example, if the highlight reading indicates 1/60 at f22 and the shadow reading 1/60 at f2·8, select an exposure about half–way between (1/60 at f8) for the best possible compromise.

Colour films have far less latitude and particularly with colour slide film you should take a reading from the brightest part of the subject and bias your exposure towards that tone, letting the rest of the tones take care of themselves. Often, too, one tone is of key importance—such as the skin tone of a face, so step in close to the face to take a meter reading. If this is impossible take a reading from the back of your hand—as long as it is lit in the same way as the subject.

▲ HIGH CONTRAST: brightly lit subjects with large dark or light areas and few intermediate tones often have a brightness range too great for colour slide film. Decide which end of the range you can sacrifice, or choose less contrasty lighting. If other areas need more than two stops either way with slide film, detail is lost in highlights if you expose for dark areas (left) and in the shadows if you expose for the light areas (right).

▶ AVERAGE OF TWO READINGS: to show detail throughout the entire contrast range (the difference in light and dark tones) you must compromise. Take a reading from important light and dark areas of the subject, and expose mid–way between the two readings. Most black and white films accommodate about seven stops difference between highlights and shadows, while colour slides can cope, at most, with only two or three stops because of the film's limited latitude.

Making the most of your camera

Cable release socket

Film plane index

Flash X sync socket (with cover)

Infra-red index

Memory lock button

Apart from the shutter release, film winder, focusing and exposure controls, even the simplest cameras have a few additional knobs and switches that are either safety devices or provide an extra degree of control. Used correctly they may not only make picture taking more reliable but can also increase the versatility of the camera.

Here's how to use the extras most commonly found on modern cameras, and in some cases what you can do if your own camera lacks them.

Depth of field preview

Many cameras have a fully automatic aperture diaphragm which allows the user to focus and take exposure readings at the lens's widest aperture setting. When the shutter is released the aperture automatically stops down to whatever has been set on the aperture ring.

A depth of field preview button or lever closes down the lens to the taking aperture without disturbing the settings you have previously made. This is usually only found on a single lens reflex camera and allows you to study the range of sharp focus through the viewfinder before making an exposure. The facility does have limitations however, because using it causes the viewfinder to appear much darker, and at very small apertures (f22 for example) it may be difficult to see the image.

When photographing a face, most

▲ Once you have focused the subject a pair of figures for the aperture in use show the range of sharp focus in the composition—this is depth of field.

EV compensation dial

Depth of field scale

Depth of field preview

Self timer switch

Battery check lamp

Shutter lock

There is a wide variety of camera controls and you should be familiar with their use if you want to make the most of your camera.

people focus on the eyes. At fairly close distances the ears and tip of the nose may be out of focus. Using a depth of field preview allows you to check if this is happening and lets you know if you should select a smaller aperture to increase the depth of field. Conversely, you may wish to separate the main subject from a confusing or distracting background by using a wide aperture. It is possible that, although you have selected a fairly wide aperture to complement a particular shutter speed, there may still be sufficient background sharpness to spoil the picture and detract from the three-dimensional effect. Check this with the depth of field preview, and open up a stop or so if necessary.

Manual and pre-set diaphragm lenses allow you to close the aperture manually and watch the way more of the subject becomes progressively sharper as the aperture becomes smaller. Fully automatic diaphragm lenses fitted to cameras with no depth of field preview are not quite so simple to use if you specifically want to determine the exact range of sharp focus.

Nearly all lenses for SLR cameras have a scale of figures additional to aperture and distance scales: these figures run in pairs either side of a central reference mark. This is a depth of field scale which shows the photographer the range of distances in sharp focus.

Once the lens has been focused and the aperture set, look at the two figures on the focusing distance scale which line up with the pair of marks for your set aperture. These are the nearest and farthest subject distances which will be in sharp focus. For example, with a 50mm lens on a 35mm camera set at f16 and focused at 2 metres, the depth of field extends from 1·5 to 3 metres. Most photographers gain a fairly accurate idea of the depth of field range for particular apertures and focusing distances by experience. However, even the most knowledgeable will need to check depth of field on occasion, particularly in close-up work when the range of sharp focus may be only millimetres.

Using a wide aperture limits depth of field, while a small aperture extends it.

Infra-red index

When taking black and white infra-red photographs special focusing adjustments must be made because infra-red rays do not behave in the same way as visible light. The point of focus for infra-red radiations is further from the back of the lens than it is for white light, and a small degree of focusing compensation is necessary to produce sharp infra-red photographs. In fact the lens must be adjusted as if the subject were slightly closer.

Most lenses have a red mark, the infra-red focusing index, next to the focusing scale. The lens should be focused on the main part of the subject as normal. Note the distance on the focusing scale and move the focusing ring so that this distance lies opposite the red mark.

Zoom lenses are often provided with several indices for infra-red, each annotated with the focal length to which it applies.

If no infra-red index is provided you can still make your own focusing adjustments. Focus on the subject and then give a small twist to the focusing ring as if the subject were a few centimetres closer to the camera.

By stopping down to f11 or f16 sufficient depth of field will be provided to overcome problems at all but closest focusing distances. These adjustments are not necessary with colour infra-red film.

Infra-red indices on zoom lens

Infra-red index on fixed focal length lens

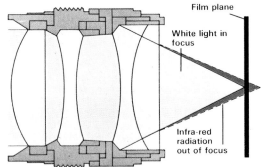

▲ Most lenses show infra-red focusing correction with a red mark. Zoom lenses have several.

◄ Infra-red rays focus farther from the back of a lens than visible light.

► Small focusing changes or small apertures give sharp infra-red pictures in black and white.

Mirror lock

The rear elements of some extreme wide angle lenses extend a long way into the body of the camera, and with a reflex camera may be struck by the mirror when it flips up during exposure. You could only use this type of lens fitted to a camera with a device for locking the mirror up and out of the way. With the mirror locked up through-the-lens viewing is obviously impossible, and an accessory viewfinder fitted to the hot shoe is a reasonable compromise.

The mirror lock is also useful when you want to reduce noise and vibration to the minimum. If you lock the mirror after composing and focusing, the mirror remains motionless during exposure. The mirror lock can be used when a motor drive is fitted to the camera to obtain the maximum number of frames per second of which the motor drive is capable. The fraction of a second taken up when the mirror rises and falls can make as much as one frame per second difference, which may cause you to miss an unrepeatable shot.

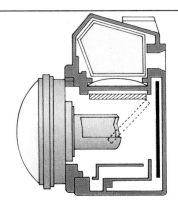

◄ With a reflex mirror locked up a motor drive can operate at maximum speed. Some wide angle lenses cannot be fitted unless the mirror is locked out of the way.

▼ Left: a mirror in its normal position; (right) locked up obscuring the viewfinder.

Shutter lock

A shutter lock obviously prevents the camera from being fired accidentally and wasting frames. But the shutter lock often also switches off the batteries and thus conserves them.

The mechancial locking types can also be used to obtain really long exposures rather than using a cable release. The shutter speed dial is set to 'B', the shutter released and held down, the lock set, and released when exposure time is completed.

If you don't have a shutter lock on your camera, make sure that you leave the shutter untensioned when the camera is put away—even if only overnight. Then if something knocks against the release, a frame cannot be wasted and in most cases the battery drain caused by continued pressure on the release button is avoided.

▶ A mechanical shutter lock rotates into the lock position. Making a habit of locking the shutter when the camera is in transit can prevent battery drain and wasted frames.

Film plane index

This is usually found on a camera top plate. The index shows the exact location of the film within the camera and thus enables accurate measurements and calculations to be made. It is most useful for close-up work when you may want to measure bellows extension or extension tubes to help you work out magnification and exposure. Close-ups are difficult to focus with a non-reflex camera because the focus cannot be checked through the viewfinder. Instead the distance from the subject to the film must be measured accurately. Some cameras which do not have a film plane index have a serial number engraved on the top plate. The top of the figures often corresponds to the location of the film plane inside the camera.

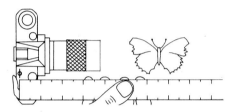

▲ Using the film plane index as a reference mark can help you make exact exposure and magnification calculations.

► All film plane indices closely resemble the one on the Chinon CE-4.

Battery check

With so many modern cameras depending on electronics, battery power is vital. It is a good idea to test batteries from time to time, especially since silver oxide and manganese alkaline types last for so long and then suddenly give up. Use the battery check button before each main picture session, but do not be tempted to overdo the testing or you may drain the batteries prematurely.

If you don't have a checking facility, most manufacturers recommend that camera batteries are replaced after a year of *normal* use. If you are in doubt about battery condition, replace them. Never store equipment for more than about one month with batteries inserted—they may leak and corrode the inside of the equipment.

► Many modern SLR cameras have a visible battery check device (some also have an audible check signal). If the battery power is sufficient to give accurate exposure information the red lamp glows when the button is pressed.

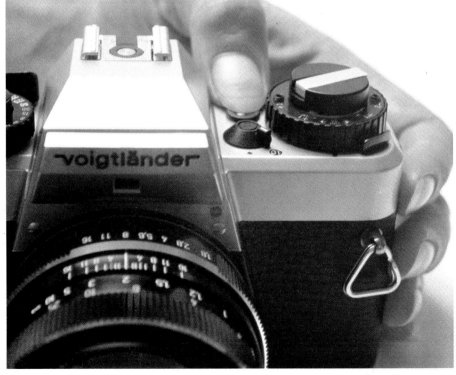

Rearsight features

Many viewfinder rearsights are fitted with grooves or a screw-in collar to accept accessories such as a right-angle finder. They also accept eyepiece correction lenses which help the spectacle wearer.

Spectacles can be a nuisance and prevent the photographer from getting his eye close to the finder and therefore from seeing the entire screen from corner to corner, including exposure information. The back of the viewfinder can also scratch spectacle lenses. Fitting a dioptric correction attachment to the rearsight, which exactly matches your spectacle prescription, is a possible solution. They are available from some camera manufacturers to suit a range of long- and short-sighted vision, but can also be made by an optician if special correction is necessary. Some SLR cameras have a limited range of correction built in to the rearsight.

Many automatic metering cameras have a small shutter which can be moved over the inside of the viewfinder eyepiece by operating a lever. The shutter prevents light from entering

through the eyepiece and affecting the exposures. This is more likely to happen when the camera is mounted on a tripod or being used on delayed action when the photographer's eye is not there to shade the eyepiece. The meter cell inside the camera responds to this extra light and it may result in under-exposure. If your camera doesn't have an internal eyepiece blind you can probably buy an external cover which clips into the viewfinder rearsight grooves (if provided). An alternative is to make your own blind from opaque card or tape.

Spectacle wearers can overcome the problem of light entering the eyepiece because of the distance between eye and viewfinder being greater than for non-spectacle wearers by buying a rubber eye-cup. The cup screws or clips on to the rearsight, and although it won't eliminate light entering from behind the camera, it will reduce it and in addition makes use much more comfortable.

▶ A grooved or threaded viewfinder rearsight can accept a number of useful accessories. A rubber eye-cup on the Voigtländer VSL3 – E makes viewing comfortable for the spectacle wearer.

▼ Familiarize yourself with how to check and change the batteries. They must be fresh and correctly inserted if the camera is to function properly.

Film memo holder

A simple way of reminding yourself what type of film is loaded in your camera is to slip the end of the film carton into a special size frame which is provided on the back of many cameras. Forgetful people without film memo holders could quite easily tape the carton end to the back of the camera or slip it into the ever-ready case. Some cameras have an adjustable dial which you can set to remind you whether you have loaded black and white or colour film, and whether it is balanced for daylight or tungsten light.

▲ The Rollei 35S has a film memo dial which can be adjusted for colour or black and white negative film, and daylight or tungsten colour slides.

◀ Film memo holders are usually just the right size to take a 35mm film carton end, and often have a film speed table.

There are many different exposure controls which may be included on your camera apart from shutter speed and aperture selectors. Here you are shown exactly how to use them.

Exposure memory

Even the most accurate through the lens exposure meter can be fooled by a subject surrounded by large dark or light areas, subjects which are predominantly back lit, or those against unusual backgrounds. These can influence the meter, providing false information about the light level. Thus the main subject is over-exposed if the meter reacts to a large expanse of black background and, conversely, under-exposure of the subject results if it is back lit or surrounded by a large bright area.

Some cameras have a built-in exposure memory which ensures that the subject is given the appropriate exposure to show detail regardless of the surroundings. To use the memory facility effectively take a meter reading close up to the subject, or even from a substitute object of the same tone as the main part of your photograph, and lit in the same way.

Often the exposure reading is taken by gentle half-way pressure on the camera shutter release button—this activates the méter circuits. Holding the button in the same position while moving away to photograph the entire subject keeps the camera set to whatever aperture and shutter speed have been pre-selected during close-to light metering. The exposure is made without releasing this gentle pressure on the shutter release.

The disadvantages of this method are that if you 'let go' the memory is over-ridden and you are back to square one. Care must also be taken neither to release the pressure sufficiently for the camera meter to take its reading from new information, nor to squeeze a little too hard, trip the shutter and waste a frame. This type of exposure memory or exposure hold is most commonly found on 35mm non-reflex cameras.

Some sophisticated cameras have a special memory button which is less precarious to use. The memory button may be the type which is held in once the light reading has been made; or some electronic cameras retain the exposure memory for several seconds after once pressing the memory button. In the latter case a viewfinder light signals that the memory is in operation.

▲ ▶ Several automatic cameras have a special shutter release or perhaps a separate button which enables the user to hold a meter reading and prevent a change in lighting conditions from affecting the exposure settings.

▲ The camera's built-in meter has responded to the strong back light causing the child's face to become dark and lacking in detail.

▼ Detail is shown by taking a light reading from close to the child's face and holding in the exposure memory button, while repositioning the camera.

Exposure compensation

Many automatic SLR cameras have a means for overriding the meter's settings to compensate for 'difficult' lighting conditions with certain subjects. This is usually in the form of a dial providing two full f stops compensation over and under that set. The settings are often graduated in ⅓ or ½ stop steps and can either be marked −2, −1, +1, +2 or x¼, x½, x2, x4. In both cases the respective settings indicate two stops less exposure, one stop less, then one stop more and two stops more exposure than that set.

For back lit subjects, or subjects against a bright background the dial should be set to *plus* (that is *more*) compensation. This provides detail in the main part of the subject and the amount of compensation required depends on the amount of back light.

A dark background or large dark unimportant areas of the picture seem to occur less frequently, but *minus* compensation (by giving *less* exposure) gives full detail in the main or lighter parts of the subject.

Some cameras have back light compensation only, and this often provides fixed 1½ stops more (plus) exposure.

If your camera lacks the EV (exposure value) compensation dial you can

▶ EV compensation scales are usually only found on automatic SLR cameras. The Chinon CE-4 gives ±one stop and only the ⅓ stop steps are marked. The Contax 139 can provide ±two stops compensation

achieve the same degree of exposure control, and more, by adjusting the film speed dial. Move the film speed indicator to half the ASA of the film in use to increase exposure by one full stop. For example if you are using 100 ASA film, set the film speed dial to 50 ASA. This tells the camera that less sensitive film is being used so the built-in meter automatically compensates. Doubling the film speed setting decreases the exposure given by one full stop—if you are using 100 ASA set the dial to 200 ASA.

It is of course vital that the dial is returned to its correct setting when returning to 'normal' photography with lighting which needs no compensation. Some cameras have a signal in the viewfinder to show when dial-in compensation is in use, but there is no signal to remind you that you have adjusted the film speed dial. If you forget to readjust the compensation control or film speed dial subsequent frames will be over- or under-exposed.

▲ Also capable of ±two stops, the Minolta XG2 has its EV scale marked more simply. Minus under-exposes while plus over-exposes. x¼, x½, x1, x2 and x4 are equivalent to −2, −1, 0, +1 and +2 respectively.

▼ Select minus compensation when an important light area (the distant buildings) is surrounded by a large dark area. Here a straight exposure has lost that important detail.

▼ The minus EV setting has considerably darkened the foreground and provides much more detail in the lighter subject areas. It is used less often than 'plus EV'.

Multiple exposures

Most modern cameras make it impossible to make a double exposure unintentionally. But sometimes double or multiple exposures provide unusual and interesting results.

A few cameras have a switch or lever to allow the shutter to be retensioned without advancing the film to the next frame. This makes accurate register of the subject components possible and gives the most successful multiple exposures.

Some cameras with this facility also manage not to advance the frame counter. If your camera's frame counter advances every time the shutter is cocked, make sure to make a mental or written note that one or more of the frames is double or multiple exposed so that you don't take the film from the camera before you have used every frame. This means that the frame counter may indicate frame 38 on a 36 exposure film for example.

Pressing in the rewind release button while advancing the film wind-on lever may be possible with some 35mm cameras without a multiple exposure device. This cocks the shutter but as

◀ Many strange effects can result from a double exposure such as this ghostly apparition.

▶ Top: cameras with a multiple exposure switch facilitate a double or multi-exposure, especially if the frame counter is simultaneously cancelled. Remember to cancel the switch to return to normal photography.

▶ You don't need a special double exposure button. With most 35mm cameras you can hold in the rewind release button while operating the advance lever. If you are careful this cocks the shutter without moving the film, essential for accurate register of all subsequent exposures on that frame. (The frame counter usually moves, so keep track of the actual frame number.)

Delayed action

Delaying the tripping of the shutter for several seconds after pressing the shutter release has several advantages. The photographer can mount the camera on a tripod and take a self-portrait, or perhaps include himself in a group photograph. He might also set up a photograph (perhaps a candid shot) and walk away while the exposure is made. As well as helping with shy subjects this can be used to prevent the photographer's shadow from appearing in the picture.

Some cameras have a variable delay, usually between two and 10 seconds. Many cameras use a clockwork timer to regulate the countdown time, while others have a totally silent electronically controlled rundown, often monitored by a flashing red light on the front or top of the camera body.

On some cameras it is possible to cancel setting of the delay either before or during the countdown period, but on others, once the delay mechanism is set you are obliged to use it. Make sure you know what type of delay timer is fitted to your camera.

For cameras with no built-in timers a mechanical delayed action device can be purchased separately. It attaches to a cable release, or can be screwed into a cable release socket, and you can set the delay you want.

▶ Above: mechanical delayed action timers are still the most common type. Some can be set for a varied delay.
Below: electronic timers are gaining in popularity. Countdown is often silent and indicated by a red light.

the film take-up spool sprockets are thus disengaged the film does not move to the next frame. There is a risk that the film may move slightly which could alter the composition, or may even cause overlap with the next frame. Try the technique first with a test film. You will enjoy greater success if you operate the film advance lever slowly and gently.

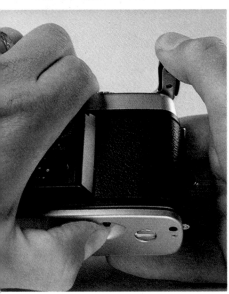

Cable release socket

The shutter release of many cameras is internally threaded to accept most makes of cable release and long air release. On a few cameras the cable release socket may be found elsewhere, such as on the side of the lens housing. The cable release can be used for timed exposures with the shutter speed dial set to 'B' (the long time setting which holds the shutter open all the while the shutter release is depressed). Some releases can be locked to hold the shutter open for long periods—several minutes or hours.

Many photographers use a cable release whenever the camera is mounted on a tripod. This reduces the risk of camera shake when using slow speeds.

It is also helpful to use a cable release for a complicated set-up. This means you don't have to find room to work your hand between camera and nearby lights to fire the shutter, and eliminates the danger of disturbing camera, lights or subject. You may also get better portraits if you remove your eye from the viewfinder after focusing and composing and fire the shutter with a cable release. This tends to put the subject more at ease.

▼ The location of a threaded socket can vary but, wherever it is, inserting a cable release is preferable for long exposures to prevent camera shake. It is often found within the shutter release button.

Flash synchronization

Most 35mm cameras have flash con-tacts built in to their accessory shoes on the top plate. They are called hot shoe contacts, and do away with the need for a separate cable to connect the flash gun with the camera shutter.

The metal pins should be kept clean to provide good contact for the flash gun —hot shoe covers are inexpensive items. Focal plane shutters must be set at the correct synchronization speed, usually around 1/60.

Most SLR cameras have a separate coaxial socket to accept a sync cable from an electronic flash gun. This allows more versatile flash lighting because the flash can be removed from the accessory shoe by using an extension sync cable. The coaxial socket is usually marked 'X'.

Sometimes it is possible to use two flashes—one mounted on the accessory shoe and one connected by sync cable—to fire simultaneously. Check this with the camera handbook first.

'FP' sockets are seen less frequently these days, but refer to older type flash guns and flash bulbs. X and FP sockets delay opening of the shutter until the flash has reached the peak of its light output.

Knowing how to use all the features provided on your camera helps you get the most from your equipment. If you are not sure what a particular dial or lever is intended for, this probably means that you have not read (or were not provided with) the handbook.

If you are not sure of something, spend some time going through the operation of the control with the handbook.

▲ Whether your camera has two separate flash sockets or a dual purpose one you must ensure that you use the correct one to synchronize with flash. Electronic flash units are the most common and sync with 'X' settings.

35mm non-reflex

35mm eye-level viewfinder cameras

These cameras, although larger than most 110 cameras, are still extremely compact, relatively simple and light enough to slip into a pocket. They need few accessories. The lens is permanently fixed to the camera. Some have built-in exposure meters and flash units, which eliminate the need to buy these extra items.

Many of these cameras have range-finders which are coupled to the lens focusing mechanism. This means that the lens can be focused accurately while looking through the viewfinder, saving time and avoiding mistakes through guessing distances. But decide which of these features you really need. A high quality lens on a well made camera may be a better solution than a host of extras and a poor quality lens. Here the photographer can choose how much of the process he wants to control and how much he wants the camera to do for him.

The biggest single advantage of these 35mm compact cameras is the variety and lower cost of the film they use. Also the format is large enough to make good enlargements.

1 selenium cell exposure meter
2 coupled range finder
3 viewfinder
4 film rewind
5 hot shoe for flash

6 exposure meter scale
7 shutter release
8 film wind on

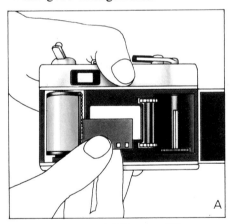

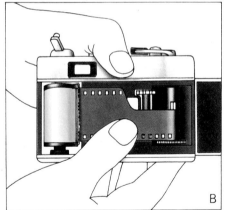

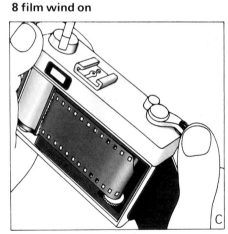

How to load 35mm film

Open the back of the camera, usually by releasing a catch on the side or by pulling up the rewind knob until the back clicks open.

With the rewind knob still pulled up, place the 35mm cassette into the free space on the left of the camera body so that the tail of the film lies across the back of the lens. Push the rewind knob down so the cassette is held firmly. (A) Pull the tail of the film gently out of the cassette and insert the free end into the slot in the take-up spool on the right of the camera. Make sure it is pushed as far as it will go into the slot

and the lower row of perforations on the film mesh with the sprockets is beside the empty spool. (B)

Using the film wind and shutter release, wind the film on until the upper row of perforations also mesh with the appropriate sprockets.(C) Close the back of the camera and wind on the film for two exposures, or until the frame counter on the camera reads 'one'. The film is now in position.

How to unload 35mm film

To unload the film first press the small rewind button, often mounted on the base of the camera (sometimes this is a small lever marked R on the camera

top, back or front). This engages the rewind mechanism. Keeping your finger on the button, turn the rewind knob in the direction marked by an arrow, usually counter-clockwise.

When the film is fully rewound into its cassette you will feel the pressure on the rewind knob cease.

Open the camera back and remove the cassette. Never do this in bright sunlight.

Note: If, while you are rewinding, the film appears to have jammed, take the camera into a darkroom (or to a camera shop) and unload it there. Do not open the camera in the light or the roll of film will be ruined.

Advantages of 35mm

35mm film has several advantages over the smaller sizes.

● The larger negative size of 24 x 36mm means that the image recorded on the film is bigger. This means it needs less enlarging than the 110 for a given size print, giving better detail.

● Apart from the factory processed Kodachrome colour slide film, all 35mm films can be home processed. The majority of enlargers are made for this size of film, or the larger 6cm square.

● There is a wider choice of film for 35mm cameras than for any other type, both in colour (for prints or slides) and black and white. The range is large, giving the photographer the opportunity to choose the best possible film for the subject.

● As important as the negative size of 35mm film is the loading system used by these cameras. The film is held in place by sprockets which fit perforations on the edge of the film and is held flat by a pressure plate in the camera back. This gives a sharper image than cartridge loading films, but it does take longer to load and unload the film.

Rangefinders

Rangefinders measure the distance between camera and subject and are fitted to many 35mm viewfinder cameras. The measuring scale is coupled to the lens so that merging two

▲ The rangefinder window in a camera is usually placed near the top of the body in line with the viewfinder.

▲ The selenium cell seems huge compared with the tiny silicon cell on the 110 camera.

images in the viewfinder automatically focuses the lens.

There is a bright spot in the centre of the viewfinder on this type of camera. As the focusing ring on the camera is turned the image at the bright spot will appear split in two unless the lens is correctly focused.

On 35mm cameras these rangefinders are generally accurate up to about 8m; after that the properties of the lens ensure that the picture will be in focus.

Exposure meters

A large number of 35mm viewfinder cameras have built-in exposure meters, some in addition to the rangefinder previously mentioned. These produce an accurate exposure either automatically or when the photographer lines up a needle in the viewfinder. Some of the latest models use coloured lights, called LEDs, to tell you when the exposure is correct.

There are various types of exposure meter, shown by the two examples opposite. The Olympus Trip 35mm has a selenium cell surrounding its lens; this is fairly large and can power itself, but it is not sensitive to low light conditions. The battery powered CdS and silicon blue exposure meters are smaller and much more sensitive.

The angle of view measured by the meter is usually between 15 and 30 degrees and gives an average reading across the centre of the composition in the viewfinder.

Points to better pictures

Keep the camera and lens clean with a soft brush. Make sure that there is no dust, dirt or pieces of metal in the camera body. These can scratch the film.

Red-eyed subjects are sometimes inevitable if the flash unit is built in too close to the lens. To minimize this effect ask your subject to look at a bright lamp for a few seconds—to reduce the size of the pupils—and then quickly take the photograph. Alternatively, photograph the subject from one side and not looking directly at the camera.

Try using the camera vertically instead of horizontally. The subject in your viewfinder may be one which is better composed upright, like a portrait.

Whenever possible move in closer to the subject with your camera. This makes for bolder compositions with less irrelevant background; but be careful with people, their faces can distort. Squeeze the shutter release gently rather than jabbing at it and jarring the camera which may spoil the sharpness of your picture.

One of the best ways to improve your photography is to go out and take photographs. Experiment with black and white photographs and ask the processor for contact prints. This saves money and you can have any pictures you really like enlarged at a later stage.

Find the closest distance at which your camera will focus sharply. It may be marked on the focusing scale and seen in the centre spot of the rangefinder, or you may have to get into the habit of guessing distance.

Look at the depth of field scale (if you have one) on the lens of the camera. This useful guide is sometimes hard to identify. It tells you how much of your picture will be in focus at any aperture setting. You may find that a higher f number on the dial will bring the background into focus.

Find the point on the depth of field scale at which everything will be sharp to infinity at a medium aperture like f5·6. Knowing and remembering this setting means that you can take a sharp picture of something unexpected when there is no time to focus accurately.

If your camera does not have a built-in exposure meter, read the manufacturer's guide which comes with every film package, and think about buying an exposure meter. Experience will help you accurately estimate exposures, but a light meter is more reliable for difficult lighting situations.

Interchangeable lens cameras

Interchangeable lenses

A camera which is reasonably compact, easy to operate, and can take a whole range of lenses opens up dozens of new possibilities for any photographer. Telephoto lenses for sports action pictures and better portraits, wide-angle lenses for depth in sweeping landscapes and pictures in cramped spaces, or close-ups of insects using a macro (close-focusing) lens. The penta-prism SLR camera can provide all these things. It is the most popular interchangeable lens camera, widely used by amateurs and professionals alike. There are others with inter-changeable lenses—for example med-ium format SLR cameras and some viewfinder cameras—and these are discussed in detail later on.

Special features of the SLR

The advantages of the SLR camera to the enthusiast are enormous. It is unrivalled for flexibility and can be used in nearly every photographic situation. If you can afford it, there is a lens, filter, or accessory to fit each occasion; but every SLR camera has certain basic features which make this flexible approach possible.

The range of lenses: when you buy a 35mm SLR camera it usually comes with a lens of about 50mm focal length. This photographs a view familiar to the

▼ The bayonet mount on this lens slots into the camera body, linking the two. The red spot on the lens lines up with another on the camera. The two are locked together by twisting the silver ring to the right.

human eye and is called a normal or standard lens. But on either side of the 50mm lens there is a large number of lenses extending to wide angle on the one hand, and telephoto on the other. First start with a 40–55mm standard lens and get used to the camera before deciding on your next lens. Your choice of an additional lens will depend on the sort of pictures you really like to take. Are they portraits, buildings or landscapes, close-up photographs of flowers and insects, or recording the excitement of sporting events? The answer will help you choose your next lens, but always buy the best quality you can afford.

The viewing system: the SLR has a unique viewing system. The image in the viewfinder is the same image seen by the lens. The viewfinder shows how much of the subject will be photo-graphed, whether the lens is focused correctly, and the effect of the chosen f number or a filter. In fact, you can preview the finished picture before pressing the shutter. A pentaprism (five-sided prism) mounted between the viewfinder and the focusing screen shows the image both right way up and right way round, whether the camera is held horizontally or vertically.

TTL metering: exposure metering in an SLR camera can share the advantages of seeing through the lens by taking the light reading through it as well. This feature is called through the lens or 'TTL' metering. Instead of using an external 'eye' the TTL meter reads from inside the camera system and thus works perfectly with all types of

lenses and attachments.

Exposure control: getting the correct exposure is a combination of f number (aperture size) and shutter speed for the amount of light available. To help the photographer most SLRs have a built-in exposure meter which measures the brightness of the light entering the lens. The right choice of shutter speed and f number will make a needle in the viewfinder line up with a marker (or a small light shine). The exposure is then correct.

A large number of SLRs have auto-matic exposure control which makes things even simpler for the photo-grapher. There are two kinds of automation: aperture priority and shutter priority. Both have their advantages and the one you choose depends on the sort of photographs you want to take.

Aperture priority tends to suit still subjects in which accurate control of depth of field is important, such as landscapes and portraits. It is up to the photographer to set the f number he wants, and the camera automatically sets the correct shutter speed.

Shutter priority gives the photographer control over the shutter speed—a better solution for capturing move-ment. Once the shutter speed is set the correct aperture is selected automatic-ally and shown in the viewfinder.

Some of the most expensive and sophis-ticated models have both shutter and aperture priority settings. You can switch from one setting to the other at the flick of a lever, getting the best of both worlds.

Even on cameras with automatic

▼ The picture below shows the aperture/shutter/auto priorities of the Canon A-1.

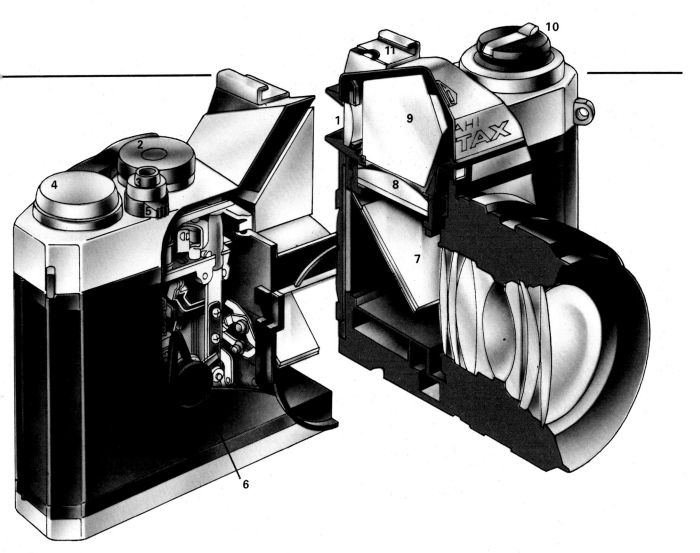

1 Viewfinder
2 Film speed (ASA) and shutter
   speed dial
3 Shutter release
4 Film wind
5 Shutter lock
6 Self timer
7 Reflex mirror
8 Focusing screen
9 Pentaprism
10 Film rewind
11 Hot shoe

exposure control there is usually some provision for manual override. Once they have some experience, many photographers feel that they like to have total control over the camera's choice of settings.

Many SLRs with built-in meters still have manual control of aperture and shutter. You set the shutter speed to suit your subject—1/125 for still subjects and up to 1/500 for something moving—then alter the aperture settings until the exposure meter needle (or signal light) in the viewfinder indicates the correct exposure. This works equally well if you set the shutter speed first.

Lens mounts

The lens-to-camera attachment is very important on SLR cameras. It must be easy to fit, light-tight, and link up smoothly with the camera's controls. There are two basic types of lens mount—screw thread and bayonet.

Screw thread mounts: found on the older or less expensive SLR models. Their great advantage is standardization. All screw thread lenses fit any make of 35mm camera body made for this type of lens mount.

Bayonet mounts: this mount is much quicker to use and is supplanting screw thread. Unfortunately, each manufacturer has a slightly different system, but most specialist lens makers can supply adapters to suit the different models and fit them for you.

Disadvantages

There are times when an SLR is not the best camera to have, but these tend to be specialized situations. The focal plane shutter and the movement of the mirror make the camera noisy. During exposure there is a momentary loss of the image in the viewfinder—a problem during long exposures. It has more moving parts and is, therefore, more susceptible to damage from rough handling than a viewfinder camera. The shutter cannot synchronize with flash at high speeds (useful when using flash in daylight).

An SLR outfit is more expensive to insure and does require you to take care of it, but most of the equipment can be traded in at a good price if you decide to change to a newer camera. And, with this system, you can often keep a favourite lens adapted for use with the new camera body.

Although heavier and bulkier to carry around, especially with more than one lens, than the 35mm rangefinder cameras, the SLR is still remarkably compact for its performance. All the accessories, as you collect them, can fit into a purpose-made gadget bag and can bring within the grasp of the average photographer a wide range of subjects previously considered to be confined to the specialist.

Before buying an SLR

- Do you want lenses which screw on to the camera body or which have bayonet mounts? Bayonet is faster, but screw thread lenses are generally cheaper.
- Do you want built-in, through the lens metering or a hand-held exposure meter? It is better to buy a camera with TTL metering and get a hand-held meter later on.
- Do you want to be able to change the focusing screen for a different type, or is the one seen in the viewfinder easy for you to focus sharply?
- Some cameras are heavier than others, some are now very much smaller. The larger, heavier models tend to be more robust, but the lighter, more compact ones are easier to carry with you. Try the camera and controls to make sure they are comfortable and in the right place for you.
- There are two types of focal plane shutter. The modern, electronic shutter works vertically and is often made of metal. It will synchronize with flash at 1/125. The older, rubberized cloth type, although quieter, works horizontally and can only be used with flash up to 1/60. If you are planning to use flash in daylight the vertical shutter is better.
- Is the image in the viewfinder bright enough and easy to focus, and is the exposure information displayed clearly?
- Are you going to want to add a motor-drive or autowind unit at a later stage? Maybe you would like to be able to use the camera with a bellows attachment for nature photography or in a laboratory.
- Does the camera have a depth of field preview button? This allows you to see the effect of the aperture before the shutter is released.

▼ This autowind, fitted to an SLR camera, has (from the right) a rewind switch—marked R, a dial to select single frame autowind (S) or continuous (C), and two dials which control the number of continuous exposures and frames per second.

▲ This photograph was taken in a zoo using a 200mm telephoto lens and a fast shutter speed to catch the movement of the polar bears romping.

◄ With a normal lens on an SLR camera you can focus close enough to make interesting pictures with tiny animals, flowers and insects, like this ladybird crawling along some privet berries.

The Leica M4-2 is a rangefinder camera with a full range of lenses. Leitz produced the first 35mm camera in 1925. Built with great precision, the camera was light and gave high quality results on the motion picture film then used. The design evolved to include a full range of lenses, coupled rangefinder, shutter speeds from 1 second to 1/1000, exposure meter and reflex housing for telephoto lenses. All lenses now feature a bayonet mounting system.

The advantage of this type of camera is that it is small, quiet, robust, and there is no loss of the image during exposure. Some people find it easier to focus in poor light.

The lenses you can buy range from 21mm to 135mm, focused through a coupled rangefinder. Framing marks in the viewfinder appear automatically as the lenses are changed, including automatic adjustment for parallax. Longer telephoto lenses focus through a reflex housing.

There are many earlier interchangeable lens viewfinder cameras still being used today, alongside similar models like the Contax or the Canon. The other cameras made of this type are Russian—the Kiev and FED44—and are available at low cost with lenses from 28mm–135mm.

▲ The Leica M4-2 above is a classic camera. It has been used over the years by some very famous photographers, among them Henri Cartier-Bresson.

▼ This stunning desert photograph is pin sharp from foreground to horizon. A wide angle lens emphasizes the tremendous depth and also the dramatic sweep of the dunes.

▼ The Pentax A110 could be the forerunner of a new type of camera. It has all the features of a fully automatic SLR and the advantage of being truly pocketable. You can buy the camera with its 24mm normal lens, or with the entire range of accessories. In addition to the filters, lenses and lens hoods shown there is an auto-winder and a close-up lens for the 24mm.

Building up an SLR outfit

The biggest attraction of a 35mm single lens reflex camera is its versatility. Not only is it a useful piece of equipment in its own right, but it can be the 'heart' of a complete camera outfit. You can add things like extra lenses, filters, a flashgun, a tripod, as and when you feel you need them, to help you get the results you want.

Smaller items—a blower brush for cleaning lenses, or a cable release, for example—also form part of the serious photographer's equipment as the collection builds up. And, of course, you will need a gadget bag, or a carrying case to keep everything in.

The right priorities

Don't be put off by the vast array of camera accessories on the market—you won't need them all. Obviously you need to sort out priorities and decide what to buy now and what to leave for later. This will mainly depend on:
• Your style of photography. Think about the items you really need to help with the type of photography you concentrate on, be it landscapes, portraits, still life or sport.
• Your budget. A cheaper item, such as a filter, can open up new fields, even if you can't yet afford to invest in more expensive extra lenses.

Inexpensive basics

First, think about the smaller items for the outfit. *A lens hood* (rubber or metal) not only protects the front of the lens from damage but helps to prevent 'flare' when shooting towards the sun. Camera shake can be a problem, so *a cable release* is useful whenever long exposure times require

◀ **An ideal basic outfit? This is the range of equipment many keen amateurs might hope to own after two years or so.**
1 **Gadget bag**
2 **Collapsible tripod**
3 **80–200 zoom lens with macro focusing**
4 **Electronic flashgun**
5 **Camera body with 50mm lens**
6 **Extension tubes**
7 **Second camera body with 24mm lens, motorwind, and cable release**
8 **Rubber lens hood**
9 **Flash extension lead**
10 **Selection of filters**
Additional items shown are films, batteries, a lens cap, and cleaning tissues. You might also carry a notebook and pencil, a puffer brush, and a small screwdriver set.

the camera to be mounted on to a tripod or support. Camera care equipment, such as *a blower brush, lens cleaning tissue* and even a small screwdriver set for on-the-spot repairs (a loose screw on the lens, for instance) all have a place in the outfit too.

Camera bags

You will need some sort of carrying bag for these first basic accessories. At first a medium-sized soft shoulder bag is enough to carry the camera, lens hood and filter, spare film, lens cleaning tissues and hand-held exposure meter—if your camera has no TTL metering. It is helpful if the bag has an outside pocket of some sort to keep the small items from getting damaged by the bulkier ones. Just make sure the various things are well wrapped in dusters to stop them banging about.

Some people keep their camera in its ever-ready case.

As you add more items to your outfit a special camera carrying case is more suitable. Most are made from reinforced real or simulated leather, and contain cut-outs or removable inserts to secure various pieces of equipment. Most have carrying handles as well as shoulder straps, so that the case can be carried easily while you are taking photographs.

There are various ways you can make sure your equipment is securely held in the case, and overleaf we show how a typical camera bag can be adapted to your precise needs.

Finally, and very much for the larger outfit, there is a range of more expensive aluminium attaché cases with foam rubber inside, which can be cut to hold the equipment firmly. These offer good protection, but they can be the most expensive. Avoid the cheaper ones made of foil-covered plywood which is lighter, but does not offer as much protection. Bear in mind that, because these aluminium cases are brightly finished, they tend to be conspicuous—and may possibly attract a thief.

Choosing filters

There are many different types of filter on the market, but the basic outfit need only contain four or five. Most photographers start off with a simple skylight 1A filter which cuts through ultra violet 'haze'. Unlike a normal UV filter, it is also colour corrected, so it can be used for black and white *or* colour film. The skylight filter can be kept on the camera all the time to stop dust and dirt spoiling the lens.

A polarizing filter will counteract reflections from glass or other similar surfaces, darken the sky, and make colours more vivid.

Various coloured filters—red, green, blue, yellow—can be used for effect in black and white work. In a landscape shot, for instance, a yellow filter will make the sky darker, an orange filter will exaggerate the effect, while a red filter darkens the sky still further. With colour film, these filters give an overall colour cast to the picture, which can be effective.

Colour correction filters are useful for either colour negative or transparency film. They enable you to take daylight pictures with tungsten (artificial light) film, and vice versa.

So a few filters will make a worthwhile yet reasonably inexpensive addition to your camera outfit. You might want one or two of the simpler special effects filters, as well. The starburst turns a single light source into a repeated star shape, and a soft focus filter can be used to soften portraits.

Lenses

The most important additions to the camera outfit are the extra lenses. If you have always used a standard lens on your camera, you may not find it easy to decide which would be the best lens to buy next. Obviously, you want to start with the one that will be the most versatile for your type of photography. As a first buy, most photographers choose a wide angle lens (28mm) or a telephoto lens (135mm). If you like taking scenic landscape pictures or you want to include a wide area without having to step back with the camera too much, then a wide-angle lens is a good choice. A 28mm lens is the most popular type of wide angle. Lenses of 24mm and wider give more image distortion and can give an interesting special effect but, with care, they can also be of general use. For portraits, sport and other general types of photography, buy a 135mm telephoto lens. Most of them are lightweight, easy to use and reasonably priced. Later, you can invest in a longer focal length lens (200mm or more) for distance shots.

On the other hand, many photographers now buy a zoom lens as an alternative which means that they get, in effect, three or more lenses in one compact unit: which also means there's less weight to carry about. Both wide

angle to normal (28–50mm) and short-telephoto to long-telephoto (80–210mm) zoom types are available, and some even offer a close-up, 'macro', setting. A zoom lens may well be cheaper than a set of three or four lenses of fixed focal length.

Some independent lens manufacturers make interchangeable mounts so that, if you decide to change your camera later on, you can keep your lenses and simply buy another mount.

Camera supports

A tripod, or a similar form of camera support, is essential for any long exposure shots. There are many tripods on the market, from table-top models to heavy-duty studio stands. Look for one which is sturdy but lightweight and portable (most are made of aluminium). Quick release legs and an adjustable pan and tilt head are useful features. Simpler and more portable camera supports include a monopod (a single leg tripod) or a G-clamp, which attaches to a table or similar surface and has a tripod screw to support the camera in any position.

Looking ahead

As your photography develops you may want to add items such as a flashgun for indoor photography or fill-in lighting outdoors, or perhaps a motor-drive for fast action photo-

graphy, if your camera will accept one. At a later stage, you could get an extra camera body, so that you can shoot black and white and colour at the same time, or use two different lenses without having to keep changing them. But remember to buy only the items that you will really need, otherwise you could end up with a gadget bag full of expensive hardware which you never use.

Hiring equipment

It is always worth discussing with your local photographic dealer the possibility of hiring certain items—either for very occasional use, or before you decide to buy. You may feel that the high cost of a long telephoto lens or a more powerful flash unit would not be justified by the number of times you would use it.

Insurance

Once you start accumulating valuable equipment, it is wise to consider insuring it all. Although there are separate policies for camera equipment, most companies advise amateurs to add their equipment on to an existing household contents policy. With an 'all risks' extension, the equipment should be covered for accidental loss or damage, even on location. But check with your insurance company, or a broker, for more details.

Equipment to buy for . . .			
Subject	**Lenses**	**Filters**	**Other items**
Landscapes	Any wide angle (24–35mm) Telephoto (100–200mm)	Skylight 1A Polarizing Coloured (red, yellow, green etc)	Tripod Cable release
Portraiture	Telephoto (85–105mm) Short tele-zoom (70–150mm or similar)	Skylight 1A Colour conversion (80A or 85B) Simple effects (starburst or soft focus)	Tripod Cable release Flashgun
Still life	Lens with macro facility (usually zoom or telephoto)	Skylight 1A Polarizing Colour conversion (80A or 85B)	Tripod Cable release Screw-on close-up lenses Flash gun
Sport	Telephoto (135mm or 200mm) Long zoom (70–210mm, 100–300mm or similar)	Skylight 1A Polarizing Coloured (red, green, yellow etc)	Shoulder or hand grip (with build-in cable release) Autowinder or Motordrive

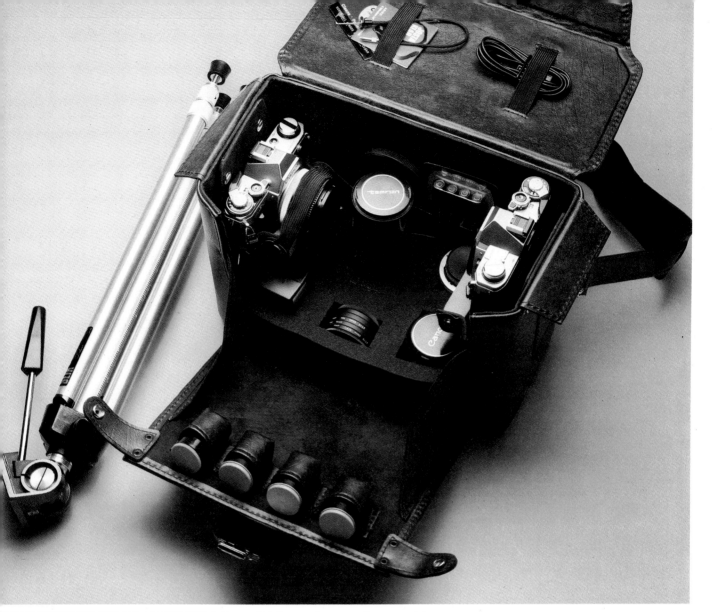

▲ All the equipment shown on the previous spread packs neatly into this Bush & Meissner gadget bag with room to spare for further additions. But lenses and other expensive items could be damaged by knocking into each other so it is worth making a foam base for the bag, tailored to fit each piece of equipment. Adapting a bag in this way is easy and cheap.

Buy a piece of plastic foam 7–8cm thick and trim it to fit tightly into the bottom of your bag; then follow the instructions set out on the right. Take care, when you plan the layout, that larger objects do not obstruct built-in pockets already in the bag. If you need to add an extra piece, stick the foam with any all-purpose household glue.

◄ Keep at least one camera body loaded with film and with a lens attached, so it is always ready to use. The extra front flap on this bag means you can get at all your equipment quickly.

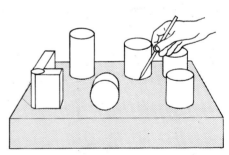

▲ Arrange equipment carefully on top of the foam base and trace round each item with a felt pen.

▲ With a craft knife, cut the foam round the lines marked and remove to leave storage spaces.

77

Automatic 35mm SLR cameras

One example is shown from each category of automatic 35mm SLR cameras.
1 Shutter priority, manual override
2 Multi—mode, six exposure modes
3 Aperture priority, manual override
4 Aperture priority, no manual facility

Incorrect exposure is the most common cause of spoiled pictures. Automatic exposure systems, however, offer the simplest, most convenient means of consistently getting the exposure right for most subjects and lighting conditions. More important, automation allows you to concentrate on the most important aspect of photography—the subject.

There are two basic types of automatic exposure control: shutter priority and aperture priority (sometimes called shutter— or aperture–preferred). In both cases the photographer sets one control and the camera computes the other. A few cameras have a fully automatic arrangement programmed to select both settings.

As with any separate or built–in light meter, the automatic exposure system must be pre–set with the ASA speed of the loaded film for accurate exposures. In other words, set the film speed dial correctly before you begin taking photographs.

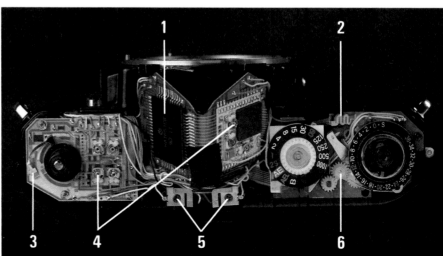

▲ An inside view of what makes automation possible—electronics. A complicated array of circuits and wires control the functions of the multi—mode Fujica AX–5. Don't be tempted to tamper—a costly repair may result.

1 Main control centre (micro chip)
2 Contacts for shutter release button
3 On/off and delayed action switches
4 Meter and shutter speed resistors
5 Hot shoe/dedicated flash contacts
6 Cogs for reverse frame counting

Shutter priority

The photographer chooses a shutter speed suitable for the subject and the effect required, and the automatic system selects and sets the correct aperture. The aperture settings are stepless (not limited to full or half stops) to give precise exposures even in rapidly changing light conditions.

Advantages: the user can choose a sufficiently fast shutter speed to arrest movement of a subject, or to avoid camera shake under poor lighting conditions. Intentional blur can also be produced to create the impression of movement by selecting a slow speed.

Disadvantages: you tend to get shallow depth of field in dim lighting; much greater depth of field results when the light is strong. If a particular aperture is required to control depth of field, the shutter speed dial must be adjusted until the viewfinder meter display shows the aperture you need. This delays picture taking.

Light metering, viewing and focusing can all be carried out with the lens at full aperture, but only lenses with the correct couplings can be used to ensure that the lens closes down to the automatically selected aperture for each exposure. Fixed aperture lenses such as mirror lenses therefore cannot be used on 'automatic'.

Applications: the system is ideal for the sports or wild–life photographer whose work depends to a great extent on using the correct shutter speed to freeze movement, and for photographers who want to introduce a controlled degree of blur.

Set for
shutter priority
automatic

▲ When stopping the action counts, a shutter priority camera comes into its own. You select a sufficiently fast shutter speed and the correct aperture is set automatically according to the lighting conditions.

▶ Shutter priority automatic use is only possible with the lens aperture ring set on 'AE'. Rotate the shutter speed dial to select the most suitable speed for the subject. Moving the ring off 'AE' switches to manual exposures.

Aperture priority

The photographer sets the aperture of his choice and the automatic exposure system sets the appropriate shutter speed for the lighting conditions and the film in use. The shutter speed scale in the viewfinder only gives an approximate indication of the speed selected because most automatic aperture cameras have stepless shutter speeds. This means that speeds are infinitely variable throughout the range instead of only those fixed settings marked on a dial.

Advantages: the system is ideal for immediate control over depth of field. Large apertures can be set to limit sharpness, making a subject stand out from an out of focus background. Small apertures can be set enabling most of the subject to be sharp in the photograph. If a lens has a fixed aperture (for example a mirror lens) an aperture

Set for aperture priority automatic

priority camera will still give automatic exposures by varying the shutter speed.
Disadvantages: you can get blur and camera shake in dim lighting, and frozen action pictures in bright conditions. When a particular speed is required, to avoid camera shake for example, you have to juggle with apertures until the appropriate shutter speed shows in the viewfinder. This takes time, and one advantage of automation—speed—is lost.

◄ With an aperture priority automatic camera select 'A' (for automatic) on the shutter speed dial. The correct shutter speed is automatically set to match the aperture you have selected. Move the dial off 'A' for a full range of manually selected exposures.

▼ Aperture priority cameras are ideal for controlling depth of field.

Applications: aperture priority cameras are by far the most common automatics, and they can be used for a wide variety of subjects. They are ideal for work involving accurate control of depth of field, for example close–ups using extension tubes when the lens is mounted some distance from the camera body, or even for microscope work when the camera lens isn't used at all.

Multi–mode cameras

Some cameras can be switched to either aperture priority or shutter priority, and may have additional exposure facilities. For example:

● automatic flash exposures
● automatic exposures with the lens stopped down
● fully programmed automatic exposures where the camera selects both aperture and shutter speed
● manual control of exposure

Advantages: obviously a multi–mode camera is extremely versatile. It has all the advantages of shutter and aperture priority cameras, but can be set to 'programmed' (P) to allow the photographer to concentrate totally on composition.

Disadvantages: multi–mode cameras are more expensive than their simpler counterparts, but their only real disadvantage is that, until you are familiar with all the controls and viewfinder

Set to programmed exposure

▶ With up to six choices of exposure mode (including manual) a multi–mode camera may at first seem complicated, but familiarity breeds confidence. Here 'P' (programmed) has been set.

▼ On 'P' the camera sets both shutter speed and aperture, so you need only compose and focus. In allowing quick operation 'P' is ideal for candid shots.

Automatic setting (no manual option)

▲ Automatic—only aperture priority cameras are easily identified by the lack of a shutter speed dial. When you have set an aperture the camera automatically sets the correct shutter speed. 'B' for timed exposures and a flash setting are also provided. In this case 'M90' is for flash, and also provides a mechanical emergency shutter speed in case the batteries fail.

◄ The 'dedicated' or 'integrated' flash gun is designed for maximum convenience with automatic cameras. When both the camera and flash are set to automatic, and the flash is fully charged, the correct shutter speed to synchronize with flash is set automatically. This ensures that you do not inadvertently set too fast a shutter speed, and spoil your flash shot.

displays, photography can be confusing.

Applications: these cameras are designed to cope with almost any photographic situation. A multi–mode camera can be used for most types of photography as well as becoming a 'family camera', mode selection depending on the ability or interest of the user.

Manual override

Many automatic cameras can also be used completely manually. Whether there is a moving needle or LED (light emitting diode) display in the viewfinder, on the manual setting you adjust the camera controls until a 'correct' exposure is indicated, just as with a manual exposure camera, giving you full control over exposures.

For manual exposures with a shutter priority camera you move the lens aperture ring off its automatic setting. With aperture priority cameras, you turn the shutter speed dial from the automatic position to set a selected speed. Both types of camera usually have a locking device to prevent this from happening accidentally.

Automatic override

No automatic system can cope with all lighting and subject conditions, or allow for the photographer's personal preferences. Most automatic cameras have some means of modifying the settings made by the exposure system, while retaining the automatic facility (in other words without having to switch to manual operation).

An exposure compensation scale often surrounds the film speed dial, and adjusting this gives a little more or a little less exposure by effectively changing the film speed setting. Setting '+1' or 'x2' (depending on how the scale is marked) gives one stop more than—or double—the metered exposure, while '–2' or 'x¼' provides two stops less than—or one quarter of—the metered exposure.

Automatic–only cameras

A number of aperture priority automatic cameras do not offer manual control. Some automatic exposure override is normally featured, although in some cases this is limited to a fixed 1½ stops increase in exposure for backlit subjects.

Although there is no conventional shutter speed dial, a control on the top plate is usually marked in the following way: 'A' for automatic exposures, 'B' for long exposures, 'X' or '60' for a flash synchronization speed. There is often an 'off' position, and sometimes settings for one or more mechanical shutter speeds.

Flash guns

Some manufacturers market special 'dedicated' or 'integrated' flash units specifically for use with their range of automatic cameras. The flash is mounted on the camera hot shoe and the camera and flash are first set to 'auto'. When the flash is fully charged the camera is automatically set to the correct flash synchronization speed. All you have to do is to choose a suitable aperture.

Most automatic cameras accept a large number of electronic flash guns, but some of them lack an X socket. An extension sync cable cannot be used, and unless prepared to buy a hot shoe adaptor with extension cable, the photographer is therefore limited to hot shoe mounted flash photography.

Battery power

Automatic, electronic cameras rely on battery power not only for metering but also to control the shutter. So if no mechanical speeds are provided you cannot use the camera at all without batteries. Although a few automatic cameras have one or more entirely mechanical shutter speeds, several do not—in particular some of the auto-matic–only models. For this reason most models have a battery check so that you can see if all is well before a photography session.

Remember that meter displays, delay-ed action devices and exposure pre-views, for example, all place a heavy drain on battery power. Resist the temptation to use these unnecessarily, and switch off power when the camera is not in use.

Choosing an automatic SLR

● If in the past your photography has involved first selecting the shutter speed, a shutter priority camera is ideal. A manual override facility helps with difficult situations.

● If depth of field (or lack of it) is your most important consideration, an aperture priority automatic camera is the obvious choice, manual override giving extra versatility.

● If you are not concerned with manual exposures, an automatic–only camera will suit you.

● A multi–mode camera is extremely versatile. It suits the most advanced enthusiast with diverse interests, and can be set to 'programmed' so that even a child can take correctly exposed photographs.

While there is little point in spending money on a sophisticated camera with features you are never likely to use, try to find a model which you can 'grow into' rather than one with which you will quickly become dissatisfied.

VIEWFINDER DISPLAYS
Because you do not have total control over exposures it is vital to know that a correct exposure will be set. The type of viewfinder display varies from camera to camera. The simplest type is found in the Pentax MV1 which gives exposure information through coloured lights. Compare this with the more complicated bank of LEDs in the multi–mode Fujica AX–5. Generally a shutter priority camera gives a read–out of automatically selected apertures, while an aperture priority model supplies shutter speed information.

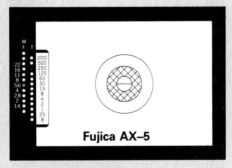
Konica FS–1

▲ A red LED shows the automatically selected aperture in this shutter priority camera.

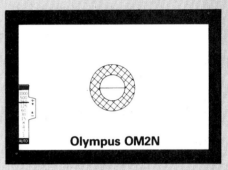
Olympus OM2N

▲ The shutter speed scale appears only when this aperture priority camera is set for automatic exposures.

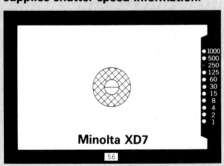
Minolta XD7

▲ On aperture priority the selected aperture is shown as well as a shutter speed scale (with LED indicator).

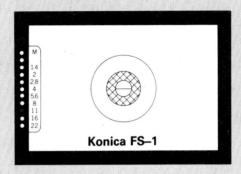
Fujica AX–5

▲ In programmed use this multi–mode camera viewfinder shows the aperture and shutter speed automatically set.

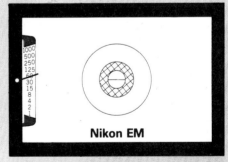
Nikon EM

▲ A needle shows which shutter speed will be automatically selected by this automatic–only camera.

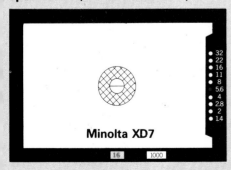
Minolta XD7

▲ On shutter priority, confirmed by a green '16', the set speed and automatically selected aperture appear.

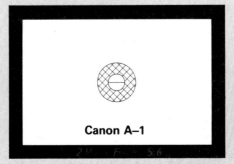
Canon A–1

▲ This unusual digital display gives complete exposure details whatever mode is in use (here 'F' stands for flash).

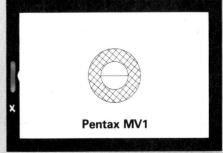
Pentax MV1

▲ A green LED confirms a correct exposure, red warns of over–exposure, yellow a shutter speed below 1/30.

Using a medium format SLR

Like the TLR camera already mentioned, medium format SLR cameras use 120 (or sometimes 220) roll film (see page 98). Though more expensive than the TLR camera, the medium format SLR camera has largely taken over this larger format market, especially in professional circles. It is similar in operation to the 35mm SLR camera, but on a larger scale. Lenses are easily interchanged, extension tubes and bellows can be used and there is a wide range of available accessories. The viewfinder does not suffer from parallax which occurs with TLR cameras, caused by the viewing and taking lenses seeing the subject from slightly different angles. The format is the same as for TLR cameras; 120 roll film is used and, depending on the camera, the negative sizes are: 6 x 4·5cm giving 15 exposures on a roll; 6 x 6cm giving 12 exposures, 6 x 7cm giving 10 exposures. The 6 x 6cm format is still the most popular and has the advantage that the camera does not have to be turned on its side.

Advantages

Professionals and some serious amateurs tend to use these cameras rather than 35mm ones because the bigger negatives and transparencies give better quality in many circumstances: to make a standard 30 x 25cm enlargement from a 6 x 6cm negative, for example, calls for a degree of enlargement of about 5½ times; to make the same size print from a 35mm negative you would have to enlarge it 10 times. If both cameras are loaded with emulsions of the same speed the smaller degree of enlargement must give better prints with finer grain, greater sharpness and less obvious dust spots—in fact, even if the medium format camera was loaded with 400 ASA film and the 35mm one with 125 ASA film, the medium format negatives would still usually produce better quality.

Disadvantages

However, though the medium format SLR undoubtedly gives better quality than a 35mm SLR with many subjects, it has several major disadvantages. An outfit consisting of a camera with normal, long focus and wide angle lenses is much more expensive, heavier and bulkier than a similar 35mm outfit. The lenses have less depth of field at a given aperture because of their longer focal lengths.

How it works

The basic design of these cameras is traditional—light entering the lens is reflected upwards by a mirror lying at an angle of 45° on to a ground-glass focusing screen. After composing the

The rectangular format and pentaprism of Mamiya's 645 simplifies composition. The Mamiya RB67 has a rotating back to allow full use of the 6 × 7 format. Shutter priority automatic Rolleiflex SLX has a built-in winder and uses the 6 × 6 format. All cameras use 120 film.

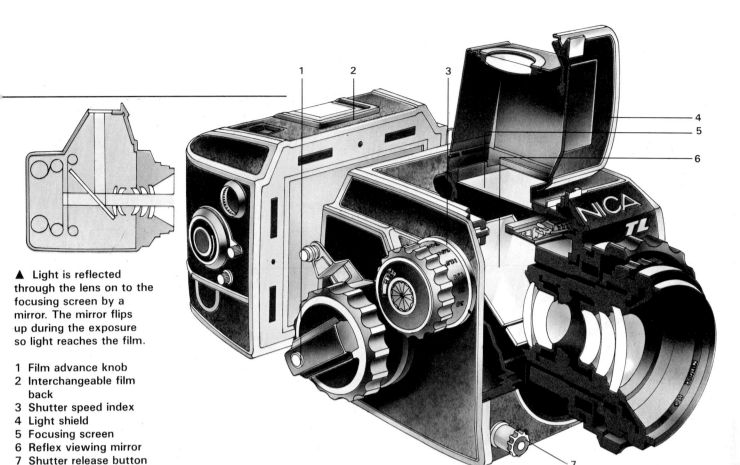

▲ Light is reflected through the lens on to the focusing screen by a mirror. The mirror flips up during the exposure so light reaches the film.

1 Film advance knob
2 Interchangeable film back
3 Shutter speed index
4 Light shield
5 Focusing screen
6 Reflex viewing mirror
7 Shutter release button

picture and focusing, the shutter release is pressed, the mirror flips up underneath the ground-glass, preventing light from entering the body through the eyepiece, and the exposure is made either by means of a focal plane shutter or between lens shutter.

Loading film: cameras such as the Hasselblad and Bronica use roll film loaded into interchangeable magazines so that when you come to the end of one film there is only a brief delay to change magazines before you start exposing the next roll of film. It is also possible to change from colour to black and white in the middle of a roll without risk of fogging either film. Other cameras such as the Rolleiflex SLX and Bronica ETRC use 'chargers', the film being loaded beforehand into lightweight frames that are dropped into the back of the camera in the same way that a cartridge is loaded into an Instamatic camera. However, the charger cannot be changed in the middle of a roll. Some cameras, such as the Pentax 6 x 7, are loaded in the conventional manner.

Each loading system has advantages and disadvantages. Magazines let you work rapidly or change emulsion types in the middle of a roll, large capacity magazines and a variety of other backs are available but they are expensive, bulky and heavy. Chargers are very much lighter and can be changed slightly faster than magazines but they cannot be removed until the whole roll has been used.

▲ The Pentax 6 × 7 looks like a scaled-up version of a 35mm SLR, such as a Nikon, but probably weighs three times as much. It is popular for advertising work because the whole of the 6 × 7cm negative can be used for prints. The camera has an interchangeable viewfinder and lenses.

▲ Hasselblad 500C/M is a classic 6 × 6cm camera. It has a wide range of lenses, each with its own shutter, uses interchangeable magazines and several types of viewfinder. A variety of accessories includes a meter prism finder, rapid winder, flash bracket, magazine and lens hood.

Viewing: the basic viewing system is a waist-level ground-glass screen giving an image that is the right way up but reversed from left to right. This is satisfactory with 6 x 6cm format cameras which are held in one position only but impractical with the oblong 6 x 4·5cm and 6 x 7cm ones because the act of turning the cameras on their side to take vertical pictures makes the image extremely difficult to view and compose. Therefore these cameras are generally used with pentaprisms, so that the viewfinder image is seen both right way up and right way round. They are especially suitable for 6 x 4·5cm cameras since the pentaprism is reasonably light; with a 6 x 7 camera it is heavy and bulky and may not cover the whole area of the frame. All these pentaprisms are more bulky and expensive than their 35mm equivalents. Some cameras have an exposure meter built into the viewfinder system to give through-the-lens metering.

Shutters: some medium format reflex cameras have focal plane shutters, others have between lens ones, while the Hasselblad 2000 FC can use either (although the focal plane is more common) unless the Compur-type lenses are fitted. The focal plane shutter, which is built into the camera body, has the great advantage that you only need the one shutter for all your lenses. It is easily coupled to the film wind and has a high top speed.

The disadvantage is that a focal plane shutter can only be used with electronic flash at comparatively low speeds, such as 1/30, making it difficult to use flash in daylight.

The between lens shutter can be used with flash at any speed but each lens you use must be fitted with its own separate shutter, adding greatly to the cost of the outfit. In addition, the coupling and mechanical operation of the camera is more complicated.

When you take a picture with a focal plane shutter reflex, as soon as the release is pressed the lens diaphragm closes down to the stop you have previously selected, the mirror rises and the shutter is then released—a fairly straightforward sequence. With a between lens shutter reflex, on pressing the release the shutter closes (it has to be open for viewing and focusing), the lens is stopped down, the mirror rises together with a 'capping plate' that prevents light from reaching the film while you are focusing, and finally the shutter operates and the exposure is made. Though it all takes place in a fraction of a second the sequence is much more involved than with a focal plane shutter.

Lenses

Medium format cameras offer a reasonably wide choice of lenses. The standard 80mm lens is similar to a 50mm lens for a 35mm SLR; 45mm is equivalent to a 28mm wide angle lens; and a 150mm is similar to a 100mm medium telephoto lens.

Typically, a standard 80mm lens in a focusing mount fitted to a 6 x 6cm camera focuses down to something under a metre; if you want to move closer to the subject, extension tubes, close-up lenses or a bellows unit is needed. Exceptions are the Rolleiflex 66 and the Mamiya RB67 which have built-in bellows focusing, allowing you to take extreme close-ups without any accessories. The aperture of the standard lens is usually limited to f2·8 (though an f1·9 is available for the Mamiya 645). But, as good quality can be obtained on fast film, this limitation is not too important.

Buying a medium format SLR

Though medium format cameras are popular for advertising and commercial work using electronic flash or a rigid stand, their size makes them less suited to casual, hand-held photography. Before buying a camera of this type it is wise to ask yourself if the better quality you will obtain justifies the extra effort and cost involved, particularly if you intend eventually to commit yourself to a complete system. If you use colour transparencies you will have a limited choice of projectors, you will probably have to mount your own slides, and you will not be able to use the popular Kodachrome 35mm film. In other words, while medium format cameras are suitable for professional work or for use by serious amateurs in search of top quality, they are not so suitable for the amateur who takes pictures for fun. Professionals too are increasingly turning to the 35mm SLR.

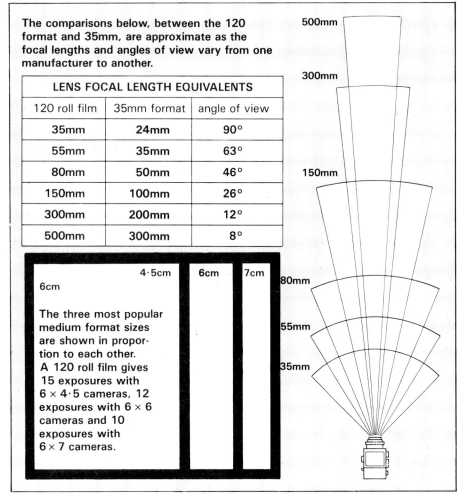

The comparisons below, between the 120 format and 35mm, are approximate as the focal lengths and angles of view vary from one manufacturer to another.

LENS FOCAL LENGTH EQUIVALENTS		
120 roll film	35mm format	angle of view
35mm	24mm	90°
55mm	35mm	63°
80mm	50mm	46°
150mm	100mm	26°
300mm	200mm	12°
500mm	300mm	8°

The three most popular medium format sizes are shown in proportion to each other. A 120 roll film gives 15 exposures with 6 × 4·5 cameras, 12 exposures with 6 × 6 cameras and 10 exposures with 6 × 7 cameras.

4·5cm   6cm   7cm
6cm

500mm
300mm
150mm
80mm
55mm
35mm

Roll film produces square or rectangular pictures depending on the camera being used. The landscape (above) was photographed with a 6 × 7 camera using the full frame to compose the picture. The square picture (far left) was taken with a 6 × 6 camera. The image could be cropped slightly to make a more pleasing vertical shot. The ruins (left) were shot with a 6 × 4·5 camera, turned on its side for a vertical picture.

Choosing a 35mm SLR camera

With its accurate viewing and focusing system, through–the–lens (TTL) metering, and interchangeable lens facility providing scope for almost every picture–taking situation, it is easy to see why the 35mm SLR is a popular general purpose camera. There is a vast number to choose from, and the competition in terms of specification, quality and price is keen.

There are a number of points to consider before spending your money.
● What is the most you can afford to spend?
● What type of exposure metering do you want?
● Is the viewfinder easy to use?
● Are the controls convenient?
● Are the shutter speed and aperture ranges adequate for your purposes?
● Does the camera allow you to build up a worthwhile system (particularly lenses)?

Price

Decide on your price limit, and stick to it. Only you can know how much you can afford to spend, not the person from whom you are buying. It is worthwhile spending an hour or so scanning through dealers' advertisements to see how much prices vary for the camera you would like to buy. Remember that the price of a camera often reflects the price of accessories you will want to add later. Try to think ahead; can you afford a system?

Exposure measurement

Almost all SLRs today have TTL metering, and light readings are taken from light passed by any focal length lens. (External or hand–held meters can be time–consuming to use.)

A full aperture metering camera can take light readings with the lens set at its widest aperture. The viewfinder therefore remains bright for ease of focusing and composition, and is closed down to the correct aperture only when the shutter is released.

Stopped–down metering means that an accurate reading can only be taken at the working aperture and, although cheaper, this system is not as convenient to use as is full–aperture metering.

Manual or automatic?

Do you want the built–in meter to give automatic or manual exposure settings? With a manual camera the photographer has to decide on the combination of aperture and shutter speed to provide a correct exposure. This gives the photographer total control, but time can be lost in setting both camera controls. Automatic exposure systems can be far quicker to use.

If you decide to buy one of the many cameras offering automatic exposure setting, consider whether you prefer aperture or shutter priority systems (see page 78). Multi-mode cameras

have a choice of both systems; some can also programme both settings without the photographer having to do anything except set the film speed, compose and focus. Automatic use means that if lighting conditions are constantly changing the exposure is instantly and automatically adjusted.

Viewfinder

The SLR is built around its viewing system, so the viewfinder is an important feature. A large rearsight enables spectacle wearers to see the whole screen clearly—if a rubber eye cup can be fitted this is often more comfortable to use.

Focusing screens vary in construction, some being brighter and more evenly illuminated than others. Dim, uneven focusing screens can hamper accurate focusing.

A few cameras have interchangeable screens and viewfinders, but most people can manage quite happily with the ground–glass screen, microprism circle and split image centre spot commonly seen in many modern SLR cameras.

Also often shown in the viewfinder are the shutter speed, lens aperture, or both. Over– and under–exposure warnings and correct exposure signals are almost always featured. Such complete viewfinder information shows the exposure situation at a glance.

Some manual cameras only have a

▲ The 42mm screw thread lens mount is now usually only found on cheaper manual cameras. To ensure correct focus the lens must be completely screwed in. Changing screw-in lenses can be time-consuming.

▲ Many cameras in all price ranges have bayonet lenses. First align the two reference dots: three claws on the lens then mate with three slots in the camera mount. A short twist locks in the lens for full exposure coupling.

▲ ▶ Metering at full aperture ensures a bright viewing image whatever aperture is set, but depth of field is difficult to judge without a preview.

▲ ▶ Stopped-down meter readings always darken the viewfinder image according to the aperture set; depth of field can be seen but focusing may be difficult.

◀ Whether you choose full-aperture or stopped-down metering, exposure results should be identical. Decide if you want economy or convenience.

correct exposure indication, with no other exposure information provided. This system demands that you know the camera well enough to judge which shutter speed and aperture you have set without removing your eye from the eyepiece.

Pointer needle meter displays can often be interpreted more accurately than light emitting diodes (LEDs), so that with experience you can deliberately make small exposure adjustments, perhaps only ⅓ stop, without looking at the aperture or shutter speed dials. Black needles can, however, be much more difficult to see than LEDs in dim light, or against a dark subject area.

Handling

Once you have decided on the type of camera you would like to buy by checking price and specification, you will probably have a short–list of two or three different cameras. From then on your choice becomes far more subjective, and you can only make your final decision based on how you feel about the handling of each camera.

Size, bulk, weight and layout of controls are all matters of personal preference. Some people prefer a shutter

A small, light camera is not necessarily superior to a large, heavier one; base your choice on how you feel about holding and handling both types.

speed dial to be on the camera top plate, for example, whereas others like a shutter speed ring to be around the lens mount. Both types are available.

A bright viewfinder and ease of fine focusing are equally important—but you can only judge if these aspects are up to your standards by going to a dealer and handling a number of cameras.

Spend a little time with each of your short–listed cameras in your hands to feel how the film advance lever, aperture and shutter speed controls, automatic and manual metering, and depth of field preview operate.

Shutter

If you take action pictures the camera's fastest shutter speed is important. Top speeds of 1/1000 (more rarely 1/2000) can freeze fast motion. If much of your photography is in low light then the choice of speeds at the slow end of the range is more important.

Speeds may be controlled electronically or mechanically. Automatic electronic cameras often have a shutter speed range down to 8 or 16 full seconds, and shutter speeds can be infinitely variable (or 'stepless') through the range. If a mechanical speed is also provided (some cameras have more than one) you can make an exposure even if the batteries fail—but

the meter will no longer operate.

Most focal plane shutters synchronize for flash at 1/60 or slower, but some allow use of 1/125 to give more exposure choice when you use fill–in flash.

Noise and vibration are important considerations, especially to the wildlife or candid photographer, and lack of vibration is especially important when using slow speeds or telephoto lenses.

Powered film advance imposes extra strain on mechanical shutters and mirror movements, and cameras have to be constructed more robustly to cope with this. While most bodies are robust enough to cope with the modest 2fps rate of an autowind, stronger construction is needed for the more rapid shooting rates required by motor–drives. Go on brand reputation and whether the main body and controls have a substantial feel to them.

Lenses

The majority of 35mm SLR cameras have bayonet fitting lenses. Few now retain the once universal 42mm screw thread because, although the lenses tend to be slightly cheaper, it takes longer to unscrew one lens and screw in another than the more rapid twist–lock bayonet action.

Bayonet fittings for different camera brands vary, and specific types are

rarely (if ever) interchangeable between different makes of camera. The major exception is the Pentax-K bayonet design from Asahi which is now featured on several other camera names. There are also ranges of lenses by independent manufacturers made to fit cameras of varying bayonet designs. You almost always have to buy a camera with its standard lens. This is often 50 or 55mm in focal length, but 40 and 45mm standard lenses with their slightly wide angle view are gaining in popularity.

Common maximum apertures, in order of cost, are f1·2, f1·4, f1·8 and f2. A wide maximum aperture gives a slight exposure edge in dim light, but you may prefer to use a fast film than to buy a more expensive lens which, in practical terms, can only give perhaps an extra half stop.

Lenses often sell on reputation—but for good reasons. It is therefore better to go for well–known makes when choosing lenses rather than the cheapest one you can find. Take bulk and weight into account when buying additional lenses—both should complement the camera body.

If you aren't obliged to buy the standard lens with the camera body, consider buying a zoom which takes the 50mm focal length in to its focal length range. It will doubtless cost more than a

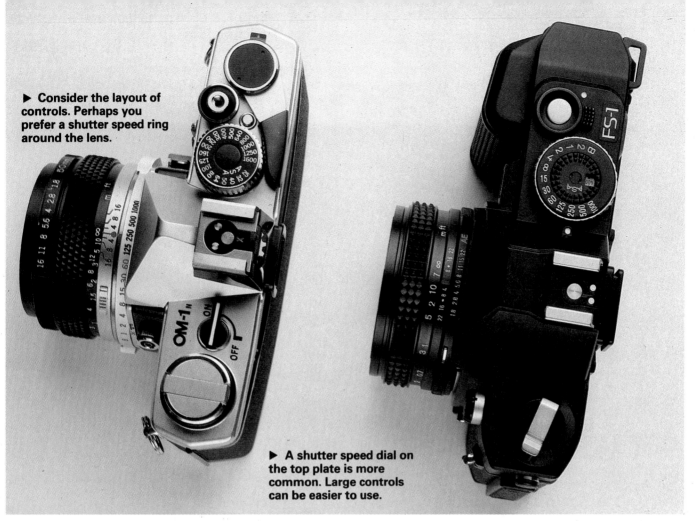

► Consider the layout of controls. Perhaps you prefer a shutter speed ring around the lens.

► A shutter speed dial on the top plate is more common. Large controls can be easier to use.

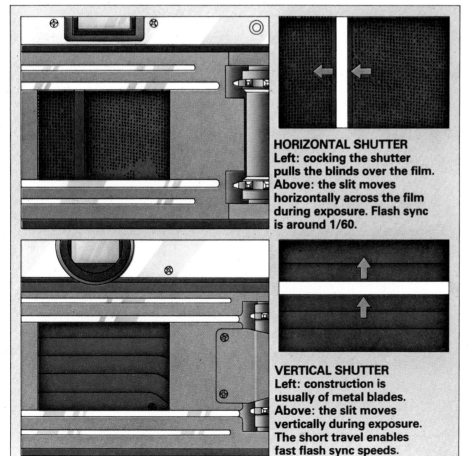

HORIZONTAL SHUTTER
Left: cocking the shutter pulls the blinds over the film. Above: the slit moves horizontally across the film during exposure. Flash sync is around 1/60.

VERTICAL SHUTTER
Left: construction is usually of metal blades. Above: the slit moves vertically during exposure. The short travel enables fast flash sync speeds.

standard lens, but by no means as much as several lenses encompassed by the zoom range.

Choosing

Consider first that the camera will be the heart of your outfit, so ensure a good range of reasonably priced lenses and accessories are readily available from the manufacturer and from independent makers. Even more important, make sure that the camera suits your requirements, that it is comfortable to hold, and that the controls are of a suitable size with clear lettering where applicable.

Operation should be easy, not a task. Don't be too influenced by flashing coloured lights, bleeping signals, and a 'professional' finish. These can be useful, but none of them make better pictures. Remember that the more LEDs there are, the greater the drain on the batteries—batteries can be expensive.

Bargains can often be had by buying a second–hand camera. Many dealers offer discount on new equipment and this can provide a useful saving. In any event, don't expect to combine the maximum discount with the maximum of after–sales service. It is rarely possible, and your dealer's advice as you progress is usually worth your paying that little extra.

Underwater equipment

Underwater photography is rapidly gaining in popularity, but without doubt it is a difficult area in which to achieve success because of the physical problems involved. You can take impressive photographs in shallow water with simple snorkelling apparatus, but for depths greater than about four metres you must know how to dive safely (never dive alone). With experience you will develop an eye for successful underwater pictures, but before you reach that stage you need to kit yourself out with suitable underwater equipment and understand how to use it.

Underwater housings

To keep water out of your camera you need a water–tight housing. As well as keeping working parts dry, underwater housings enable all necessary controls to be operated with the housing in place. Some housings have over–sized control knobs to make this easier. Commercial makes are available for 110, 35mm reflex and non–reflex and roll film cameras.

Shallow water housings. At a depth of only 10 metres the pressure is twice that on the surface. The pressure has the effect of trying to collapse the housing and to force water through any faulty seals there might be. Cases designed for use at maximum depths of up to 10 metres are relatively cheap. Any make of 35mm SLR camera (fitted with a standard or similar length lens) fits in the Ewa Marine housing. The casing is flexible plastic and controls are operated through a rubber glove set into the housing.

Transparent polycarbonate cases allow you to look through the camera's reflex viewing system (but only with the eye a few centimetres from the eyepiece). You can also spot any leaks before the camera itself is flooded (sea water rapidly corrodes camera mechanisms).

Deep water housings. There is much more choice in this category, but they tend to be more expensive than shallow water versions. Cases are readily available for use down to 100 metres— the deepest that most Scuba divers go. The immense pressure of deep water makes a 'rubber glove' design impractical because the glove can easily rupture under pressure. Important considerations when choosing a deep water housing are whether the casing allows reflex viewing, whether the camera controls are easy to operate, and whether the camera porthole (the transparent plate through which the

▲ *Mike Portelly* photographed this shoal of tropical fish with a Hasselblad in a deep water housing. Equally impressive pictures are possible with basic equipment and an understanding of the problems.

▲ Left: the Scubi-35 is a complete shallow water outfit consisting of a non-reflex 35mm camera and flash in a polycarbonate housing. Right: a shallow water housing for a 35mm SLR camera.

DEEP WATER HOUSINGS

When taking your camera more than 10 metres down you need a deep water housing. They are expensive but protect the camera from corrosive sea water and increased pressure. With such housings you can take pictures to a depth of at least 100 metres.

▲ Most deep water housings have a choice of ports. A dome port is on the camera, a flat port is shown beside it.

Deep water housings are available for most reflex camera formats.
1 The Hasselblad (6 x 6cm) housing can be used at 250 metres down.
2 The RB67 Marine is designed for the Mamiya RB67 (6 x 7cm) reflex camera.
3 This 35mm housing is for a Nikon camera, but others are available.

ROCK POOLS

You don't need to dive deep or travel far to take successful shots under water. Flexible camera housings are inexpensive and can be used with most 35mm SLR cameras (right). A rubber glove set into the casing allows adjustment of controls. Most shallow water housings can be used at 10 metres. Below right: many opportunities for impressive underwater pictures present themselves in shallow rock pools. You can easily capture them by snorkelling. Far right: *Peter Scoones* came across these colourful anemones in a British rock pool (photographed with available light).

camera lens 'sees') is interchangeable. Rigid alloy cases require a special prism for reflex viewing. This can be supplied as an integral part of the housing, or many photographers use an external sports finder frame. Leaks tend to be more difficult to see, but alloy housings are more robust than plastic housings: some can be used 150 metres deep.

Purpose–built cameras

The Nikonos III is one of the few available cameras built specially for underwater use. No casing is needed because all internal parts of the camera are watertight. It is a fairly basic manual 35mm non–reflex camera without a built–in meter. There is no rangefinder for focusing so you have to estimate focusing distances, and the viewfinder is a direct vision type which may cause parallax problems at close subject distances. An external sports finder frame can be fitted for easier viewing through a diving mask. The shutter release incorporates a film wind–on lever, so both operations can be done with one hand. It can be safely used down to about 50 metres.

A range of lenses is available—35mm (which is supplied as the standard lens), 15mm, 28mm and 80mm. Both the 35 and 80mm lenses can be used on land too, but the 15 and 28mm can only be used under water. Lenses cannot be changed under water.

▲ The Nikonos III is shown mounted on a bracket with a typical underwater flash gun and light meter. An external viewing frame is fitted to the camera. A close-up attachment and framing device are shown on the right.

◀ This is the photographer's view of an underwater light meter. Controls and figures are large to aid use underwater.

Lenses and ports

Light is refracted (bent) more in water than in air, which makes underwater subjects appear closer (and therefore larger). When a lens is used behind a flat underwater porthole its angle of view is reduced. The magnification of the subject and reduction in angle of view causes a 15mm lens to become equivalent to a 20mm lens when a flat port is used. Likewise, 35mm is equivalent to 45mm, and 80mm to 120mm under water. Using a wide angle lens with a flat port also produces edge distortion and blurring because light has to pass through a thicker piece of plastic at the port edges.

Use of a dome–shaped porthole on camera housings helps solve the problems. The spherical shape of the dome ensures that light from all directions passes through it at right angles. Refraction of light is eliminated, and the angle of view of the fitted lens is unchanged. Domes are

a form of 'corrective optics' and some water corrected lenses use similar principles. Dome ports or water corrected lenses are a better choice than flat ports because distortions are far less noticeable.

Water contains many suspended particles such as sand, tiny animals and air bubbles, all of which absorb and scatter light, reducing visibility

and lowering the contrast of photographs. It always pays to get close to a subject to reduce diffusion caused by a large expanse of water between the camera and the subject. Wide angle lenses (15–28mm with 35mm cameras) are the best choice because of their wide angle of view and ability to focus fairly close. Alternatively, use close–up equipment.

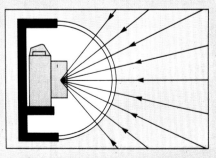

▲ With a flat port the lens's angle of view is decreased; frame edges may be blurred as light passes through a thicker surface at the port edges.

▲ A dome port maintains the lens's angle of view and minimizes edge distortion because dome thickness is consistent throughout.

A wide range of additional accessories is available, including extension tubes and clip–on converter lenses to increase lens acceptance angle.

Lighting

If you are using natural light, try to time your photography so that the sun is overhead, and the water is calm. Reflection and refraction from the surface is then minimized. The deeper you go the greater the reduction in light intensity because it is absorbed by water. Even in clear water on a bright day, and using 400 ASA film, it is difficult to get acceptable results at 30 metres or so. Because the light intensity can vary so much it is important to take a light meter with you.

Purpose–built underwater light meters are available. They can be attached to your equipment with a commercially made bracket if one is not supplied. A cheaper solution is to put an ordinary light meter into a custom–built case, or perhaps in a sealed jam jar.

An external light source puts back light absorbed by the water, and restores lost colours (particularly reds). It also allows the use of shorter exposure times and smaller apertures to eliminate camera shake and increase depth of field respectively.

The simplest form of artificial light to use is a torch held by a diving companion. Special underwater floodlights can be used, but most photographers prefer to use flash if natural daylight is inadequate.

Electronic flash units are available for a wide variety of camera housings, and are attached with special waterproof connections. Many of these are regular land units housed in transparent underwater casings. A number of flash brackets are also available to enable the flash to be mounted well off the camera at an angle of about 45° to the subject. Using flash closer to the camera would illuminate particles in the water, thereby scattering light and reducing contrast. Angling the flash reduces this scattering effect, and gives more modelling and contrast to the photograph.

It is best to make a series of tests with your lighting equipment before you start taking pictures seriously. Take photographs of an underwater subject (perhaps a diver holding a colour test card) at varying distances and depths. Use each lens aperture in turn to determine the appropriate settings and to see how well your equipment performs. Make notes on an underwater

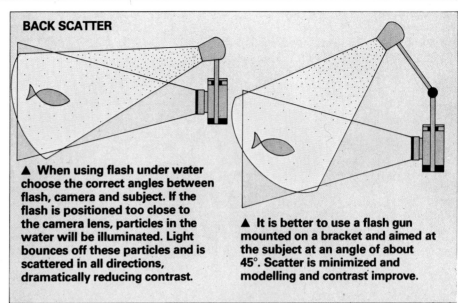

BACK SCATTER

▲ When using flash under water choose the correct angles between flash, camera and subject. If the flash is positioned too close to the camera lens, particles in the water will be illuminated. Light bounces off these particles and is scattered in all directions, dramatically reducing contrast.

▲ It is better to use a flash gun mounted on a bracket and aimed at the subject at an angle of about 45°. Scatter is minimized and modelling and contrast improve.

▲ Flash compensates for light absorbed under water and restores lost colour, but the flash may not have the same coverage as your lens. In this picture you can see exactly which areas have been lit by flash by the colours revealed.

slate. If you carry out tests in a swimming pool remember that murkier sea water will demand increased exposures for good results.

Colour correction

In anything deeper than about two metres of water, colour photographs can be disappointingly low in contrast with a strong blue or green colour cast. This is because water acts as a colour filter which absorbs orange and red light.

At depths between two and five metres you can compensate for the blue cast by using the appropriate colour correcting filter (red). Filters reduce the amount of light reaching the film so that exposure times have to be longer. Below five metres the colour cast is probably too strong for correction, in which case supplementary lighting becomes necessary.

In clear blue water, such as is found in the Mediterranean, or in coral seas, a red correction filter is best. In water where visibility is 10 metres or less, a magenta filter is generally better to correct the resulting green cast.

Colour correcting filters are available in different strengths. The Kodak colour compensating (CC) range is available in 5, 10, 20, 30, 40 and 50 CC units. A rough rule of thumb for choosing the best filter is to add 10 CC filter units for each metre of light travel through the water. For example, when a diver is two metres below the surface and one metre from the subject, the total light path is 2 + 1 metres = 3 metres. Using 10 CC units per metre, 30CC filtration is needed, and this is often standard when taking natural daylight pictures near to the surface.

Slight under-correction is preferable to over-correction—a blue or green cast is generally more acceptable than a red or magenta one because the eye expects underwater scenes to appear slightly blue. Use of a yellow filter for black and white photography close to the surface helps to improve contrast.

Equipment maintenance

Take precautions to ensure good maintenance of your underwater equipment. Keep it out of the sun on the boat. Rinse everything thoroughly in fresh water after use to remove salt residue. Blot off water droplets, paying particular attention to the port, and inspect and re-grease all seals with silicone grease.

Open out the housing and remove accessories before putting the equipment into storage. Extra care should be taken in inspecting electrical connections and you should have them checked out by an expert if you are in any doubt. Check the housings for leaks before you start on an important assignment.

▲ Left: *Peter Scoones* photographed this seascape using natural light. Because water always absorbs red light an overall blue cast results. Right: by using a red compensating filter over the lens and increasing exposure you can replace some lost red tones and convey a more natural colour impression.

▶ At 5 metres down (or less) use a red or magenta compensating filter to eliminate blue or green casts respectively, depending on the water colour. Add 10CC filtration for each metre of light travel through the water. At 2 metres down and 4 metres from the subject you need 60CC (6 x 10); the same filters are used when 4 metres down and 2 metres from the subject. An increase in exposure time is necessary to compensate for reduction in light reaching the film because of the filters used.

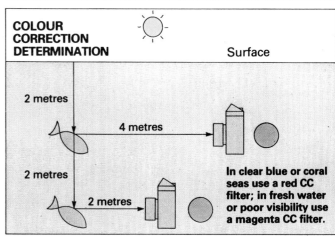

COLOUR CORRECTION DETERMINATION

Surface

2 metres

4 metres

2 metres

2 metres

In clear blue or coral seas use a red CC filter; in fresh water or poor visibility use a magenta CC filter.

Points to remember

● Get close to the subject to minimize light scatter, loss of visibility and reduced contrast.

● Use a wide angle lens to take in a large subject area and to enable you to focus close. Close–up equipment will help.

● If you don't have any underwater lighting equipment, take all your photographs close to the surface. The two hours either side of noon provide the best lighting.

● Use the appropriate colour correction filter to prevent a blue colour cast (only effective down to about five metres).

● When using flash, mount the unit on a flash bracket to enable the flash to be used at an angle. This replaces lost colours, provides modelling, and adds contrast to the photograph. The short duration of flash also stops movement (of a fish, for example).

● Check your equipment and look for leaks before you dive.

▶ **Get in close and use flash for sharp vivid pictures such as this clown fish swimming between anemone tentacles.** *Peter Scoones*

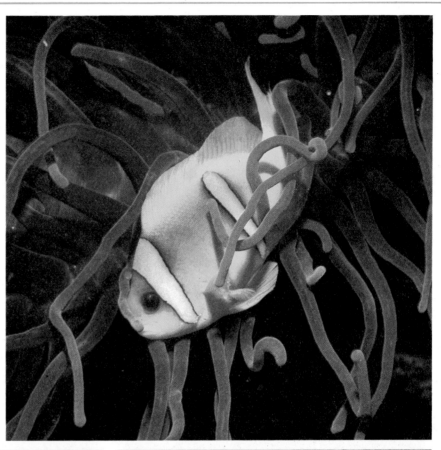

▲ **Although this photographer is carrying a lot of equipment it is all neatly mounted on a bracket, keeping clutter to a minimum and making photography easier. Note the flash angle and close camera-to-subject distance.**

▲ **This pencil sea urchin was photographed as shown on the left. The Nikonos III was used with a close-up attachment. The two rods control minimum lens-to-subject distance. You can achieve similar results with an SLR.**

All about film

Using the correct film can make all the difference between a disappointing picture and a highly successful one. So it is important to know the full range of films available for your camera—or the one you may be thinking of buying next. It is a question of matching the film to the type of photography you are doing. Some films are better for poor light conditions or fast-moving subjects, others can reproduce the tiniest detail of a flower. Some colour films produce colour prints, others produce slides for the projector: there are films for daylight and indoor electric (tungsten) light. Some you can process yourself, others must be factory-processed.

When buying a film you need to decide on:
• **Type** do you want colour prints, colour slides or black and white prints?
• **Size:** is the film available in the correct size for your camera?
• **Exposures:** how many are needed?
• **Speed:** is it the right film for the particular lighting conditions?

The most common sizes available today are 110 cartridges, 35mm cassettes, and 120 roll film. 110 is fairly limited in types and speeds available, while the other two come in a much wider range. So if you plan to buy a new camera, bear this in mind. This article deals with the more standard types of film. Film for instant-print cameras, view cameras and other specialist films are covered later.

Packaging

Film is always sold packed in light-proof wrapping in a box marked with its *size, type, speed* and *number of exposures*. It is available in three main forms—cartridges, cassettes and roll film.

Cartridges: 110 and 126 (Instamatic) films are packed in plastic drop-in cartridges. These are the easiest films to load, but are only used with the less expensive eye-level viewfinder cameras. The drawbacks with them are that each exposure costs more than on other types and the cartridge cannot hold the film firmly enough against the back of the camera to produce really sharp pictures. Speeds and types, in both colour and black and white film, are limited.

35mm cassettes hold double perforated film. They are used in some eye-level viewfinders, rangefinders and in most SLR cameras.

Roll film is used in TLRs and large-format SLRs, and some older models of viewfinder cameras. It is protected by a backing paper which is longer than the film and so protects it from light at the beginning and end.

Film and backing are supplied wound tightly on to a spool with a wide flange to protect the edges of the film.

Picture format

The camera you use determines the format and size of the negative. The format will either be square or rectangular. The square formats are 126, 127 and 120 (6 x 6cm) roll film, and all the rest are rectangular.

Size

The actual size of the negative affects the quality of any enlargements: the larger the size of each negative, the better the quality of the enlargement.

Even so, the quality of most modern films is such that large prints can be made from small negatives. Even a 110 cartridge negative, taken on a camera with a good quality lens, can be enlarged up to 20 x 15cm without loss of detail. Poster size prints can be made from 120 roll film with similar detail.

Cartridges
• *110 film:* the small negative is difficult to view without enlargement; contact prints are of very limited value. 12 or 20 exposures.
• *126 film:* uses film 35mm wide with single perforations. Used in some eye-level viewfinder cameras. 12 or 20 exposures.

35mm cassettes
• *135 film:* this size gives the widest variety of film types. 20, 24 or 36 exposures. It is also available in bulk lengths for loading into cassettes in the darkroom.

A few cameras take half frame negatives, using the same cassettes but giving double the number of exposures.

Roll film
• *127 film:* used in older eye-level viewfinder cameras. 12 exposures.
• *120 film:* according to the camera, this film allows negative sizes 6 x 6cm (known in the past as 2¼ square). 12 exposures. Also comes in 6 x 7cm (10 exposures), 6 x 4·5cm (15 or 16 exposures), and 6 x 9cm (8 exposures). Used in TLRs, roll-film SLRs (like the Hasselblad), and some older types of viewfinder cameras.
• *120 double perforated film:* negative size 6 x 6cm. Used in roll-film SLRs. Only available in bulk lengths for loading into special magazines.
• *220 film:* exactly the same negative

sizes (6 x 6cm) as for 120 film, but the film is twice as long, giving 24 exposures, and has no paper backing.

Take care

- **Film date** When you buy a film check the date stamp on the package. Out-of-date film may be all right, but you have no recompense if the film is faulty.
- **Avoid heat** Don't leave film where it will get too hot, such as the back window or dashboard of a car. Films tend to deteriorate in humid conditions, or when subjected to chemical fumes.
- **Light protection** Put each exposed roll of film back in its lightproof wrapping or tin until it is processed. Remember, exposed film deteriorates more quickly than unexposed, so have it processed promptly.
- **Loading/unloading film** Never load or unload film (particularly fast film of 400 ASA or more) in bright light, but only indoors or in deep shadows.
- **Dust and dirt** Before you load a new film always check that there is no dust or dirt inside the camera. These can scratch the film.
- **Jammed film** If you feel sudden resistance when winding on the film do not force it: take the camera into a darkroom. Open the camera back and reposition the cassette. You may have to improvise a darkroom by using a coat or jacket, a cupboard, or even by crawling under the bedclothes.
- **On holiday** It is best to buy film before you go. Often more expensive abroad, and you are sure of having up-to-date, well-stored film of the type you want.
- **Used film** Always bend the end of exposed film over (or wind it right into the cassette) so that you don't re-load it as a new film.
- **Packing film** When travelling, make sure that films are not packed into baggage that will be x-rayed— this applies to exposed and unexposed film equally. Keep it in your hand baggage and ask the security officer to check it by hand.
- **Processing** Have films processed as soon as possible after finishing the roll, as exposed film deteriorates more quickly than unexposed film, particularly if left in hot conditions.
- **Loading** Make sure that the film loads smoothly on to the take up spool, that none of the perforations are bent or torn, and that both sets of perforations mesh smoothly with the sprockets before closing the camera back.

FILM FORMATS

The range of picture sizes shown actual size. (They are generally described by the dimensions printed alongside, although in practice some cameras give slightly smaller pictures as shown.)

110 cartridge
(13 x 17mm)

126 cartridge
(28 x 28mm)

35mm
cassette
(36 x 24mm)

35mm cassette
half frame
(18 x 24mm)

120 roll film
(6 x 6cm)

127 roll film
(42 x 42mm)

120 double perforated (6 x 6cm)

120 (6 x 7cm)

99

Film speed

The term speed describes how light-sensitive film is. A 'fast' film reacts very fast to light, a 'slow' film is less sensitive so needs brighter light or a much longer exposure. Different film speeds cater for different types of photography. A medium speed film is suitable for general everyday pictures; fast film is used in low light conditions or for moving subjects; slow films are used where very fine detail is required. Check carefully what range of film speeds is available for your camera. There is a wide range of different films available for 35mm cameras while 110 film is generally available only in medium and fast speeds.

Why photographs look grainy

Light-sensitive film carries millions of silver halide crystals and it is the size and number of these crystals that determine the speed of the film. The crystals—or grains—on fast film are much larger than those on slow film, which means the print or transparency will look 'grainy'—as though printed on sandpaper. With smaller prints the effect is not very noticeable, but the more a print or slide is enlarged, the more the grain shows up.

Colour film works the same way as black and white film although the effect is often less noticeable because most colour materials are slower.

Speed ratings

Film packs are usually marked with two speed ratings—ISO/ASA (International/American) and DIN (German). The table, right, shows equivalent ASA and DIN speeds. With ASA the doubling of speed is shown by the doubling of the number; with the DIN system the doubling of speed is shown by an increase of 3. For example, 400 ASA film needs only a quarter of the light needed by 100 ASA film.

Ratings for colour and black and white film differ slightly: see chart below.

COLOUR	ASA/DIN	B&W	ASA/DIN
Slow	25/15		(none)
	32/16		32/16
Medium	64/19	Slow	64/19
	80/20		80/20
	100/21		100/21
	125/22	Medium	125/22
	160/23		160/23
Fast	200/24		200/24
	400/27	Fast	400/27

Medium speed film

This is the best general-purpose film for most everyday subjects. It is sensible to get used to using one particular film before experimenting with either slower or faster films. Medium speed films give a useful compromise between speed and grain, and negatives enlarge up to about eight times the dimensions of the negative.

▲ Slow films are used in good lighting conditions, especially when slow shutter speeds are possible. These films produce a fine-grained image with plenty of detail and contrast. A slow colour film like Kodachrome 25 (ASA 25) used here, gives a bright, crisp image with fine detail.

► Fast films are used in poor lighting conditions or when fast shutter speeds are needed to stop movement. The faster the film the coarser the grain. This enlargement from part of a 35mm negative on a 400 ASA film shows how image quality suffers on fast films.

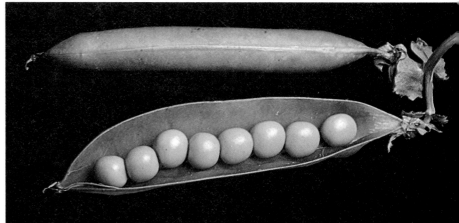

Fast films

These are for use in low light conditions either indoors, early evening or on dull winter days. Fast films can generally handle most subjects either where the light is bad or where a fast shutter speed is necessary to stop movement. But higher film speed means that pictures look grainy if the negative is enlarged more than about eight times, and there may be some loss of detail.

Even faster black and white films are available and are covered in a later article on Specialist Films.

Slow films

Slow film gives sharp detail and a fine grain-free image, and is therefore particularly useful for big enlargements. It is really best for static subjects such as landscapes, buildings, or still life. Remember that a slow film needs longer exposure time, which increases the risk of camera shake, so these films are often used with the camera on a tripod.

Setting the film speed dial

On cameras that have some form of automatic exposure control you should set the speed rating of the film you are using on the film speed dial. Check this each time you load a new film.

Some 110 cameras are designed to take either 100 ASA cartridge or the faster 400 ASA film, and the camera automatically adjusts the shutter speed as the faster film cartridge is inserted.

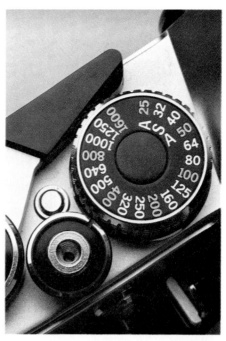

► The film speed dial must be set to the ASA rating of the film on cameras with automatic exposure control.

▼ The coarser grain quality of a fast film used in poor light need not be a drawback: but in this sunset shot the grain adds to the misty atmosphere.

Choosing colour film

First, you need to choose between a colour film that produces prints (negative film) and one that produces slides for the projector (also called reversal or positive transparency film).

▲ Top: colour print film produces colour negatives as shown here, and then prints. Below: slide film gives colour slides for the projector.

Print film has greater latitude—is not so fussy about light conditions—than slide film and slight adjustments to colours can be made when printing. Print film is universal, which means it can be used in both daylight and artificial light provided they are not mixed. Speeds range from 80–400 ASA.
Slide film is processed direct into colour slides and is therefore cheaper than print film, which has to be developed and then printed. But, unlike a negative, slide film gives only one slide for each exposure. Duplicates can be made, but they are expensive and there is some loss of quality. It is cheaper and better to take more shots in the first place if you think you will want more than one copy of a particular subject.

Slide film requires more exact exposure but gives excellent quality colour images full of detail and brilliance when projected. Film speeds range from 25–400 ASA.
Tungsten versus daylight film
Slide film is colour balanced for use in either artificial light (tungsten) or in daylight, so it is important to match the film to the lighting conditions. Try to avoid mixing the two sorts of light in one picture.

If you use the wrong film, the colour balance is affected: daylight film used in electric light produces slides with a strong orange-yellow cast, while tungsten film used in daylight gives a blue cast. Colour correction filters are available for all cameras except most cartridge-loading models so, if you have a roll of daylight slide film in the camera and then want to take a few shots indoors, you can just fit the correct filter.

Electronic flash and blue-tinted flash bulbs give the same coloured light as daylight, so you can use daylight film both indoors and out.

Pictures taken at sunrise or sunset also have a warm orange-yellow cast. If you want to avoid this, pictures should be taken well after sunrise and well before sunset. Alternatively, a simple filter will reduce this cast.
Processing
Most colour films, with the exception of Kodachrome, can be home processed, but it is wise to master black and white processing first.
Prints from slides
It is perfectly possible to have prints made from slides, but they are expensive because the processor has to make the equivalent of a negative, called an inter-neg, or use special paper.

Choosing black and white

It is useful to have at least two speeds of film. A medium 100 or 125 ASA gives a good compromise between speed, grain and detail while 400 ASA is useful for moving subjects or low light levels. However, only 100 ASA film is available for 110s.

Black and white slide film is available, but this is usually used for lectures. Standard film speeds range from 32–400 ASA.

Uprating your film

If you do your own processing, or have a helpful processor, it is possible to take photographs even when your exposure meter tells you it is too dark. With a 400 ASA film you set the film speed dial to 800 ASA (called uprating), giving you an extra stop or letting you double your shutter speed. When you process the film you increase the development time to compensate for this under-exposure. This is explained in a later article.

IN DAYLIGHT
1 Daylight film used in daylight gives the correct colour rendering.
2 Tungsten balanced film used in daylight gives a blue cast.
3 This can be corrected by using an amber colour correction filter, but the film speed will be slower.

IN ARTIFICIAL LIGHT
1 Tungsten balanced film used in artificial light produces the correct colour balance.
2 This yellowish cast is produced with daylight film in artificial light.
3 This can be corrected by using a blue colour correction filter.

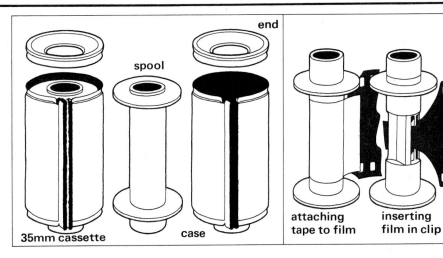

35mm cassette   spool   end   case   attaching tape to film   inserting film in clip

Loading your own cassette

By loading your own cassettes with bulk film, you can save up to 50% in costs. Bulk reels of 135 film come in lengths of 5m, 17m and 30m, packed in a light-tight can and wound on a cardboard or plastic core.

1·5m will give	**36** exposures
5m ,, ,,	**120** exposures
17m ,, ,,	**408** exposures
30m ,, ,,	**720** exposures

You will need:
A bulk reel of film or pre-cut lengths of 36 exposures (refills)
A clean, empty cassette or a reloadable cassette
Scissors
Two drawing pins
Black masking tape

Light on
1 To separate the cassette spool and case, tap the knob projecting at one end sharply on a table; or prise the end off carefully with a bottle opener, blunt knife or your thumb. (Avoid Kodak crimped on cassettes—they are very hard to open.) Some re-loadable cassettes have screw-on caps.
Inspect the felt jaws of the cassette carefully. Discard any cassette that is dirty or dented.
Check to see if the centre of the spool contains a spring clip. Remove any old pieces of film in the clip and check, with a piece of dud film, that the clip will hold the end firmly. If so, you won't need tape to fix the film to the spool.
2 For short lengths of film, measure off the length required and mark each end with a drawing pin. Fix a 3cm length of masking tape near one of the drawing pins so you can find it in the dark. Make sure your hands are dry and clean when handling film, and only touch the edges.

Practise the next steps in daylight first, with any length of dud or exposed film. With the actual film, work in *total darkness*—in a darkroom, in a blacked-out cupboard, or under the bed clothes at night.
In total darkness
3 Take the bulk reel of film out of its can, holding the film by its edges. Stick the end of the film to the centre of the spool with tape and wind the film firmly round the spool in the way it curls naturally ('emulsion in'). The emulsion side feels matt. If your spool has a spring clip in the centre, shape the end of the film to fit the slot with a pair of scissors.
For short lengths, measure off the length required against the drawing pins and cut the film.
For 36 exposures, wind on the film until you can feel that the spool is almost full and then cut the film. Don't overfill the spool or the cassette may jam.
Always remember to put the bulk reel back in its can and close the lid carefully, taping it in place.
4 When the film is fully wound on to the spool, slot over the outer case, leaving the end of the film projecting through the felt jaws of the cassette. Squeeze the case and snap or screw on the end. You can now relax and switch on the light.
Changing bags
If you have not got a room or cupboard that you can make lightproof, changing bags are available from photographic shops. These need practice to use with ease. Be very careful to remove dust and check everything inside before you start. Daylight film loaders are also available but they are probably only worth buying if you load dozens of cassettes every month.

Special films

Photography covers a vast subject area and with the choice of black and white print film, colour prints and slides in a varying range of emulsion speeds there aren't many subjects with which you cannot cope.

For general subjects and techniques most people are quite happy with ordinary black and white or colour films. However, there are a few other types of film geared towards more specialized techniques. Some of the films are not readily available over the local photographic counter, and you may be obliged to place a special order, or even to buy more than you need.

Tungsten film such as Kodak Ektachrome 50 Professional (Tungsten) or Kodak Ektachrome 160 (Tungsten), is slide film designed for taking photographs in tungsten light (photographic lamps rather than photofloods). The quality of tungsten light is distinctly red biased: if daylight film is used with photographic lamps the result is orange and warm in tone. For some subjects this may actually enhance the effect by giving a warm romantic image, but if you want to recreate natural colours, tungsten film is essential.

● For photofloods an 81A filter over the camera lens gives correct colour balance with tungsten film. If you are using normal room lighting, tungsten film gives slightly better colour balance than that produced on daylight film, but it will still be warm in tone.

● If you have your camera loaded with tungsten film and want to take pictures outside (in daylight) you must use an 85B filter over the lens. If you don't then the photographs will be unacceptably blue and cold in tone.

● The processing method is as for any other slide film; you can process your own films or have them done commercially through the usual outlets.

● 35mm and 120 sizes are available.

▲ Tungsten film and tungsten light: tungsten film is exactly balanced for the red bias of tungsten lights. Grey and white show colour casts most easily but here rendition is correct.

▲ Tungsten film and daylight: noon daylight is much bluer than tungsten. Tungsten film is balanced for a high red content and the effect is therefore blue when lit with daylight.

▲ Daylight film and tungsten light: if you use tungsten lights and daylight film the effect is usually too red. Tungsten film exposed in tungsten light and an 85B filter gives the same effect.

▲ You can use tungsten film in daylight only if an 85B filter is fitted over the camera lens. The amber filter corrects the blue quality of daylight and makes the subject colours appear correct. An increase in exposure is needed.

▲ If you omit to use the correct filter when taking daylight pictures on tungsten film all colours are reproduced incorrectly. The subject takes on an overall blue colour cast which is usually unacceptable.

▲▼ Tungsten film is the best choice for mixed source lighting. Neon tubes appear red, highlights lit by the sun are blue, and the fluorescent lit interior is green. Only areas lit by tungsten light reproduce correctly. The model below is lit by daylight and by tungsten, which results in a strange blue cast on one side of the face and the correct tone on the other.

▼ Tungsten film has reproduced the station sign in the correct colours. No other light source in the picture is compatible with this film, but the result is better than on daylight film.

Black and white reversal film is simply a slide film. Just as a black and white print portrays a multi-coloured subject in varying shades of grey, monochrome reversal film produces a black and white slide for projection. Clear areas represent white parts of the subject, opaque black areas correspond to unlit shadows, and varying shades of grey replace in-between tones.

Compared to a brilliant, well-exposed colour slide, the black and white alternative looks pretty dull.

However, it is useful to copy old black and white prints which are perhaps taking up a lot of room, but of which you would like to keep a record. Storage space can then be kept to a minimum and you still retain those old memories.

The slides can be projected just like colour slides, and many people use them for lecturing.

The speed of black and white reversal film is generally slow (around 32 ASA)

and the grain must be fine to allow maximum detail to be reproduced. Reversal film gives a good range of tones.

● Agfa's Dia-Direct is an example of the few black and white reversal films available. It is only found in 36 exposure 35mm cassettes and the price of processing by Agfa-Gevaert is included. Ordinary slow speed, fine grain black and white films can be reversal processed by using special chemicals and techniques. The large number of different chemicals and the various

▼ Dia-Direct is a black and white slide film with a full tonal range and good contrast. It can be used to copy continuous tone originals such as black and white prints (top strip) to minimize storage space, or for lectures. It can also be used to take slides (below) as you would with any other film. Some consider them lacklustre compared to colour slides.

development stages are rather involved however, and you will probably prefer to have pre-paid processing.

Black and white copying film has only limited use for the amateur. For example you can use it to make records of original drawings and paintings to allow you to circulate examples of your work without the risk of losing the originals. The copying films available are in general slow speed, and a tripod or special copying stand is essential to steady the camera and prevent shake. The normal contrast characteristics and fine grain properties of the films allow them faithfully to reproduce tone and detail present in the original. This is called a 'continuous tone' film.

● For copying colour originals on to black and white you need a film which is sensitive to all colours of the spectrum—this is called 'panchromatic'. If the subject is already in black and white (such as a print) a film which is only blue sensitive is adequate.

These colour slides were copied in a slide duplicator using a slow speed, fine grain film with a good contrast range. Black and white negatives were produced and prints made. For copying colour originals a panchromatic film must be used, but for black and white subjects blue sensitive film can be used. Detail is lost and contrast is always increased whenever a slide or print is copied.

Choosing a wide angle lens

▼ Wide angle lenses from various manufacturers differ in design. Despite variations in size and shape wide angle lenses do have common features.

1 28mm extra wide angle lens
2 24mm extra wide angle lens
3 17mm ultra wide angle lens
4 18mm ultra wide angle lens
5 28mm extra wide angle lens

Look at this page from about 15cm away. Keep your eyes fixed on the dot below:

Don't move your eyes to look. Can you see your hands? Can you read anything apart from the words near the dot when your eyes are fixed on it? The answers should be yes and no, in that order.

Even with your eyes fixed on the dot and the page held as close as 15cm away, you still have some vision beyond the edge of the page—a full 180°. But only the central few degrees are really sharp enough for reading or seeing clearly.

The human eye has a wide field of view, and a wide angle lens does exactly the same thing. But in a photograph you expect to see sharp detail all over, not just in the centre like the human eye. The eye can move its sharp spot round but the camera can't; the lens must record detail corner-to-corner.

Wide angle lenses have a shorter focal length compared with the film size they use than standard lenses have. A 24mm lens is 'standard' for a 110 pocket camera (film size 13 x 17mm) but wide angle for a camera taking 35mm film (24 x 36mm). The shorter the focal length of the lens, the smaller the image it produces of an object at a given distance—you can get more surrounding image on as well.

But it's not quite that simple. An ordinary short-focus lens would produce that smaller image, but it would be surrounded by a dim area of unsharp picture—no good if you want the true wide angle recording of detail edge-to-edge. So lens designers have evolved special wide angle lenses which focus rays from the extreme edges of a wide field of view instead of losing them or bringing them to an imperfect focus. They have a series of glass elements which gradually bring the rays round the very sharp angles needed to focus them, using deeply rounded curvatures to gather the light. This usually means they can reproduce detail sharply between angles of 60° and 115°.

Retrofocus lenses

Wide angles with short focal lengths need to be very near the film—a 25mm lens would ideally have its optical centre about 26mm from the film, with some glass in front and some behind. But most 35mm SLRs have bodies about 43mm deep (lens mount to film)

▲ A wide angle lens allows the photographer to change his view point and composition without moving much—a couple of paces changes the angle of a subject as much as 90°.

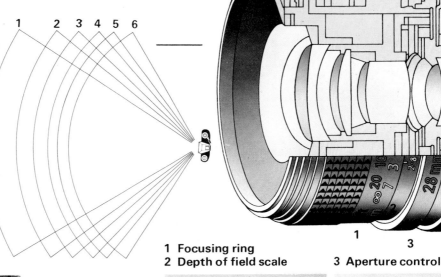

Focal lengths of wide angle lenses for 35mm SLRs

1	35mm wide angle	63°
2	28mm extra wide	75°
3	24mm extra wide	84°
4	20mm ultra wide	94°
5	17mm ultra wide	102°
6	15mm extreme wide	115°

These focal lengths and angles of view are approximate and differ from one manufacturer to another—a 15mm extreme wide angle lens can have an angle of view as wide as 180°.

1 Focusing ring
2 Depth of field scale
3 Aperture control

▲ View as seen through a standard 50mm lens on a 35mm SLR.

▲ A 35mm wide angle lens has a wider angle of view and gives greater coverage.

▲ A 24mm extra wide angle lens appears to push the scene even further back.

▲ A 17mm ultra wide lens creates perspective problems.

and mirrors which need about 30–35mm of clearance to swing up. To make the use of wide angles (35mm focal length or under) possible on SLR cameras, a retrofocus design is used. Most of the wide angle light-gathering is done by a set of glass elements at the front of the lens which contract the size of the scene in front—rather like binoculars used backwards. A set of rear lens elements resembling an ordinary camera lens 'sees' this reduced wide angle view and projects it on to the film.

Like all camera optics, these designs are complex and the dividing line between the front group and the rear group is often blurred or non-existent. But in some types you can look through the front group and see a diminished world, and use the rear separately to take photographs.

Choosing a lens

With wide angle lenses covering between 63° and 115°, there is some distortion on the wider angles. For a 35mm SLR, a 35mm focal length covering 63° may not be wide enough if your standard lens is 50mm; 28mm covering 75° would be a better choice. A 24mm covering 84° is going to extremes and, unless you particularly need this coverage with its risk of image distortion, the 28mm is the most sensible all-round choice.

Picture making

Wide angles increase your view of the overall scene but alter the effect of perspective in the picture. If there's a statue in front of a building it will appear to loom up out of all proportion as you move closer, while the background remains much the same.

These lenses give you more of the horizon, more of the sky—things you can't get by stepping back from a subject. But don't forget that you can move closer to nearby subjects—people, buildings, cars—provided you keep the subject away from the edges of the lens to avoid distortion. Wide angles give you a panoramic background automatically, but moving closer lets you keep the main subject as large as with a standard lens.

You can also move round subjects to vary that panoramic background. If you are 15 metres from a subject using a 200mm telephoto lens, you have to circle round a long way to move 90°. But with a wide angle you would be only 2 metres away, and a short walk would move you 90° round. Fewer obstacles get in the way at 2 metres, too.

From 3 metres away, dropping on your knees for a low viewpoint has little effect on how you see a standing figure —you look up at about 15°. But from 1 metre, dropping to your knee gives an angle of 45°. The closer you are, the greater the effect of small changes in camera position. Even the range of positions available by moving from side to side, kneeling, or taking a single step have great effect with wide angle lenses.

Using a wide angle lens, you can choose a close detail for the foreground with a given background and then, by moving round a bit, choose another detail without changing the background. So moving 2 metres might change the scene from one with flowers in the foreground to one with scrap iron, but without altering the background significantly. The great depth of field of a wide angle lens means you can keep both foreground and background perfectly sharp. Holes in walls, interesting windows, breaks through undergrowth, and so on, will frame your picture sharply if carefully used.

If small changes in viewpoint make big differences, extreme viewpoints—from on top of a wall, or from the ground— have an unbelievable effect. A 24mm lens on a 35mm SLR gives vertiginous views from only 2 metres up, and a 17mm used from ground level makes a crowd look like giants. The familiar converging vertical lines can be exaggerated by ultra-close viewpoints to make ordinary two-storey buildings seem like tower blocks.

If you use converging lines for effect, design the picture so that the lines run out of it in a balanced way—not symmetrically, but with a clear central vertical axis and without leaning over to one side. To make your verticals perfectly straight, hold the camera precisely vertical. You may need to climb on a chair to compose an interior correctly, or photograph a building from a first floor window across the street. If you have a tripod, swing the camera round to line the screen edges up with verticals to check for exact parallelism. Even better, buy a camera-top spirit level to fit your accessory shoe.

For the candid photographer, wide angles let you pre-focus the lens at about 2 metres, set the aperture to f8 and get good results anywhere between 1·5 metres and 2·5 metres. This is ideal for rapid-reaction snaps in the street, in crowds, or when people think you are too close to photograph them.

To see the world in wide angle terms, always relate foreground and background and move your viewpoint round to juxtapose them. The wide angle world is dependent on small key details as well as global views. The good wide angle photographer looks closely at these details despite the apparent affinity of wide angles for overall scenes.

Practical aspects

Exposure metering: because wide angle lenses take in a larger view there is more chance of including a big shadow patch or an expanse of bright sky, giving extreme contrasts or unbalanced areas of bright and dark.

Generally, SLR through-the-lens (TTL) metering systems give accurate or slight under-exposure with wide angles. Over-exposure is rarely a problem unless you photograph a small light detail on a black background. For accurate wide angle metering, move in close to take the reading or aim the camera/meter down to eliminate excess sky. In contrasty scenes pitch the exposure for the parts which are most

▲ A wide angle lens can be used very effectively for a portrait. From close to the subject an almost overall view is obtained. *Tomas Sennett*

► These extremely dramatic figures were photographed from close to the ground. Because of the way a wide angle lens distorts perspective the figures and the palm appear to be converging. *Jon Gardey*

▼ By photographing the subject from nearby with a wide angle lens the torso appears less dominating, drawing attention to the hands and the action of the subject. *David Kilpatrick*

important to you.

Focusing screens: despite popular belief, most modern SLRs are very easy to focus even with wide angles like 20 or 18mm; their microprisms work perfectly. Screens which show a high proportion of the real picture area (over 92%) and allow you to see really sharp detail in the corners, are best.

Depth of field: short focus lenses, including wide angles, have great depth of field. You can often take a photograph of two subjects a long way apart and get both of them sharp if the lens is stopped down. Sometimes this great depth is hard to avoid and pictures become muddled, so do not hesitate to use a setting like 1/1000 at f5·6 if you need to cut out the 'total focus' effect of 1/125 at f16.

Depth of focus: inside the camera, depth of focus at the film plane is very limited with wide angles. There is no room for error so if the film is not positioned correctly you won't get a sharp image.

Convergence and divergence: the close viewpoints and wide view of short lenses can make perspective seem exaggerated. Aim up and buildings seem to stream up to a vanishing-point, or lean; aim down and things grow up like mushrooms; aim along and a road or rail track sweeps away dramatically. Use this deliberately by using strong angles, or avoid it carefully by keeping your camera dead parallel to buildings for perfect verticals. Never accept slightly converging verticals and always balance your picture.

A feature available on some 35mm SLR wide angle lenses is the facility to shift the lens to correct converging lines.

Filter threads: because wide angles depend so much on mount design to avoid cut-off corners, and may use large front glass areas for best performance, filter sizes can be inconsistent even within a range. However, you should be able to find 35mm, 28mm and 24mm lenses to match your standard lens filter kit. You may be able to get 20mm lenses too, but for sub-20mm wide angles larger filters are universal.

Watch out for

● Filters, lens hoods and other accessories on wide angles—they may cut off the corners of the image. Your SLR screen may only show 88% of the true picture area, so mistakes like

this won't be spotted until you see the photograph. Buy the slimmest filters possible and the correct lens hood—if in doubt, take some test shots with the lens set at infinity and the smallest aperture.
• Wide angles may have large areas of glass—avoid scratching them. Use a lens hood if possible, and a UV filter.
• Avoid shooting into the sun with the sun just out of the frame. If you have a depth of field preview, always check that the wide angle is not throwing up flare when working against the light.
• Cheap wide angles may turn straight lines into slight curves, especially near the edges; they may not be very sharp in the corners, and may not take good close-ups.

◄ The curve of this round-fronted building is further emphasized by a wide angle lens which, because of the vertical format, here creates converging verticals in the perspective.

► The great depth of field of a wide angle lens makes it possible to compose a picture with a strong foreground while retaining background detail as well.
Tony Evans

▼ The figure merging with the tree is distinctly set off by the flat background.
Michael Boys

Medium telephoto lenses

When you look at a scene, it doesn't matter very much to your eye whether an important part occupies a tenth of your view or over half of it—in fact, to see something comfortably it needs to be at a suitable distance, not too close. A face is just as 'important' at 3 metres as it is at 1 metre, and nobody looking at a house or tree from the other side of the road would feel compelled to cross over to get a better view.

That is because your eyes can pick out very small areas of detail and 'read' them, ignoring the rest of the scene. Only when something is very small and very distant do we find aids like binoculars or a telescope useful, because the subject has gone beyond the limit of our visual resolution— that is, beyond the point where we can pick out fine detail.

There is also a limit to the amount of fine detail which can be contained in the small area of a photograph. If you take a colour slide of a distant subject there is no point in projecting the slide on to a screen and then looking at a small area standing close to the screen. It makes sense for the subject to fill most of the picture, so that the finest possible detail can be seen without distracting surroundings. It is not simply a question of moving in on the subject—this isn't always possible. A long focus or telephoto lens is the answer, because it has the effect of bringing the subject closer.

A long focus lens has a longer focal length than a standard lens for any given film size. It produces a bigger image of the subject (a higher magnification). A special optical design has been devised to produce compact lenses which can reduce the size by up to half. This design is called 'telephoto'. Today the term is so widely used to describe any lens giving a magnifying effect that 'telephoto' tends to refer to any long focus lens, and not just those using a compact design.

With all telephoto lenses, a doubling of the focal length produces twice the image size on the film. Lenses up to 200mm for 35mm SLRs (equivalent to about 350mm on a large format SLR) are included in the medium range; the longer telephotos, as well as zoom lenses, are dealt with in separate articles.

To choose a medium telephoto lens you have to decide on its main function. If your standard lens is 50mm and you do a lot of portraits, then 85–105mm could be the answer; 135mm gives you freedom in candid shots and 200mm gets into the action in sports photography. For general photography a good choice is a telephoto of around 100–105mm.

Picture making

Standing in one place with a 135mm lens (on a 35mm SLR), you could photograph more than 20 entirely separate views without overlapping. That even allows a few degrees to spare between each shot if you just keep moving round through 360°. If you add to that your ability to aim the camera up or down as well, then there could well be over 60 completely

MEDIUM LENGTH TELEPHOTO LENSES FOR 35mm SLRs
1 100mm
2 135mm
3 100mm macro
4 200mm
5,6 telephoto converters
7, 8 lens mounts to fit lenses from independent manufacturers on to various cameras.

200mm MEDIUM TELEPHOTO LENS FOR 35mm SLR

1 focusing ring
2 distance scale
3 depth of field scale
4 aperture setting
5 bayonet fitting

Centre: the angles of view shown for various focal lengths are approximate as they can vary slightly in lenses from different manufacturers. The longer the focal length of the lens, the smaller the angle of view is. Maximum apertures are slower and depth of field also decreases. Angles are measured on the film frame diagonal.

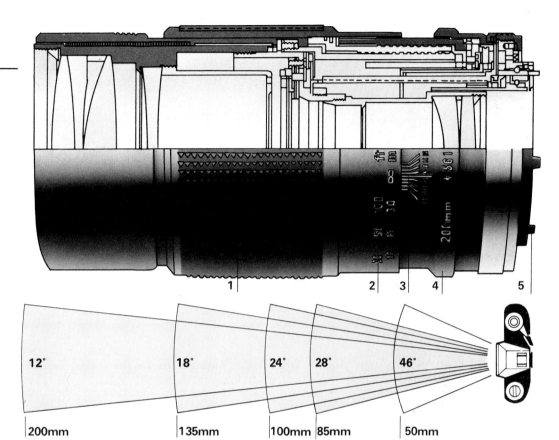

▲ **85mm lens** with this focal length on a 35mm SLR there is no obvious compression of planes.

▲ **100mm lens** moves the subject closer and the effect remains fairly normal.

▲ **135mm lens** —the background is slightly out of focus and obviously a 'tele' vision.

▲ **200mm lens** throws the background out of focus and the compression of perspective is strong.

Minimum focusing distances for medium telephoto lenses

Sometimes it is useful to have some idea of what lens to use in a given situation. In the cases below, portrait and full length are vertical compositions and 'car' gives a rough idea of how well an average car fits a horizontal frame side-on.

Lens	Portrait	Full length	Car
85mm	2m	4·5m	9m
135mm	3m	7·5m	15m
200mm	4·5m	10m	21m

These are examples of the distances you would need to have in order to manoeuvre and get a good shot. So, as you can see, there is little point in trying for a comfortably composed portrait with a 200mm lens in a room measuring less than about 6 metres, unless you want both you and the subject to be crammed against the walls.

Eventually you will get to know how much your own telephoto lens includes, and you can begin to see the world in telephoto terms—it is no longer necessary to actually fit the lens before you know if the subject is suitable. A very good idea is to walk around for an afternoon with the telephoto lens on your camera. It will familiarize you with the lens and show you how to be more selective.

different views from one standpoint. And if you use a 200mm lens, the number obviously increases. This is where selectivity comes in.

The key to successful telephoto photography is the ability to select those small areas in the scene round you which make good photographs—details, faces, 'landscapes within landscapes', groups of objects or people. But once you have spotted a subject for your telephoto lens you may have to move a long way to one side, or move closer in, to get the right angle and the best frame-filling composition. Because of this, telephoto shots are often the kind which you just see and shoot—the small incident, the interesting detail—as opposed to the kind which you visualize and then manoeuvre round to compose.

Shutter speeds for hand holding: where wide angle lenses allow you to use slow speeds with little more than a firm stance, telephotos of 85mm and over on 35mm cameras, and the equivalent on large formats, begin to show up any camera shake as unsharpness.

• The rule of thumb is the same for all lenses—use a shutter speed with a 'number' not less than the focal length of the lens for hand-holding. Use 1/125 with an 85mm or 100mm, 1/250 with a 135mm or 200mm. With all telephotos, especially when following action, try to use the highest speed your exposure will allow. Remember that the added weight and balance shift of a telephoto lens increase the possibility of camera shake, so use fast shutter speeds— 1/250, 1/500 or even 1/1000—whenever you can.

Holding the camera steady: to avoid shake when it is not possible to use these fast shutter speeds, use a tripod, a monopod or some other support to keep the camera steady. For mobile action shots, you can buy a shoulder-stock with a trigger shutter release and for short telephoto lenses a simple pistol grip screwed into the base improves steadiness. If you cannot use extra support of this kind, make sure that you always grip the telephoto focusing mount when shooting so that one hand supports the lens and the other the camera.

Perspective problems: telephoto lenses are highly selective, separating subjects from their background or surroundings; and drawing them closer. Perspective is flat—there are no dramatic sweeping vistas to be seen through the telephoto lens—so that the emphasis is on isolating detail. Distances are not clearly recognizable, and with longer lenses—135mm or 200mm—the distance between planes in the final picture can be very hard to assess, each one appearing like a layer of scenery dropped down behind the main subject. There is still some perspective left, of course, especially with shorter telephotos. But the general feeling given is of solidness, flatness and lack of depth. The telephoto view is something we never see naturally unless we use binoculars—there is always a foreground edge in the field of our normal

vision to give us depth. Telephoto images often cut this out.

Selective focusing: as well as being selective in picking out details, the telephoto is very selective in its focusing. The limited depth of field results in differential focus, where the subject is picked out as a crisp image between an out-of-focus foreground and background. By using telephoto lenses at fairly wide apertures such as f4 or f5·6, you can be even more selective in focusing. Distracting backgrounds can be diffused and attractive backgrounds, such as foliage behind a portrait outdoors, can be softened.

If your camera has a depth-of-field preview button it can be used very effectively with a telephoto lens. It allows you to preview the stopped-down image on the focusing screen. You can then adjust the aperture to get the exact effect you want.

Obstruction: sometimes using a telephoto lens means that things get in the way; things you can't move because they are between you and the subject—

◀ The telephoto lens was used here to compose the picture. A standard lens would not have allowed such tight composition without moving up to the trees. *Michael Busselle*

▼ A telephoto lens made this composition possible without disturbing the seals. *Ernst Haas*

▲ Any attempt to approach the subject would have disturbed the tranquillity of this scene.
Michael Busselle

◀ A medium telephoto lens can be used without a tripod providing there is sufficient light to allow a shutter speed with a number larger than the focal length of the lens being used.

▼ By focusing on the crossbar in advance, the photographer was able to concentrate on releasing the shutter at the exact moment the athlete would pass over it.

fences, branches or twigs, wire netting and so on. But if you use the telephoto lens at a wide aperture such as f4 the differential focus may make them seem to disappear altogether. Cage netting in zoos can be eliminated by putting the telephoto lens right up to the wire and working at f4 or f5·6 with a 135mm: but always check by using the depth-of-field preview before shooting.

Portrait problems: the limited depth of field causes problems when you move in close for a portrait. It is very tempting to focus on the hair or eyebrows, as they are good 'targets'. Always focus on the pupils of the eyes or the eyelashes—nothing looks worse than a well-focused nose and blurred eyes. Try to stop down your lens just enough to bring nose, mouth and eyes into sharp focus at the same time.

Panning: because telephotos have a limited depth of field, it may be necessary to focus while following a moving object. This involves panning to keep the subject in the frame and at the same time turning the focus ring enough to keep it sharp. Practice is the only way to perfect this technique. A far easier method is to preset your focus on a mark or spot which you know the subject will pass (a point on a race track, for example). You follow the subject in the normal way, ignoring the fact that it may be out of focus when you first see it through the viewfinder. As it passes the preset point you take the picture—though a good photographer presses the shutter an instant before to allow for the normal delay in our physical reactions.

The key to success is to keep the subject correctly framed and move smoothly through—follow it and keep following it even while you press the shutter. Do not stop moving the camera. If you stop when you press the shutter you will lose the subject. Slow speeds may be used with success if your speed is accurately matched to the subject—the background will blur, giving an effect of speed.

Technical aspects

Mounts: interchangeable mount telephotos are commonly available, and it is generally hard to tell the difference in quality between telephoto lenses of independent make and camera makers' lenses.

Contrast and colour rendering: telephotos may be low in contrast. Choose a multi-coated lens when possible and keep to one make only for consistent colour rendering.

▲ A medium telephoto lens allows the photographer to work without moving in too close to the subject. The subject tends to be less self-conscious. *John Kelly*

◀ Children often react to the camera without the shyness or awareness that adults have when being photographed. *Roland Michaud*

▶ By following the subject with the camera a sense of movement and speed is retained. *Suzanne Hill*

Lens hoods: many lens hoods sold with telephotos are too short. A lens hood about 75mm long can be used on medium telephotos of most types, and helps to protect the lens from dirt and knocks as well as from stray sunlight. Telephoto lenses may produce overall light flare without a lens hood if used into the light.

Filters: because telephoto lenses look at more distant subjects, any haze or mist will have a greater effect on the results. Always use haze cutting filters, such as UV and skylight filters. Never over-expose on misty days. Fog and mist cannot be penetrated but light haze can. Watch out for rising heat haze—no filter can stop this from producing poor sharpness in telephoto shots.

Filter threads: if a filter for your standard lens does not fit your telephoto lens it is usually possible to adapt the filter by using stepping rings. If using gelatin filters, of course, there is no problem as you can use a universal mount.

Exposure metering: a telephoto lens picks out a small area of the overall scene, and as a result only that area must be used to base the exposure on. If you are using a hand-held meter, a reading taken close in to the subject is desirable. If you are not able to go in close, which is one main reason for using a telephoto to begin with, a spot meter or narrow angle meter is useful. Most hand-held CdS meters have acceptance angles of about 20° and are therefore fairly suitable. With TTL metering cameras, the lens itself makes the close-up reading, and there is no major problem.

Focusing screens: telephoto lenses up to 200mm all work perfectly well with modern SLR focusing screens at full aperture—most microprisms and split-image range finders will function if the lens aperture is wider than f4·5, and few telephoto lenses up to 200mm are slower than this. To avoid 'bull's-eye' compositions a plain ground-glass screen with no central aids is useful as telephotos are very easy to focus on ground-glass, and a plain screen helps uncluttered composition.

Depth of field: telephoto lenses have a limited depth of field at wider apertures (f8 or wider) but can be stopped down to f16 with significant gains in sharpness. Never be deceived by what you see through the viewfinder at full aperture, which will eliminate distracting backgrounds by blurring them totally—always check with a stop-down preview, if possible. They may snap into focus at f11. Use differential focusing creatively to lose them, but avoid using too much—out-of-focus noses on portraits will result if you work wide open at f2·8 on a 135mm.

Lens weight and camera mounts: medium telephoto lenses can generally be used on all cameras without too much strain on mounts. If the lens you buy is equipped with a tripod bush (as are some 200mm f2·8s, and similar fast, medium telephotos), this is a clear statement by the makers that they think you should try to support the lens rather than the camera. With heavy lenses like this (135mm f2, 180mm f2·8, 200mm f2·8) avoid letting the camera hang from its neckstrap—if the lens mount does not suffer, the neck-strap attaching lugs may wear out, or the strap may break.

The versatile zoom lens

You are standing in the middle of a crowd, photographing a football match. With your 100mm telephoto lens the players look far too small when the action moves to the far goal mouth, but if you fit your 200mm telephoto lens you get cut-off heads and feet when players move near you.

You are standing on the edge of a harbour wall, photographing a light-house. You want it to fill the frame precisely, with no wasted space. Neither your 135mm nor your 200mm allows this—you need 163mm. If you could move in closer or move back, your problems would be solved—but you can't . . .

You are climbing a mountain, and don't want to be weighed down with equipment. Nor do you want to be changing lenses, as this occupies your hands, which are better used for climbing. But you want a wide angle lens for close-ups of your fellow climbers and a medium telephoto for views of the scenery.

These three problems have the same answer—the zoom lens. Zoom lenses have been called '100 focal lengths in one lens'—instead of producing a fixed image, they can 'zoom' in to magnify the image, or zoom back to get more in the frame. Zoom lenses were first introduced on cine cameras but are now almost universal on stills cameras, especially on 35mm SLRs.

Making a zoom lens is a fairly complex operation, though the principle is simple. If you change the separation between two elements (or groups) in a photographic lens, you change the focal length of the combination. But you also change other things like the distance of the film from the lens, and the f stop.

Modern zoom lenses use anything from nine to 18 glass elements, moving apart or closer together in tracks worked out by computer to change focal lengths without altering accurate focus settings or the f stop. In addition, all the usual aberrations and distortions which even normal standard lenses can have, must be eliminated as far as possible.

Cheap zooms tend to be optically compensated—that is, by careful optical design a relatively simple movement of one group in the lens does everything, zooming perfectly and holding sharp focus. But to achieve this, the lens may be bulky, have a limited aperture or poor performance.

The more expensive zoom lenses are usually mechanically compensated, with tracks allowing two or three groups to move in different directions as the lens is zoomed.

200–500mm

24–50mm

70–150mm

70–210mm

35–140mm

35–105mm

Zooms can cover an enormous range of focal lengths, like the Soligor 35–140mm and 70–150mm lenses, or a narrower range like the Rokkor 24–50mm. The long Tamron lens shown covers from 200–500mm. Many lenses have macro or close focusing settings like the Vivitar Series 1 70–210mm (it uses a push/pull zoom action) and the 35–105mm lens.

Most zooms are similar in size to the long focal length on their scale—for example, an 80–210mm zoom resembles a 200mm lens, not an 80mm. Wide angle and mid-range zooms may be even larger, though in the case of some pure wide angle zooms the reverse happens—a 24–50mm zoom is more like a 24mm than a standard 50mm. They are usually one f stop smaller than a normal prime lens of the longest or shortest focal length (80–200mm—f4·5, as opposed to 200mm—f3·5; 24–50mm—f4, as opposed to 24mm—f2·8). Regardless of size, most zooms are heavy because of the amount of glass and metal used.

Choosing a lens

To choose the kind of zoom you need, bear in mind your kind of photography.
• The family photographer needs a mid-range 35–80mm, ideal for everything from groups to portraits and children.
• The keen travel photographer might prefer a 24–50mm wide angle zoom.
• The sports enthusiast could benefit from an 80–210mm.
• The portrait photographer is better off with a 70–150mm.
But remember that the real enthusiast will pick a prime lens for his or her best pictures, because they tend to be better optically—so the wide angle man might buy a superb 24mm, and cover with an 80–200mm zoom for all those telephoto lengths he might occasionally need.
• Look for a zoom which balances well in the hand, and which has zoom and focus controls which, whatever the type, are easily distinguished.
• Focus should hold when zooming so

that there is no need to re-set it after changing focal length.
• Long zoom lenses, such as 100–300mm, should have a tripod bush for mounting the lens, not the camera.

Advantages

The big advantages of the zoom—fewer lenses to carry, no lens changing, infinitely variable focal lengths—allow the photographer to work quickly and accurately, with less leg work involved in framing the subject properly, and more freedom to select the right viewpoint or moment of subject action.

Disadvantages

The disadvantages of zoom lenses are that they tend to be heavy; they are never as light as a single focal length 'prime' lens, and are often slower in lens speed (smaller maximum aperture)

▶ Cutaway view of telephoto zoom lens. Zoom lenses are made up of groups of lens elements which move to change the focal length and focus. The optics are complex and the number of groups and elements vary from one manufacturer to another. The front elements (below right) twist to focus the lens, the centre section slides or twists to alter the focal length. The rear element is fixed.

▼ The sequence below was taken with a 35–100mm zoom lens from the same point. The first shot, at 35mm (a wide angle covering 62°) takes in the whole scene; 50mm (covering about 47°) is equivalent to a standard lens on a 35mm SLR; 80mm (angle of view about 29°) moves in closer to the climbers; 100mm (angle of view about 24°) has the effect of a medium length telephoto lens.

Focusing   Correcting

Zoom

| 35mm | 50mm | 85mm | 100mm |

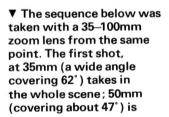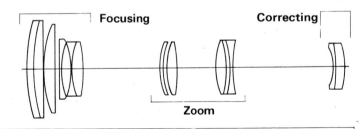

and of lower optical performance. But if they seem expensive, you only need to add up the prices of two or three single lenses to find that price, at least, is not a disadvantage.

Problems with zooms

Zooms and 'varifocals'—which are zooms which need refocusing after you change the focal length—are prone to a few major faults.

Distortion: straight lines may appear as gentle curves. noticeable with architectural subjects or copying.

Poor coverage: zooms are more likely to have fall-off in sharpness and brightness in the picture corners.

Flare: the multi-element construction of zooms can lead to flare.

Low contrast: the construction can also produce low contrast generally, even in good light.

Curvature of field: zooms may have a curved field, with the centre focusing in a different plane from the edges, especially at close distances.

Picture making

Zoom lenses allow good composition because the photographer does not have to fit subjects into a fixed magnification. They can also make a photographer lazy—he can frame-up with the zoom rather than find a good angle. To get the best shots you need to look for good angles and then use your zoom. Zoom lenses allow you to photograph from a fixed position when you cannot move freely, and also to find the positions which might not be usable with any fixed focal length lens you own.

They also save time spent changing lenses, so that you can catch many shots which you would have missed otherwise. The only exception is if you work with two cameras—for black and white and colour—one zoom between two cameras causes as many hold-ups as two lenses and one camera.

Just as you can pre-set the focus on your normal lens to catch quick shots you can also pre-set the focus control and zoom control on a zoom lens— but not necessarily to the average setting. A 70–210mm zoom is best left at 70mm, because it is much easier to view a wide field and then zoom in than it is to hunt for the subject at 200mm and pull back to frame it. But a 24–50mm zoom could be better left at 50mm.

With a zoom, you can change your viewpoint and angle quickly without losing the precise framing of the

▲ Zoom lenses are ideal for candid shots allowing the photographer to compose a shot quickly.

◄ A 70–150mm zoom lens is useful for portraits. It allows the photographer to work at reasonable distances from the subject.
Roland Michaud

▼ For sports photography, where players move from far to near, an 80–210mm zoom lens is useful. At its longest focal length it is still possible to capture the action, even from a distance.
Don Morley

subject. So moving away 2 metres does not mean getting a smaller image unless you want that to happen. Zooms give you freedom to control perspective as a result of this—notably wide angle zooms. In general photography, where you may not want to devote thought to exact viewpoints, they save time by giving a good frame-filling composition without the necessity of worrying about viewpoint.

Zooms are at their best for photographing people and children. A photographer moving round, closing in and backing off, can be off-putting to adults and children alike. With a zoom you can be less demanding and obtrusive—no more 'back a little more, please', or moving forwards for a closer viewpoint.

Zooms are excellent for sports work, where you can frame-up different points on a track or field from one position without changing lenses. You can use the pre-set focusing techniques for action work, or follow by panning, just as you can with a telephoto, and with push/pull zoom rings, you can often zoom back to catch a moving subject too. Always remember, when following a moving subject with a zoom, that both focus and zoom rings may need changing—the best answer is a zoom with one collar for both.

Zoom lenses are not ideal for landscapes and architecture, mainly because of their characteristics. Though landscape work can be done on zooms, most will give some degree of curvature to straight lines near the edges of the picture—and that includes the horizon. If no horizon is included, then zooms are perfectly acceptable, but in some cases, such as

▼ A zoom is especially useful when your subject is at all nervous. The photographer stays in one place and can change focal length as quickly as if he was focusing.

▶ When covering sporting events the photographer's movement is likely to be limited. Here a zoom comes into its own; no awkward lens changes or weight. *Julian Calder*

calm seascapes with the horizon right against the frame edge, the effect is poor. Architectural shots on wide angle zooms suffer from the same problems, accentuated by the straight lines of architecture.

A familiar effect with a zoom is the long exposure during which the lens is zoomed, producing a rushing or streaked effect. Mount the camera on a tripod, keep the main subject dead centre in the photograph, and use a small f stop so that the exposure is more than 1/8. Press the shutter while operating the zoom control, either increasing or decreasing focal length of the lens. With longer exposures, such as 10 seconds, in low light, a better effect can be had by letting half the exposure be made at a fixed setting and then zooming for the second half.

When you use a zoom, your technique can vary according to the way in which the end result will be produced. If you take colour negatives for sending away to be developed and

printed, always make a point of composing the shot exactly, but allow a little margin on the length of the photograph as most prints are not as long and narrow as the 35mm shape. For slides, you can use the full area that you see on the screen, and zooms help you to do this perfectly.

If you print your own photographs from negatives, you can plan for odd shapes—square prints, or long thin prints—by imagining the result on the camera screen. But using a zoom still helps you get the sharpest and least grainy prints by making full use of the negative. And if you zoom carefully, composing accurately, you will not need to change enlargement during a session. So you can keep to standard exposure and filtration settings for all the shots on your roll of film.

Practical aspects

Exposure metering: there is no need for special methods when metering zoom lenses—they behave just like prime lenses of their focal length. But

you can use the zoom facility to take selective meter readings or cut out bright sky areas before setting the correct focal length.

Focusing screens: because zooms are sometimes of low aperture—the f5 100–300mm for example—focusing screen aids, such as split image wedges, may not work. For long telephoto zooms a plain ground-glass screen is the best solution. Otherwise, expect zooms to be a little harder to focus generally than other lenses. A bright screen is best.

Aperture changes: many zooms have a variable maximum aperture—that is, 35–100mm, f3·5 to f4·3, meaning that at 35mm the lens has a maximum aperture of f3·5, but at 100mm this drops to f4·3, a half stop change. Always check whether the rest of the scale—f5·6, f8, f11, f16, f22—is linked to this change or not. In some types of zoom, setting f8 at 100mm would actually give you f9·5 because there is no compensation. In others, it would give you f8 correctly. Open aperture

124

▲ A zoom lens made it possible to shoot this picture cutting out the photographer's shadow. *John Garret*

◀ Expressing movement with a zoom; alter focal length during a long exposure to give double blur. *Gerry Cranham*

▶ Panning and altering the zoom setting gives another impression of speed. *John McGovren*

▼ A wide angle zoom at shortest focal length.

metering systems automatically compensate—but flashguns, for example, do not.

Changes in depth of field: remember that you should always pre-view your depth of field at working aperture and working focal length. It changes if you zoom, and checking it at 80mm does not help you judge the result at 135mm.

Changes in focus setting: although zooms are meant to hold accurate focus when you zoom, many do not. There is a slight variation, within acceptable limits. However, if you focus quickly at 70mm and then zoom, without checking, to shoot at 210mm, there may be enough error to give you a bad picture. So always either focus at the longest focal length, or at the setting you use to take the picture.

Lens hood, flare and filters: always use a hood if possible, and avoid shooting into the light without first checking the stopped-down effect, as flare patches may appear with many zooms. Check that hoods and filters do not cause cut-off at short focal lengths by taking a picture set at infinity and fully stopped down.

Filter threads: most zooms now have moderately normal filter fittings—tele-zooms may have threads as small as 49mm but are more usually around the 55–62mm mark. In camera makers' series of lenses, the zooms often have the standard thread. Mid-range zooms and wide angle zooms, however, are far more likely to have very large filter threads—62mm, 67mm or even 72mm. Filters in these sizes sometimes have very thick rims which can cut off corners, so check before buying.

Mounts: most zooms today come from independent makers, and nearly all of them are available in the popular camera fittings and with interchangeable mounts. Because zooms from independent makers are often just as good as camera makers' lenses (if available) and normally a fraction of the price, buying an intermount lens is a very good policy. Even if you change your other lenses when you change your camera, you can keep the zoom.

Long telephoto lenses

Although the human eye is capable of picking out very small subjects from a great distance, it can rarely see the detail on the subject clearly—we recognize things partly because we know what they are when we see them, rather than because we see them perfectly. Even a vague glimpse is enough to tell a bird-watcher what type of bird is flying far overhead, from movement and shape, although the visual image may be nothing more than a tiny silhouette on the eye's retina.

That is all very well for recognition, but for study and close observation we need magnifying systems, such as binoculars and telescopes, to see detail. In photography the same problem arises and the solution is much the same—you could certainly pick out a distant car with a 50mm lens on a 35mm SLR, but if you want to read the number plate or recognize the driver, much more detail is needed.

The answer for this sort of photography is the high power or extreme telephoto lens. These lenses involve optics which photographers call 'long toms' if built with glass lenses, and 'big cats' (catadioptric) if mirrors are used, as in the case of reflector telescopes.

The big problem with long lenses is bulk—a 1000mm lens should, in theory, be a full metre long and is hardly the sort of thing that can be held comfortably. Another problem is the maximum aperture. An f4 1000mm

lens would have a front glass at least 250mm in diameter before the metal rim was fitted. Add length and weight to such big, heavy mounts and glass elements, and a third problem is created—no camera could hold the lens properly and the average tripod would not be strong enough.

There are two solutions which combine to make the 'long tom' a viable lens. The first of these is the telephoto construction which collapses the light path to make the lens smaller—perhaps half or less its focal length. Secondly, very long lenses have limited apertures, such as f6·3 or f11. Accepting this limitation gives a lens small enough to use normally. Even so, to keep their size within reasonable bounds, most long telephoto lenses use a tripod mount on the lens, not on the camera, so that the weight is balanced better.

Conventional long lenses

These long telephoto lenses are rarely more than 45cm long, and usually take filters which are less than 82mm in size (or special rear mount filters). Conventional telephoto lenses are available with various features.

Internal focusing lenses do away with the cumbersome focusing collars round the front of the lens and require no heavy mechanics. These lenses can be very sensitive to small changes, making them useful for rapid focusing.

Squeeze grip lenses have a pistol-type

grip which alters the focus setting as you squeeze, so that an action photographer can follow action and focus in one movement, while keeping a hand free to release the shutter.

Fluorite element lenses use crystal lenses instead of glass to make very light, compact, highly corrected telephotos; for example, a 300mm f2·8 would not be unduly heavy. High-speed telephotos for sports work have apertures like this, or f4 for a 600mm, and normally use fluorite or non-glass elements in the lenses.

Mirror lenses

These lenses use optical mirrors to fold the light path by reflection, as well as glass elements to focus and correct the image. This produces more compact lenses than the conventional lenses. Typical mirror lenses are about 15cm long and very light, with a focal length of 500mm and a fixed aperture of f8; though lengths from 250mm f5·6 to 2000mm f16 are available. These lenses, known as 'big cats' (catadioptric), have a fixed aperture. Another design of mirror lenses, known as solid catadioptric, allows even more compact lenses, but they

▶ Long telephoto lenses with the angle of view in brackets, from the left: 500mm (5°), 1000mm (2·5°), 400mm (6°) and 800mm (3°). The 500mm and 800mm lenses incorporate the catadioptric design.

▲ A 50mm standard lens with an angle of about 46° gives an overall view of the church.

▲ A 300mm lens, used from the same spot, has a narrower angle of view and has the effect of being closer.

▲ A 1000mm lens, with an angle of view of about 2·5°, isolates detail from a distance.

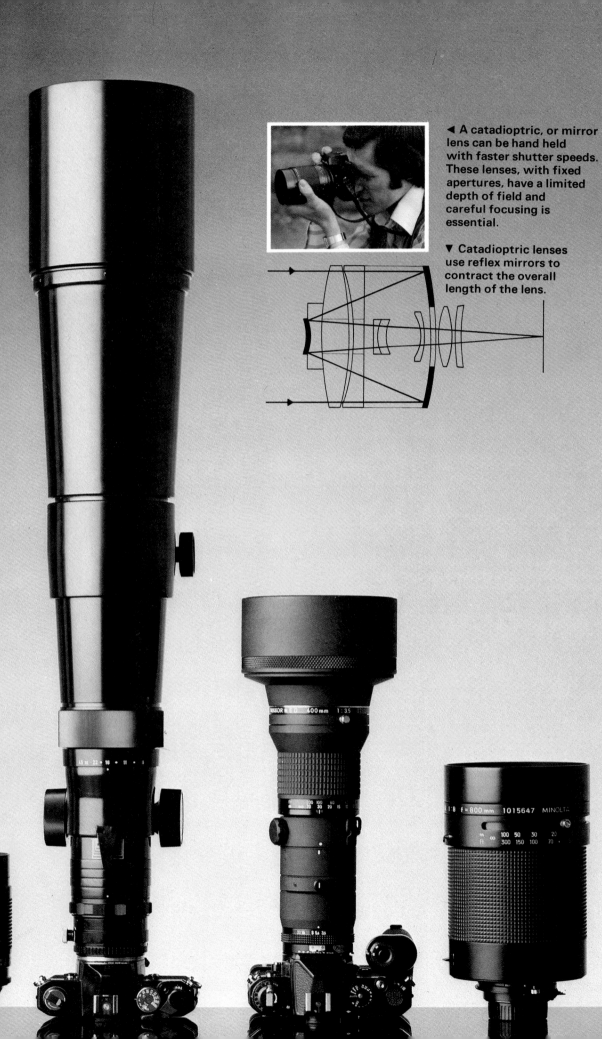

◀ A catadioptric, or mirror lens can be hand held with faster shutter speeds. These lenses, with fixed apertures, have a limited depth of field and careful focusing is essential.

▼ Catadioptric lenses use reflex mirrors to contract the overall length of the lens.

are heavier. Reflector telescopes are also available; these are similar to mirror lenses and can be used as such. Mirror lenses have O-shaped apertures and out-of-focus light points print as doughnut shapes.

Choosing a lens

Long telephoto lenses are useful for specific things. Generally, use 300–500mm for wild birds, motor cycling, car racing, sports, and air shows; 500–1000mm for water sports and wild life.

Bear in mind that you can use converters to increase the focal length of lenses—2x and 3x converters are available for 35mm SLR cameras (though these are not recommended for catadioptric lenses unless specially matched). So, if you have a 135mm lens you can increase it to 270mm with a 2x converter—if you can do this, a 300mm lens is obviously of little use, so buying a 500mm lens would make more sense. This in turn can be used with a 2x converter to get 1000mm.

Picture making

Lenses over 300mm do not produce any wide variety of pictorial results, and most photographers would be hard put to tell the difference between a 400mm and a 1000mm shot unless there are tell-tale signs, such as the 'doughnuts' produced by mirror lenses. The common pictorial effect is of extreme spatial compression, stacking subjects up in a compressed perspective, often with people behind the main subject looking larger than they should.

The unfocused image with long telephotos is a hidden trap. Some insignificant little road sign adjacent to your subject and way behind becomes a big blur of red, and shapeless splashes of colour are sometimes unavoidable. But this is also an asset, turning all backgrounds, unpleasant or otherwise, into diffused patterns.

Mirror lenses, with their doughnut shape of apertures, produce similarly shaped out-of-focus patterns, especially from highlights such as reflections on water, and double-edged unfocused images from other details. This can be a creative effect or a fault depending on the use made of it. Hexagonal diaphragms, normally used for economy on long telephotos of conventional design, produce hexagonal unfocused image patterns when stopped well down, and again these can be obtrusive or creative depending on the use made

▲ Long telephoto lenses distort perspective by foreshortening distance. A 300mm lens was used to photograph this vineyard. *Patrick Eagar*

▼ Using a telephoto lens made it possible to lose completely the distracting background of this dahlia hybrid. *John Sims*

▶ The doughnut shaped circles of confusion are characteristic of a catadioptric lens. By pre-focusing on a point on the track the photographer was able to get this shot at the exact moment the athlete was in focus—the runners in the rear appear out of focus due to the limited depth of field of the telephoto lens. *Gerry Cranham*

of them in the picture.

Mirror lenses are limited to one physical aperture and therefore to one depth of field, which is also less than the depth of field given by a normal lens. With a 400 ASA film in bright sunlight, 1/1000 at f8 may be one stop of overexposure, and the answer is a 4x neutral density filter which reduces the amount of light reaching the film.

With all lenses over 300mm, regardless of maximum aperture, you should be able to 'lose' wire netting or other obtrusive foreground material completely by placing the lens hood up against the wire or whatever, and opening the aperture fully. Never shoot through ordinary window glass —it produces serious unsharpness with long telephoto lenses. Bold, simple, clear subjects make the best shots, and subject counts more than photographic quality or creative skills. Finally, do remember that long telephoto lenses enable you to invade privacy and you should resist the temptation to misuse them. Very long lenses have been mistaken for guns in the past, with unfortunate results— they look aggressive, and not everyone knows what a telephoto lens is. So don't invite trouble by looking for it through an 800mm lens.

Focusing distances

The following is a guide to give some idea of focusing distances for various subjects.

Portraits: 300mm lens, 5–8 metres, depending on required size of face.

Wild birds: 500mm lens, 5 metres or closer.

Motor cycle racing: 300mm lens usually good for close-ups from the side of the track.

Car racing: 300–500mm, only useful for distant parts of track, otherwise too long for versatility.

Sports events: 300–500mm generally good from usual spectator distances.

Wild life: 500–1000mm to give good close-ups at acceptably safe distances.

Zoos: 300mm more than adequate, 500mm normally too long except for small fauna and birds, outdoors.

Water sports: 500–1000mm usually best because of distances involved.

Air shows: 300–500mm for normal flying height, aerobatics and fly-pasts.

Astronomy: 1000mm lens produces good-sized image of full moon.

Sunsets: all lengths over 300mm produce good results, but 500–1000mm shots can be very dramatic with the sun in the picture.

Long telephoto lenses have tremendous appeal in that they allow us to photograph scenes, events and people that would normally be impossible because we cannot get close enough. But, despite the compactness of modern designs, there are still problems in using these lenses that need to be understood in order to get the best from them.

Practical aspects

Highly selective subject selection—5° is a tight angle of view—combines with strong differential focus to pick out even the smallest or most indistinct subject from its background. But with a 500mm lens there is little you can do to change, for example, your composition or the angle from which you see the subject. You may literally have to get in a car and drive to the next hillside to change your view. There is no question of shifting over to the other leg and altering your angle as you can with a wide angle lens (see earlier). As a result, tele-photographers can just erect a tripod on the firmest ground within a large potential area without affecting the image much.

Similarly, you can't just make your subject fill the frame by closing in or moving back with a 1000mm lens— you would need to walk 100 metres with many subjects. So it is more important for the serious tele-photographer to have a range of lenses, such as 500mm, 800mm and 1000mm, than it is for the ordinary photographer to

own both a 28mm and a 35mm lens. Because of this, long telephoto zooms are becoming more popular.

Shutter speeds: for sharp results with lenses over 300mm always select the fastest shutter speed you possibly can, even using faster film than normal to help you get this. Always work at 1/500 and preferably 1/1000—a camera with a top speed of 1/2000 is almost essential for lenses over 500mm.

Mounting or holding the camera: always use two hands and adopt a firm stance with long telephoto lenses. Where possible, fit a shoulder stock, a monopod, a tensioned foot chain which you grip with your foot and pull against, or a pistol grip.

Before buying, always check that you can hold your eye to the camera viewfinder and use a shoulder stock comfortably, as designs vary in efficiency. The best solutions are a heavy tripod (not a standard model—these may vibrate), or a bean bag for resting the lens solidly on walls, tables and so on. Use a cable release for minimum vibration.

Tripods and mounting: choose a very heavy tripod—these may cost as much as a good SLR, with a 3-way pan-and-tilt head. Most telephotos have a tripod bush. Lenses with integral collars for tripod mounting are very convenient, allowing the camera to be rotated for changes of view and upright format without dismounting.

Mounts: interchangeable-mount long

◄ A 4x tele converter was used in conjunction with a 400mm lens, increasing focal length effectively to 1600mm, to enlarge the setting sun. *Patrick Eagar*

▲ A long telephoto lens is essential for water sports as it gets in close to the action even though this is physically impossible. *Tony Duffy*

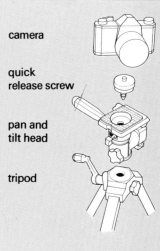

camera

quick release screw

pan and tilt head

tripod

▲ A simple tripod is more versatile with a pan-and-tilt head added. These are available separately and are very useful when panning with a long lens.

telephoto lenses are widely available, many with non-auto mounts, as it is still accepted that lenses over 400mm can have manually operated aperture controls and be usable. Always check that there is no looseness between lens and mount or mount and camera, as the weight of a very long lens will make this worse.

Camera mounts and long telephoto lenses: most manufacturers do not accept responsibility for repairs to cameras if a lens over 300mm has been attached to an SLR and allowed to hang unsupported with the camera on its neckstrap. Always carry the camera by the lens, and mount the camera by the lens on tripods.

Filters and lens hoods: many new telephoto lenses of 300–800mm use rear-fitting filters, and so do all mirror

lenses, as the sizes involved, usually about 43mm diameter, allow optically perfect filters of modest cost. Whether the filter is rear or front mounted, only the best specially approved glass filters must be used with lenses over 500mm. You will usually need one set of filters for each lens. Lens hoods, regrettably, need to be fitted to the large front element and, if not supplied, a special hood should be bought.

Metering: most long lenses have a limited range of apertures, often with very limited maximum f stops. Mirror lenses are limited to one aperture only, such as f8, and neutral grey filters must be used to reduce light transmission. Because of the highly selective angle of view, a TTL system or spot metering is essential. Allow a cut of half a stop in exposure for the best results.

▲ To stop the seagull in flight it was necessary to pan but, because of the clear sky, the blurred background associated with panned shots is missing. *Suzanne Hill*

▼ The change in perspective due to foreshortening with a 300mm lens, distorts the distance between the pier and the bathers. *Raul Constancio*

▶ Taken from high up in the spectator stands with a 300mm telephoto lens, the whole field is visible, with no loss of action. *John McGovren*

▲ Panning with a long telephoto lens creates the blurred background, giving a sense of speed and movement. *Tony Duffy*

▲ A shoulder stock incorporating a pistol grip and cable release allows more freedom of movement than a tripod.

▶ A long telephoto lens changes the perspective to the extent that all the cyclists appear to be bunched together although in reality there was quite some distance between them as they approached the hill. *Gerry Cranham*

▼ A 300mm telephoto lens pressed right up against wire netting, throws the netting totally out of focus so that it does not interfere with the final picture. *David Kilpatrick*

Focusing screens: lenses over 300mm do not usually work well with micro-prisms or split image rangefinders unless very fast (f4 or faster). Use the ground-glass ring round the central viewing aids for best results, or fit a plain ground-glass screen to the camera.

Depth of field: this is very limited with lenses over 300mm, but as a result a subject is picked out well by selective focusing. Careful, accurate focusing is essential, but it is better to accept limited depth of field than risk stopping down and having to use too long an exposure for shake-free sharpness.

Contrast and colour rendering: long telephoto lenses are generally neutral to cool in colour transmission and of moderate, not high, contrast. Cheap lenses may be very low in contrast.

Subjective contrast and sharpness: the view through a telephoto lens (mirror lenses in particular) may not appear very sharp or contrasty. However, when the results are printed or projected, there is usually a great improvement. It is still best to use long telephoto lenses on sharp-edged, brightly lit, bold subjects, rather than on finely detailed or vague shapes.

Aerial haze and contrast: the problem of water vapour, haze and heat haze in the air cannot be overcome with very long telephoto lenses. Where you may hope to get good results when using lenses under 200mm well stopped down,

lenses over 300mm become very sensitive to rising heat (which produces blurred images) and aerial haze (which produces very flat, soft pictures).

Use a UV filter all the time, and avoid using very long lenses except in crisp, clear conditions. Unfortunately, wind —which clears haze—often causes long telephoto lenses to vibrate.

Following action: move smoothly, and do not use too powerful a lens for following action—it is better to have leeway and spare area than to get a cropped-off image. Focus can be nearly impossible to follow through unless you use a special follow-focus lens with a squeeze grip—focus on a predetermined point when possible.

Tele converters

Once you discover the capabilities and limitations of your camera system you will have an idea of what additional lenses you need. Most people choose to buy one or more telephoto lenses, but these items are expensive. By buying a tele converter you can at least double your lens range, economically. For example, if you already have a 50mm lens, fitting a 2x converter doubles its focal length to 100mm; again, a 135mm telephoto lens used with a 2x converter becomes 270mm. In both cases you have two lenses in one for perhaps half the cost of a telephoto lens.

A telephoto lens consists of a group of positive (converging) elements with a group of negative (diverging) elements behind it. Adding a separate negative lens group (a tele converter) behind an existing lens therefore increases the focal length. Tele converters are comparatively inexpensive, compact and versatile.

Until recently, converters (also called extenders or multipliers) were often of poor quality. Optical quality has in general improved, and now many camera manufacturers make their own to complement their lens range. Converters are available for almost all 35mm and 120 roll film SLR cameras, and they can be used with zooms, high resolution telephoto and mirror lenses and Leica rangefinder cameras.

What a converter does

A tele converter magnifies the central portion of a prime lens image. A prime lens is any normal lens, used without attachments. A 2x converter doubles the prime lens focal length, while a 3x converter trebles it (so that a 100mm prime lens becomes 300mm). This applies equally to zoom lenses—a 70–150mm lens fitted with a 2x converter has its range increased to 140–300mm, for example.

The converter fits between the prime lens and the camera body. The focusing scale on the lens always remains correct, and you can focus on infinity. Normally all the couplings for the camera are linked through the converter so that functions like aperture adjustment and depth of field preview remain fully connected.

A converter always reduces the speed of a lens because enlarging an image makes it dimmer. A 2x converter makes a prime lens two stops slower, 3x loses three stops, and a 1·4x converter one stop. With a 2x converter, for example, a marked f11 would effectively be f22. The change in exposure

A wide range of tele converters is available to fit most camera makes.
1 Vivitar's 2x Matched Multiplier is designed for their 70–150mm zoom lens.
2 A 2x converter doubles the focal length of a lens.
3 The larger 3x converter trebles focal length.

◀ Tele converters fit between camera and lens. The lens focusing scale remains correct, and all automatic functions are usually retained.

caused by this reduction in effective aperture is automatically calculated by a TTL meter. You can also find the true f number with a hand–held meter.

Types of converter

Universal converters fit a range of cameras and are available in different 'strengths'. The cheapest type is the manual stop–down 42mm screw 2x converter with three optical elements. Converters designed to fit a whole range of lenses aim to keep aberrations to a minimum, and this often means that they will give superior performance with lenses outside their range. Zoom lens converters usually fall into the second category. Any zoom lens's performance varies through its focal length range, and most converters can only give their best performance at one particular focal length.

To get round the problem of converters which amplify lens faults and perhaps even add new ones, some manufacturers make matched converters for specific lenses (Canon fluorite telephotos and Vivitar's 70–150mm zoom, for example). The matched converter may even bring in a little correction which the prime lens might lack for one reason or another—this is the most expensive type.

Matched converters for lens ranges or individual lenses should give better saturation and contrast, more even illumination and be freer from distortion than the cheaper universal types.

▲ This photograph was taken using a 70–150mm zoom set at its shortest focal length, 70mm. Notice the framing of the subject and the size of the building in the distance.

▲ Same viewpoint, same lens, but this time used with a 2x converter with the lens set on 150mm. This gives the equivalent of a 300mm lens.

Advantages

Besides being an inexpensive way of increasing your lens range, carrying one or two tele converters with you rather than a whole assortment of telephotos means that you have far less bulk and weight to accommodate.

Because the focusing scale remains unchanged, larger image sizes than normal at the minimum focusing distance are possible. A 2x converter on a 50mm lens can give one–third life size image (on 35mm film), while using a 3x converter can increase this to about half life size.

Disadvantages

Blowing up part of an image reduces sharpness, just as enlarging a small portion of a negative does. A converter produces a softer image than a prime lens under the same conditions.

The loss in light can also give an extremely dim viewfinder image, particularly with a zoom lens, making composing and focusing difficult. A converter may introduce its own edge aberrations and distortion giving fall–off in quality at the corners of the frame. This can only be minimized by using relatively small lens apertures which may demand use of slower shutter speeds, and perhaps a tripod.

Converters are least successful when photographing distant landscapes with aerial haze. A combination of only

▲ This ornate building was photographed with a 50mm lens which takes in a fairly wide angle of view and includes distracting foreground and surrounding detail.

▲ From the same viewpoint the photographer fitted a 200mm lens, which enabled close cropping of an interesting feature on the building without including extraneous detail.

▲ A 2x converter and 100mm lens are equivalent to 200mm. Loss of contrast and edge quality are hardly noticeable when compared to the results from the 200mm prime lens (left).

modest sharpness and low contrast produced by a converter and haze in the atmosphere can give flat pictures.

Using a converter

Converters are ideal for portraits when picture corner sharpness is not too important. The kind of softness obtained from a 50mm f1·4 with a 2x converter makes a fine 100mm f2·8 portrait lens.

In sports photography using converters can pull you closer to the action, and they are especially suitable if you up-rate film for contrasty results, or use panning techniques when ultimate sharpness is of secondary importance.

Family groups and children rarely suffer from being photographed through a tele converter.

Remember that, as with all long focus lenses, pictures tend to have flattened perspective and shallow depth of field.

Close–ups are likely to be successful with converters because attention is often concentrated on the central area, there is no aerial haze, and close detail, not contrast, makes the picture.

Most converters need the prime lens to be stopped down to about f8 for the optimum results (which means a true

f16 with a 2x converter). Only specially matched converters work well at full aperture and allow high shutter speeds to be used.

Buying a converter

Buy the best quality you can afford and choose a matched converter if possible. Whatever your choice, don't expect the quality of a 100mm plus 2x to equal the performance of a good quality 200mm prime lens. Quality loss is particularly noticeable when working at wide apertures.

Buying a 2x converter gives you a 100mm portrait lens when used with a standard lens. This won't clash if you later buy a 135mm lens, and in fact gives a 270mm telephoto.

It does not make sense to buy a 2x converter and a 100mm telephoto—a 3x converter would be better because you then get 150mm from a 50mm standard, and 300mm from the 100mm telephoto.

A 2x converter extends the range of a 70–210mm zoom to a long 420mm. The range of focal lengths provided gives a wide choice with just two items of equipment. Again, don't be over–optimistic about the quality of the

▲ **Whatever converter you use, the lens focusing scale remains correct. A 3x converter fitted to a 50mm lens focused at 0.45m produced this impressive close leaf study.**

results, especially if the zoom leaves a little to be desired initially. Zooms in macro modes usually have too many aberrations to allow the use of a converter.

If you really intend to get the most focal lengths at minimum cost choose prime lenses with reasonable gaps between them—such as 135mm and 300mm—or a zoom.

Contrary to popular belief, converters work well on wide angles and macro lenses—they work on any lens which gives a sharp, bright image. But who needs a mediocre lens produced by converting 24mm f4 to 48mm f8 when your 50mm standard lens is far better? Converters are an important and versatile part of today's camera outfit, and regardless of how many lenses you may buy, and what changes you make, they always double the number of choices you have. In fact the only thing you can never do with a tele converter is to use it on its own.

◄ Converting your 50mm lens to 100mm with a 2x converter gives a convenient portrait lens with a slightly soft edge quality.

▼ *Patrick Eagar* used two 2x converters on a 400mm lens (equivalent to 1600mm) to capture this distant island in a soft hazy atmosphere.

▲ This is the type of low contrast result typically produced by using a tele converter. The scene was photographed against the light and through aerial haze and is reproduced as a soft misty view, lacking depth. A 55mm lens and 2x converter were fitted to the camera.

139

Special effects lenses

1. Bird's eye attachment

2. Fisheye attachment

5. Anamorphic
attachment

3. & 4. Wide angle attachments   4.

◀ 1. Bird's eye attachment which fits on the front of a lens, creating a round image with a black spot in the centre.
2. A fisheye attachment for a circle-image picture.
3. A wide angle attachment which increases the angle of view of a 50mm lens to 113° and of a 35mm lens to 150°. For best results the aperture setting should be f11 or f16.
4. A wide angle attachment that increases the angle of view of a standard 55mm lens to 104° and of a 35mm lens to 150°. The latter produces a circle-image picture.
5. An anamorphic attachment squeezes the image together. The resulting image is compressed and needs to be corrected to be viewed normally.

Attachments and lenses for special effects can distort the image—giving for example, a fisheye view—or they can improve the image by correcting perspective or increasing the depth of field. Prime lenses for special effects are expensive but they have specific functions. Lens attachments are less expensive and, although they do not give the same results as prime lenses, they too can create unusual images.

Wide angle effects

Although the easiest way of getting a wide angle view is with a wide angle lens (see earlier), there are attachments and lenses that can be used for extreme wide angle views and fisheye effects. For those wishing to specialize in wide angle shots there are special cameras for panoramic views. **Wide angle attachments:** a standard 50mm lens or a 35mm wide angle lens can be converted to a wide angle or fisheye lens using a screw-in afocal adapter. Afocal wide angle adapters do not change the aperture of the lens or alter its infinity focusing setting, but they do have the effect of making the focusing scale inaccurate and giving a closer minimum focus. A 50mm lens may be converted to 30mm focal length, or a 35mm lens to 21mm. Some attachments produce more distortion than others, as a fisheye lens does.
Fisheye attachments: these attachments are similar to the wide angle attachments and screw into a standard 50mm lens. With a standard 50mm lens the attachment makes it equivalent to a focal length of 8mm—the usual focal length given for a circle image fisheye. These attachments are modestly priced but the resulting lens is usually limited to an aperture of about f8 or f11. Used on a 100mm telephoto lens, the attachment gives a 16mm full-frame fisheye, but the aperture is normally limited to f22.
Anamorphic attachments: intended mainly for cine cameras, attachments such as the Isco Widerama 'squeeze' the picture to fit 50% extra image into the length of the 35mm frame. The slide or negative which results is naturally compressed in one direction, so it must be printed or projected by using the attachment in reverse, which restores it to normal dimensions. The result produces a picture with dimensions of 2·25 to 1—or over twice as long as it is high—referred to as widescreen.
Bird's eye attachments: similar in effect to a fisheye lens, the Beroflex and other bird's eye-view attachments comprise a clear perspex tube fitted to the front of the standard 50mm lens. Inside the tube there is a spherical mirror facing the lens. The camera sees a 180° circular fisheye-type image, but with all the detail of the camera and the photographer in the picture too. The photographer can be excluded from the picture by supporting the camera on a tripod and using the delayed action setting, or with a long cable release.

◀ A wide angle attachment was used with a 28mm wide angle lens to shoot this circle-image picture. The effect is similar to an 8mm fisheye lens. (The attachment used on a standard 50mm lens would produce a full-frame wide angle image.) *Lisa Le Guay*

▶ An anamorphic attachment compresses the image in one direction and must be corrected to be viewed normally (far right).

1. 8mm fisheye lens

2. 16mm fisheye lens

▲ 1. 8mm fisheye lens covering 180°
produces a circle-image picture.
Because of the shape of the lens front
filters are rear mounted.
2. 16mm fisheye lens covering 170°
produces a full-frame picture.

▶ An 8mm fisheye lens was used for
this unusual inside view of a scrum.
Gerry Cranham

▼ The horizon of this coastal scene
is characteristically distorted
due to the wide coverage of a full-
frame fisheye lens.

Fisheye lenses

Fisheye lenses (not attachments) produce full-frame or circle-image pictures depending on the focal length of the lens. For example a 16mm lens produces a full-frame picture while an 8mm lens produces a circle-image on 35mm film (both lenses have an angle view of 180°).

A full-frame fisheye lens: produces a characteristically curved image, where the straight lines normally seen are replaced by gradually curving ones, and cover 180° diagonally on the film. If you are not careful you can include your feet or hands in the picture. These lenses are normally between 14mm and 17mm in focal length and around f2·8 to f3·5 in maximum aperture. They are about the same size as wide angle lenses of this focal length but are often cheaper as they are less complicated to make. Depth of field is enormous.

Circle-image fisheyes: by using the full image-circle of the fisheye lens, with its curved lines, it is possible to include 180° or even 220° all round, in a lens capable of photographing, for example, the entire sky in one shot for meteorological uses. A normal circle-image fisheye is of 8mm focal length and may be between f2·8 and f8 in maximum aperture. Other fisheyes with special optical characteristics are available between 6mm and 12mm, but they can be very expensive (notably those covering more than 180°, which actually sees part of the scene slightly 'behind' themselves).

▲ A 28mm wide angle lens covers 74° and gives a panoramic view of a field—without horizon distortion.

▼ A 16mm full-frame fisheye lens covers 180° diagonally – more than twice as much as a 28mm lens.

Soft focus lenses

Special prime lenses are made to give a soft focus effect. Lenses today are corrected to produce sharp results, but sharpness is not always a good thing in portraits, where skin blemishes can show up badly. To overcome this and give a more atmospheric effect, soft focus lenses have a control which adjusts the glass elements so that they are wrongly spaced, producing uncorrected results with a characteristic glow or halo of diffusion round a sharp central image. The results do not look blurred (which is not the same) but hazy and romantic. Examples of current soft focus lenses include 85mm models from Fujica and Minolta and a 70 – 150mm zoom with soft focus from Tamron. Soft focus attachments, such as filters and mistys, imitate the effect of proper soft focus lenses by using treated glass or supplementary optics, but do not give as subtle a result. Soft focus generally is strongest at wide apertures, and soft focus optics can be quite sharp if stopped down to f16. These special attachments and lenses come in a wide price range. They all affect the resulting image and it is up to the individual to decide which are worth the expense. Let the subjects you enjoy photographing dictate your need for these specialized items.

Variable Field Curvature lens

Despite the computer design of modern SLR lenses, it is still hard to make a lens which always focuses its image on to a theoretically flat plane like the film. Expensive lenses having 'floating' elements which move to vary the field of sharp focus. By putting a control in to move the floating element manually, regardless of focused distance, Minolta have made a 24mm Variable Field Curvature (VFC) lens where the subject plane can be bowed or dished as well as perfectly flat, allowing subjects at the edges to be either nearer or further than those at the centre but still focused sharply even at f2·8.

Perspective control lenses

If you aim your 35mm camera directly at a building, without tilting it, you keep the vertical lines parallel. If you tilt the camera the lines lean in the resulting picture. If you cannot get back far enough even with a wide angle lens, then you have to accept converging verticals unless you have a wider coverage than a normal wide angle lens. By using a 'shift' lens you can move the lens upwards, bringing top

parts of the picture which would normally be outside the film frame into it. Precise controls enable you to move the lens exactly the right amount to bring in as much or as little of the image as needed. Of course, these movements not only bring in picture detail from outside the edge of the picture, but also lose it at the other side. Perspective control lenses are 35mm or 28mm, manually operated, and have two directions of movement,

▶ The background of this shot is out of focus as the depth of field was only deep enough to focus the vase and the flowers. The same scene photographed with a Variable Field Curvature lens has a sharp background (far right).

▼ 1. The Variable Field Curvature lens, made by Minolta, has a floating element which makes it possible to vary the field of sharp focus. It is particularly useful for close range subjects as the focusing range can be adjusted.
2. The 35mm Shift CA Rokkor lens has a shift mechanism which corrects converging verticals.
3. The Canon 35mm tilt and shift lens is similar to a shift lens in that it corrects converging verticals, but it can also be tilted or swung on its axis so that the lens is no longer parallel to the film. This makes it possible to adjust the depth of field as well.

or one plus the ability to rotate the entire lens.

Tilt control lenses

Some perspective control lenses also have an extra facility which allows the lens to be tilted or swung on its axis, pivoted so that it is no longer parallel with the film. When a lens is parallel to the film, it focuses on a plane which is also parallel to the film. If you tilt the lens the plane of focus is moved to an

1. Variable Field Curvature lens

2. 35mm shift or 'PC' (perspective control) lens.

angled position by about double the amount of tilt on the lens, and in the same direction. So, if you tilt the lens 5° downwards, the plane of focus leans backwards by 10°. At 45°, a lens on a camera held vertically would focus perfectly on the ground. In fact, the mount of the lens and other considerations limit the amount of tilt you can use, and the extra coverage built into perspective control lenses is needed for effective tilt use.

3: 35mm tilt and shift lens

▲ A 35mm shift lens was used to photograph this village scene. The same scene (left), shot without the use of a shift lens, has converging verticals. The wider the angle of view, the more the lens distorts the image. This distortion of perspective can be very effective; but usually with architectural shots, especially when photographing tall buildings, a more realistic view is seen if the converging verticals are corrected. *Mike Newton*

Tripods, monopods and other supports

Have you ever taken a series of photographs and then found that the prints or slides have all come out looking inexplicably blurred? A special occasion, impossible to repeat, becomes a hazy memory; a rare scenic view comes out looking fuzzy. Both results are not worth a slide mount or the space in the family album.

You have spent time and effort getting a good photograph, the exposure is correct and the focus is perfect, yet the end result is a disappointment. The cause is probably camera shake. This happens if the photographer moves the camera during the actual moment of exposure. Only very slight movement is enough to spoil a picture—and it is easily done, even by the most experienced photographer. But it is a problem that is easily put right by supporting the camera properly.

Resting the camera

If you hold the camera by hand for most shots it is important to know how to support it firmly. Think of yourself as a human tripod when holding the camera; stand firmly with legs slightly apart, and hold the camera rigidly in both hands with elbows tucked into your sides. This position should allow you to balance the camera firmly, but allow some movement so that you can compose the picture. When you take the picture, squeeze the shutter release slowly to avoid shaking the camera. Or bend down on one knee and rest your elbow on the other knee. In this position it is easier to hold the camera vertically. The camera can also be held reasonably steady by putting the camera strap around your neck and taking up the slack by winding the strap around one hand. Another way of steadying the camera is to attach a length of chain (available as an accessory) to it. The end of the chain is held under the foot so that the camera is under tension. This method has limited application as it can't be used in all positions and the camera can still be moved sideways.

Of course you do not always have to hand hold the camera. You may sometimes be able to place the camera on a

▲ The chances of camera shake are more likely with slow shutter speeds or when using a long lens. Use any available support to lean against in order to hold the camera steady.

◀ A combination of fast shutter speed, adequate camera support and sharp focusing produced this shot of a cyclist.

▼ This series shows: the effect of camera shake—an overall appearance of movement in one direction; too slow a shutter speed; camera held steady but wrongly focused.

wall, or hold it against a tree or lamp-post, to give it extra support. If the camera is balanced on a wall, make sure the surface is as even as possible and that there are no awkward bumps. If you are using supports you can minimize camera movement still further by using a cable release, if the camera takes one. The shutter can then be triggered through the release without the photographer touching the camera.

Cable releases

It is usually a good idea to use a cable release and some other form of support at speeds of less than 1/60.

Cable releases are available in various lengths and can be as long as 3 metres. The most common cable release is about 20cm and this is suitable for most purposes. Longer releases are pneumatically operated. Electronically operated cameras may need a special type of cable release.

Always take your camera with you when buying accessories to make sure they are suitable for your particular make and type of camera.

Reciprocity failure

With the camera on a tripod and using a cable release it is feasible to photograph in bad light with a slow shutter speed. In reality it is not so simple. Under normal lighting conditions various combinations of shutter speed and aperture can be used to expose film correctly. However, in extreme lighting conditions film does not behave as it should.

For example, if the light is very low and the meter reading indicates a long exposure, the film may be under-exposed despite using settings which are apparently correct. This is known as reciprocity law failure, and is caused by the emulsion being less sensitive to dim light over a long exposure than it is to short bursts of bright light. Exposures longer than 1/8 with colour film and 1 second with black and white will need additional exposure, but all films vary and the manufacturer's instructions usually give details. With colour there may be a colour shift as well, needing a corrective filter. This also applies with very short exposures—speeds

faster than 1/1000 and some types of flash. At both exposure extremes think of the film as being slower than its given ASA.

Tripods and monopods

These are custom-made supports which find their way into many photographers' gadget bags.

A **monopod** is a one-legged camera support, with height adjustment, and usually a spike at one end so that it can be driven into soft ground for firm support. The monopod is portable and easy to use, although most have no head adjustment for altering the angle of the camera and do not give the same firmness as a tripod.

Tripods are available in various sizes, from small lightweight models which are ideal for carrying in the gadget bag, to the heavyweight studio types. Table-top tripods are light and easy to assemble. They are most useful for indoor photography, where they can be set up on a table or chair. Because these tripods are so light they should only be used with light cameras—they are not sturdy enough for heavy models.

Small and medium-sized tripods come in a wide range and offer the photographer the most choice. Most are reasonably priced, are made of aluminium and have quick-release extending legs which means they can be set up quickly and easily. Many models have

1–5 Cable releases are available in various lengths.
6 Pneumatic release allows longer distances than cable releases.
7 Electronic shutter release allows the photographer to operate an auto winder from a distance.

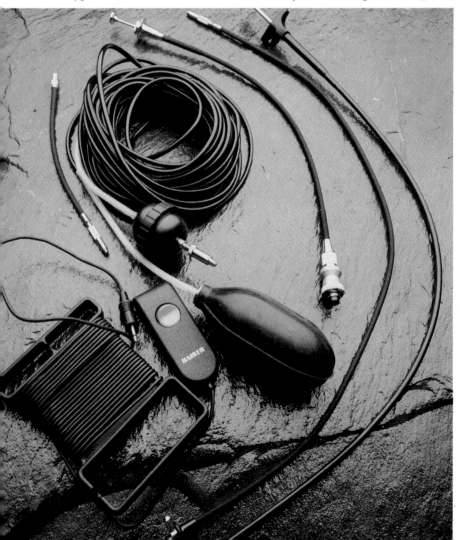

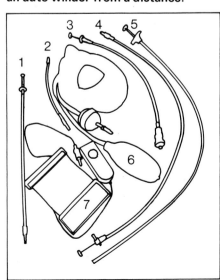

a pan and tilt head. This is an adjustable top which can be tilted back and forth and panned from side to side. The more expensive models have extra struts on the centre column of the tripod for extra rigidity. Some centre columns also have gears and a rotating handle so that the camera can be moved up and down quickly.

Some tripods also have a built-in cable release (or provision for one) so that you can trigger the shutter without touching the camera or tripod, thus lessening the risk of camera shake even more. Some tripods can also be folded almost flat on the ground for low-angle shots.

Heavy-duty tripods are designed for professionals and the advanced amateur. Because of their size, they are extremely sturdy and are ideal for supporting large cameras, or cameras with long and perhaps heavy lenses. Obviously, they are not as portable as the smaller models and are therefore mainly used in studios. Heavy-duty tripods are usually quite expensive, but offer great rigidity and firmness and a large degree of adjustment.

Using a tripod

A tripod is a very versatile camera support and with so many models available in the medium price bracket, it is the kind of accessory that every photographer should consider buying.

Despite the increasing use of highspeed film, many photographers still prefer to use slower emulsions for some of their work. With these slower films a tripod is essential in low-light situations where a long exposure is needed. At night, for example, an exposure time of a few seconds may be necessary even with fast film. Some form of support is essential when using a telephoto lens. The longer the lens, the more important the support becomes, and in some instances the lens itself is supported rather than the camera. For fast action photography, where you may need to follow a moving object precisely, a tripod with a pan head is very useful. The camera can be moved with the subject, with the photographer taking shots at random. Indoor photography is another area where the tripod is most useful, particularly when using flash. If the camera is supported on the tripod and the photographer uses a cable release, he can move away, perhaps to distract the sitter or to hold a flash for more interesting lighting. However the tripod is used, it is not just another accessory—it can be a vital part of the photographer's equipment.

● To make a medium-sized tripod more secure a weighted bag can be suspended from the central column of the tripod.

▼ **Left: a weighted bag, suspended from the central column of a lightweight tripod makes the tripod more steady as it lowers the centre of gravity. This is particularly useful in windy weather and when using a long telephoto lens.**

▼ **There are various types of table-top tripod (from left): Compact tripod which doubles as a shoulder stock. A sturdy model with pan and tilt head for any camera position. A small lightweight tripod for indoor use.**

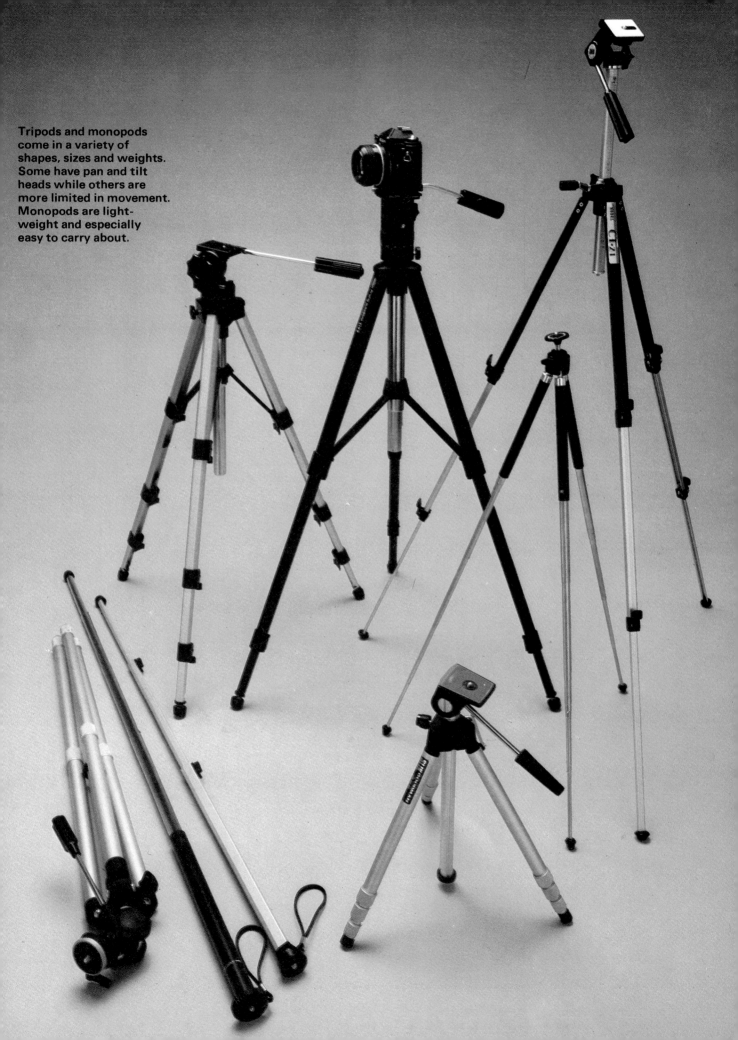

Tripods and monopods
come in a variety of
shapes, sizes and weights.
Some have pan and tilt
heads while others are
more limited in movement.
Monopods are light-
weight and especially
easy to carry about.

Other camera supports

Quite a few simple and inexpensive camera supports are available so, as this is another item to carry around, make sure you buy the one that is the most useful for the type of photography you do. Unnecessary equipment means unnecessary weight.

A **pistol grip** is a plastic hand grip which screws into the tripod bush on the base of the camera. It is usually fitted with a cable release and a trigger to release the shutter.

Rifle grips and shoulder stocks work on the same principle but have shoulder straps for even greater support and are most useful for cameras fitted with long lenses. Always check, before buying, that you can hold your eye to the camera finder and use a shoulder stock or grip comfortably—this is not always the case as designs vary in efficiency and adjustability.

G-clamps fitted with a ball and socket are also available. The clamp can be fitted on to the side of a table or a door, with the camera attached to it. It is quick to assemble and easy to carry around.

A **ground spike** is useful for low-angle outdoor shots. The spike is driven into soft ground to support the camera just above ground level.

◄ A ground spike, which also doubles as a monopod, provides good support at low angles.

► The camera strap, around the arm or neck, and tensioned by taking up the slack, helps to prevent camera shake.

▼ A suction pad used on a smooth surface holds this support steady — ideal for use in a car in a safari park.

Making a bean bag

A bean bag makes a very useful camera support. It is cheap and easily made. Two circles of fabric are stitched together and then filled with beans. Sand can be used as a filling but the fabric must be strong enough to hold it as sand is heavier than beans are. Polystyrene pellets are too light to be used satisfactorily as they do not provide enough support.

The camera is simply rested on the bean bag which is pushed into shape to support the camera in the required position.

▲ A shoulder stock with a cable release helps to steady zoom and telephoto lenses.

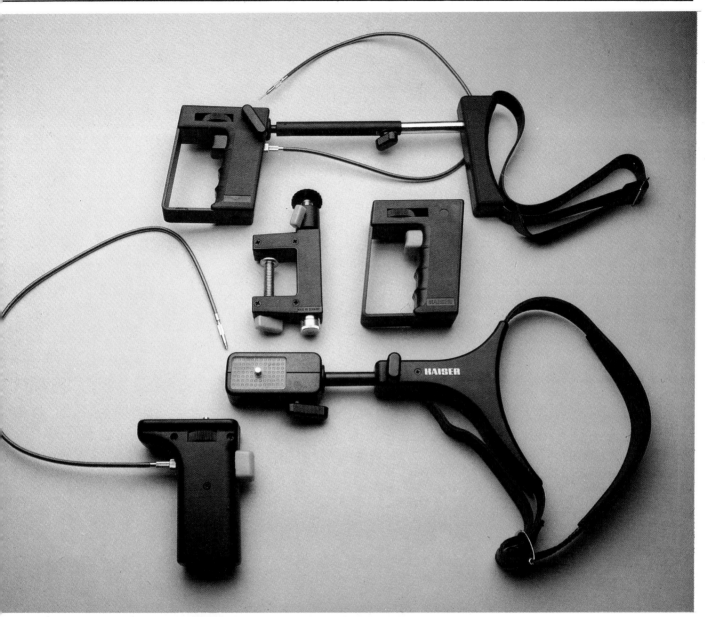

▲ Useful supports, other than tripods and monopods, include G-clamps, adjustable shoulder stocks and pistol grips. The important thing about using any of these is to make sure you can hold them comfortably to ensure successful long exposures.

◀ Far left: a pistol grip used in conjunction with a cable release enables the photographer to hold the camera and release the shutter with one hand, leaving the other hand free to do the focusing.

◀ A very versatile support is a table-top tripod which also doubles as a shoulder stock.

Close-up lenses

Close-up photography can reveal a whole new world of interest and excitement—the extraordinary or beautiful details we normally miss in insects and flowers, or abstract images and patterns to be found in nature. To capture on film the detail you can see quite easily with your eyes, the camera needs some facility to be able to focus close-up on a small object. Close-up lenses, depending on their magnification, also reveal what the eyes miss.

There is a whole range of equipment for doing this, but basically they all provide a way of taking the camera closer in to the subject than the normal closest focusing setting, usually about 45cm for the standard lens of an SLR. This makes it possible to photograph small objects from close-up, sometimes at their actual size and sometimes magnifying them, depending on the equipment being used.

This chapter starts with close-up lenses which are attached to the front of the camera's lens and then goes on to deal with extension tubes and reversing rings, macro lenses and bellows, all of which are used for close-up photography. The first two—close-up attachments and extension tubes—are the cheapest but before deciding on any particular system, consider all the possibilities.

The 35mm SLR camera has totally changed the ability of amateur photographers to take impressive close-up studies of a variety of subjects without technical difficulties. Until quite recently, photographers used to work with complex tables, viewing attachments and measuring devices in order to photograph something as simple as a rose. The SLR camera gives a precise view of the subject, however close the photographer chooses to go, right up to producing it life-size on the film, a magnification ratio of 1:1. The subject appears greatly magnified on a projection screen and even three or four times larger than life in an ordinary print.

Close-up lens attachments

By far the easiest equipment to use is the close-up attachment which screws on the front rim of the lens, and works rather like a magnifying glass. It focuses the lens at a closer distance than normal. Distances from one meter down to 10cm away are possible using a close-up attachment on a standard 50mm lens.

The advantage of these attachments is that no change in exposure is required,

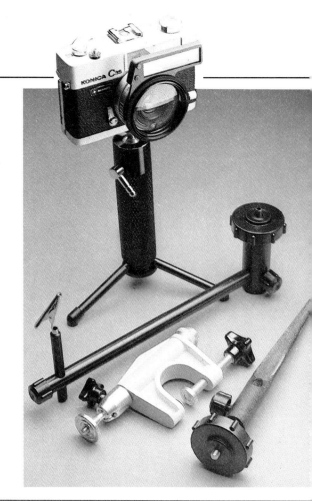

▶ **1 A rangefinder camera fitted with a close-up attachment is supported on a table-top tripod.
2 One end of the support attachment screws into the camera like a tripod and is adjustable. The clip at the other end is used to grip the item being photographed.
3 A G-clamp is a useful support for close-up work where a tripod would be too cumbersome.
4 A ground spike allows low angle shots.**

▼ **Close-up attachments are available in various strengths and with different thread sizes so they can be used on most 35mm SLR cameras. The attachments do not affect the light entering the lens so they are easy to use on cameras without TTL metering systems.**

making them easy to use with cameras without through-the-lens metering. They can also be fitted to a lens of almost any focal length, whether standard or telephoto, although wide angle lenses are not particularly successful, and they will always focus on their dioptric focal length whether on a 50mm or 135mm lens. (1 diopter focuses at 1000mm, 2 at 500mm, 3 at 333mm, and so on.) Obviously this makes for really good close-ups with telephoto lenses. The disadvantage of close-up attachments is that, because they are optical, they can cause a loss of sharpness by conflicting with the

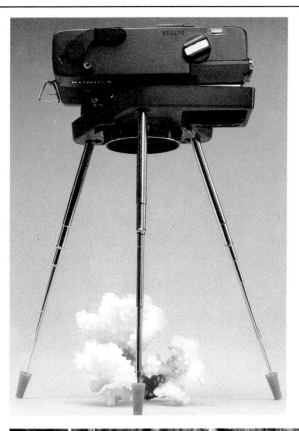

◄ A close-up attachment which incorporates extending legs supports a rangefinder camera for close-up work.

▼ Dandelions have an appealing symmetrical pattern that is enhanced by close-up shots. With a standard lens at its shortest focusing distance a group of dandelions (far left) is visible. As the strength of the close-up attachments increase so the focusing distance is decreased making it possible to move right in on an individual dandelion (below left) and a close-up of it (below).

50mm lens

plus 0·7 diopter

plus 1·5 diopters

▲ Lupins photographed with a standard 50mm lens on an SLR, 1/15 second at f8 on Kodachrome. Close-up attachments were added to decrease the focusing distance for this series of close-ups.

▼ Two shots with a 4·5 diopter attachment: f8 (left) gives sufficient depth of field for an overall sharp image; f2 narrows the depth of field so that the sides of the flower farthest from the camera are out of focus.

4·5 diopters at f8

4·5 diopters at f2

highly corrected design of the prime lens, but normally this is hardly noticeable, especially when a small aperture such as f8, f11 or f16 is being used.

Basic close-up lenses are made in various strengths, which refer to their diopters; 1, 2 and 3 diopters are the more common ones and can be bought individually. The larger the number, the closer the lens can focus. The lenses can be used in conjunction with each other; for example, the 1, 2 and 3

diopter lenses can be used together to function as 6 diopters. Make sure the strongest diopter is next to the prime lens if using 2 or more close-up lenses.

Variable close-up lenses use more than one optical element and are much more powerful, often up to 10 or more diopters, focusing the lens as close as 10cm, which produces an image about half life-size on the film. They are more expensive than ordinary close-up lenses and often give less good results but they are convenient.

Achromatic lenses are similar to 1, 2 and 3 diopter close-up lenses but usually consist of more than one element. They are designed to avoid colour aberrations and colour fringing, which breaks down the light to give a rainbow effect, producing sharper than normal results and costing several times as much as simple single-glass close-up lenses.

Practical aspects

Viewing and focusing is very critical with close-ups. The best focusing screen for close-ups is a plain ground-glass one. With SLR screens which are not interchangeable, use the ground-glass part of the screen for best results.

▶ *Eric Crichton* photographs this series. To get even lighting he uses white card to reflect light on to the subject. A flash can be bounced off the card or used to fill in. Use a tripod so that the shutter speed can allow an aperture of f8 or smaller.

plus 3 diopters

plus 4 · 5 diopters

plus 15 diopters

▲ To keep close-up photographs interesting, look for subjects with uncluttered shapes and simple backgrounds. *Paul Forrester*

◄ *Michael Newton's* giant mustard and cress was created by taking a close-up photograph and then enlarging the image.

▼ To make this rose fill the frame, *Eric Crichton* only had to use a 1 diopter attachment.

On very close distances it is usually easier to do the final focusing by moving the camera backwards and forwards.

Depth of field is often restricted to a few millimetres and it is essential to close or stop down to the smallest practical apertures. Keeping the subject flat-on to the camera helps. A depth of field preview on the camera is a great help as you can see the exact limitation.

Lens to subject distance can be a problem; with wide angle lenses the subject may be so close that the camera and lens cast a shadow on it. Using a longer lens, 90–135mm, often helps to increase separation, allowing more freedom in camera position and the arrangement of lighting, especially if this involves reflector cards.

Picture making

● When taking close-ups always remember to get really close in—there is nothing worse than a 'close-up' with lots of wasted image detail all round it. Also remember that bright, bold, simple subjects—perhaps ones

which people do not normally look at closely—will be most successful, where the camera can reveal detail coupled with strong colours, textures and contrasts.

● Always try to take close-ups in bright light, and get all the important parts of the subject sharp even if the background is totally blurred.

● Hold the camera flat on to the main plane of the subject—typical examples are a butterfly's wings or the head of a flower, both of which work best photographed straight on. If in doubt when photographing animals, focus on the eyes or head, just as you would do with a portrait of a person.

● Wind can be a problem. You do not see flowers shaking much from normal distances, but with close-up lenses or tubes fitted to your camera you will soon see that even a gentle breeze makes the subject wave around a good deal. You may need to build a small windbreak, using sheets of card, or wait for a still moment. If in doubt, shoot several frames rather than assuming that the subject is as still as it seems.

● Camera shake is also very noticeable in close-ups, just as it is in telephoto shots. A small tripod, a table-top model or G-clamp can be useful. Using electronic flash, even outdoors, to fill in the lighting, helps increase sharpness because at such close distances computer flash-guns are often working at 1/30,000 of a second.

● Look for flaws and blemishes in close-up subjects. Dust or damage shows up strongly and even relatively faint marks on a subject are revealed by the lens. A small soft brush can be useful for removing dust or natural debris from plants.

If a table-top for close-ups is set up indoors, using natural subjects or just exploring man-made objects such as old watches, a pair of cotton gloves for handling items is useful. So are bulldog clips for holding parts of a subject, and sheets of glass to support items if you do not want obtrusive background detail to appear in the picture. Even a sheet of good white paper has a texture which a close-up at 1:1 reveals.

● If book pages or drawings are being copied, remember that the viewing screen does not usually show the whole of the actual negative area, and if you can see the edges of the original on the screen, even slightly, then plenty of extra edge will appear on the final photograph. Crop as tightly as possible.

Extension tubes and reversing rings

Apart from using close-up lenses on the front of the prime lens there is another method of achieving close-ups. If you increase the distance between the lens and the film plane, much closer subjects can be sharply focused. The lens can be moved away from the film plane by using either extension tubes or bellows or a simple reversing ring. Extension tubes are dealt with here and bellows in the next section.

Extension tubes

Provided that your camera lens is removable, one or more extension tubes can be fitted between lens and body to focus the lens on subjects much closer than normal. Once an extension tube is fitted the lens no longer focuses to infinity. The closeness of focus depends on the length of the extension tube. On 35mm cameras extensions of about 10mm are the usual minimum, giving focusing distances down to about 25cm with a 50mm lens. Longer tubes such as 20mm and 35mm allow even closer distances. A set of three tubes usually has one combination giving an extension of approximately 50mm which will, with a standard lens, result in focusing as close as 10cm with a true

lifesize image on the film.

Like close-up lenses already described extension tubes make it possible to focus at shorter distances than the usual 45cm with a standard lens on a 35mm SLR.

Differences between close-up lenses and extension tubes: each method has its advantages and disadvantages. Close-up lenses are easy to carry around and can readily be attached to the lens. They do not affect the exposure, which makes them simple to use with cameras without TTL metering. Close-up lenses always focus to their dioptric focal length regardless of the lens they are used on.

The advantages of extension tubes are that they are not optical and therefore do not themselves give a deterioration in lens performance. They also allow larger magnification. But they do affect exposure. With TTL systems this isn't a problem as the meter automatically takes into account the change in light reaching the film but for the other cameras, exposure must be increased depending on the length of the extension. There are three types of tubes:

Manual extension tubes are made for many older types of SLR (mainly

42mm screw fitting models); these do not connect the automatic aperture mechanism to the camera so the aperture has to be closed manually. Normally a set of extension tubes costs more than a full set of good close-up lenses.

Automatic extension tubes connect the lens to the camera so that the automatic diaphragm on the lens functions normally, allowing the subject to be viewed at full aperture until the moment of exposure. Special sets of extension tubes are necessary for shutter priority automatic SLRs if the automatic setting is to be used. Because close-ups need small apertures for maximum depth of field, exposures are often long. Aperture priority automatic SLRs are ideal as you can decide on the aperture and let the camera do the rest provided it is properly supported. Both manual and automatic type tubes are normally bought in sets of three. This allows you up to seven variations of the tube length—by using them singly or in different combinations.

Helical extension tubes have a screw thread action so that one tube has a variable length, eliminating the need to change combinations of tubes from the normal set of three when trying to get the correct image size on the film.

A set of extension tubes usually consists of three rings which can be used in combination—a combination that doubles the focal length results in a life-size image. The tubes can be either manual or automatic. The latter allows the automatic diaphragm on the lens to function normally.

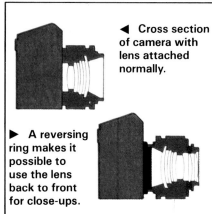

◄ Cross section of camera with lens attached normally.

► A reversing ring makes it possible to use the lens back to front for close-ups.

Reversing rings

Reversing rings can be used to mount any SLR lens back to front. Because of the way most lenses are mounted, this places it farther from the film. (Most 50mm camera lenses also give better image quality this way round when the subject is very close.) Used this way the lens does not function automatically, which means viewing at full aperture and then stopping down manually before taking the photograph.

▲ A dark blue card was placed behind the fuchsia to set it off from its distracting background and to complement the colour of the flower.

▼ A spider's web shot in the early morning. A single extension tube on a 105mm lens was sufficient for this detail on Kodachrome.
Suzanne Hill

▲ A 25mm extension tube used with a 50mm lens resulted in an image half life-size on a 35mm slide. The increased exposure factor was 2.
Heather Angel

▼ Pholiota mutabilis with bracken shot with the aid of extension tubes.
Heather Angel

Practical aspects

Exposure: the action of taking the lens further away from the film, and using only a small portion of its total image area 'blown up' by this extension, makes the image dimmer. Extra exposure is needed. Reflex cameras without TTL systems need calculation. As a rough guide, with a 50mm lens given 50mm of extra extension, exposure needs to be increased by a 4x factor—that is, two shutter speeds or f stops.

Focal length of the lens affects the size of image produced and the extra exposure needed with any particular extension tube. For example, extending a 50mm lens by an extra 50mm produces 1:1 (same size) images, but extending a 200mm lens by 50mm is the same as using a 12.5mm extension tube on a standard lens. Tubes are not suitable for use with wide angle lenses under about 35mm focal length or most zoom lenses, because of the poor image quality produced.

Viewing and focusing is critical for all close-up work—an SLR camera is really essential. With a long extension the image may appear rather dim on the focusing screen. It is often easiest to focus by moving the whole camera backwards and forwards until the image on the screen appears sharp.

Depth of field is very limited, often to a few millimetres, and not taking this into account may spoil a close-up.

▶ Photographed with a combination of extension tubes totalling 50mm, the ladybird appears life size on a 35mm slide. *Eric Crichton*

CLOSE-UPS USING A SET OF EXTENSION TUBES

▲ No lens hood was used for Eric Crichton's series of close-ups. At such a short working distance it would interfere with the lighting.

Exposure factors for extensions with a 50mm lens on 35mm SLR

The chart is intended as a guide to indicate roughly what size of extension tube is necessary to focus at different distances.

*Extension	Subject distance	Magnification	Exposure factor
12mm	30cm	.25	—
25mm	20cm	.5	2x
36mm	15cm	.75	3x
50mm	10cm	1	4x

* The length of the extension tube is approximate as manufacturers do not all use the same lengths in a set of tubes. Subject distance is a guide only; intermediate distances are covered by focusing the lens. Discrepancy is due to design of lenses which have an optical centre well behind the front element. At infinity setting with a 50mm extension a 50mm lens will focus on 10cm away from its front nodal point.

▼ Standard 50mm lens, film speed 200 ASA, f8 at 1/250

▼ plus 8mm extension tube, f8½ at 1/125

▼ plus 14mm extension tube, f11½ at 1/60

▼ plus 27·5mm extension tube, f11½ at 1/60

▼ plus 41·5mm, a combination of 14mm and 27·5mm, f11 at 1/60

▼ plus 49·5mm, a combination of 8, 14 and 27·5mm, f11 at 1/30

Close-ups with bellows

Taking close-ups with a hand-held camera is one thing—it's not all that different from normal photography and no more complicated than using a long telephoto lens. But working with more elaborate close-up equipment for shots at anything from 1:1 (same size or life-size on the film) to 10 times magnification, becomes more complex and can be expensive, though it is possible with almost any interchangeable lens SLR.

The advantages of an SLR camera are the precise viewing, focusing and composing, plus being able to check the depth of field in the viewfinder, so critical with close-up photography.

To get big magnifications, which reveal details not easily seen by the naked eye and sometimes hard to see even with a magnifier, more extension is needed between the camera and lens than you can get by using simple extension tubes. What is more, although extension tubes in sets of three allow you to change magnification without too much trouble, and bridge the gaps between tubes by using the lens focusing ring, once you move the lens 10cm or more away from the film, it would need far too many small tubes to give all the combinations needed to allow a full range of settings. Close-up lenses already described would be totally inadequate as they do not enable the lens to focus close enough even with a 10 diopter close-up lens.

The answer is extension bellows—a tubular bellows with a rigid lens mount at one end and a camera body mount at the other—mounted on a rail and allowing a full range of extensions between 30mm and 200mm.

Lenses for bellows

You are not limited to a standard 50mm lens when working with bellows—although some lenses are more suitable than others. Telephoto lenses with macro facilities allow a greater working distance between camera and subject although magnification is reduced as the focal length is increased. **28mm or 35mm wide angle lenses** of modern design and reasonable aperture —that is, f2·8 and not f2 or faster— produce excellent results used on bellows where maximum magnification is needed. However, they are best used in the reverse position.

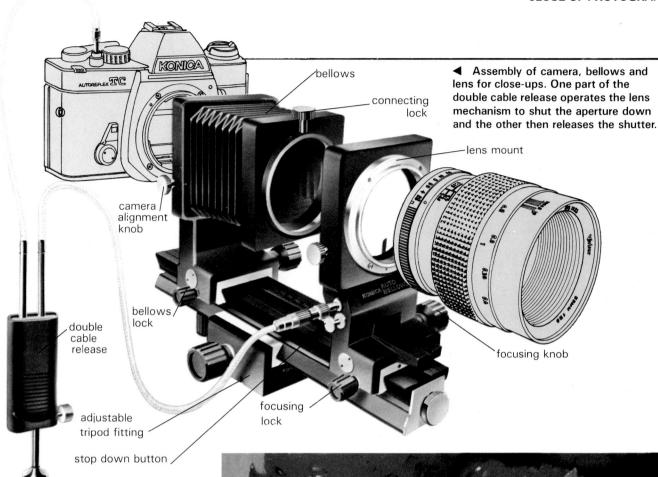

◀ Assembly of camera, bellows and lens for close-ups. One part of the double cable release operates the lens mechanism to shut the aperture down and the other then releases the shutter.

bellows

connecting lock

lens mount

camera alignment knob

double cable release

bellows lock

focusing knob

adjustable tripod fitting

focusing lock

stop down button

50mm lenses faster than f2 are likely to be unsuitable, regardless of the aperture used, and lenses of about f2 not ideal for use over 1:1. Lenses of f2·8 or thereabouts are often first rate.
50—55mm macro lenses specially designed for macro use produce good results because they are optically corrected for close focusing.
85-135mm telephoto lenses allow reasonable working distances between lens and subject. Results are variable although some 85mm f2.8 lenses are not true telephoto designs and perform very well.
100-105mm macro lenses also work well with bellows, because they give a good working distance between lens and subject.
200mm and longer telephoto lenses are generally not suitable for use with bellows; they have very limited magnification and little depth of field.
Zoom lenses with macro facilities offer a wide range of focal lengths although they rarely perform as well at the edges of the field as a fixed focal length lens does.

◀ To adjust magnification move bellow on its rail either at the front or the rear. For fine focusing move entire assembly or use lens focusing ring.

▲ A white punnet was half filled with strawberries and then photographed in sunlight using bellows to get a life-size image. The sides of the punnet reflected sufficient light to soften the shadows. *Eric Crichton*

Reversing rings: most lenses of 25–50mm, even macro lenses, can be fitted back-to-front on bellows for high magnifications, because they were originally designed to work with a short distance between lens and film and a large distance between lens and subject, that is 60cm to infinity. With bellows these distances are reversed, and turning the lens round using a reversing ring, which links the filter thread to the lens mount flange, puts the lens, once more, in its correct optical situation.

Picture making

When you take photographs at 1:1 or magnifications greater than that, you leave the world of easily-seen images and have to look for interesting subjects through the camera, rather than with your eyes alone. In nearly all macro photography it is the subject and not the composition or moment of exposure which creates the interest.

Start off by photographing inanimate objects—coral, rocks, crystal, jewellery, details of coins and so on. After that you should be able to tackle plants and outdoor subjects, but you will be surprised how much movement there is in an apparently still clump of grass. Live subjects are the last thing to try.

Always bracket macro exposures, varying both the aperture as well as the shutter speed. If you must photograph a plant or insect outdoors, where it cannot be kept perfectly still, take plenty of shots to increase the chance of a good one, and add fill-in flash if you can.

Practical aspects

SLR cameras with TTL metering need no adjustment, but other cameras require some sort of exposure factor. Exposure times tend to be long with high magnifications so, other considerations apart, a tripod is essential. Bear in mind that fast film can be used to give shorter exposures. To get maximum depth of field with a magnification of 2:1 (twice life-size) on film the lens is closed down to its smallest marked aperture, such as f16. That is an effective f64 because of the great extra lens extension (sometimes a full 150mm). With 64 ASA film, suitable for close-ups because of its fine grain, the exposure in bright sun would be either ¼ or ½ second, and with some subjects 1 or 2 seconds would be better. With a 50mm macro lens (the best type for this sort of work), you may well stop down to a marked f32—equal to

f128 at 2:1 magnification on the film. As magnification gets beyond life size (1:1) the image seen through the finder gets progressively dimmer, falling to a quarter of its illumination every time the image scale is doubled, until even a fast f1·4 standard lens will only give an image equivalent to viewing at f11 when working at four times magnification on the film.

Focusing rails: with macro photography, it is much easier to focus by moving the camera rather than by using the lens focusing ring, as this

▶ For this 1:1 image of a 1·5cm insect, dark card formed the background and an electronic flash was placed to the left of the camera. *Eric Crichton*

▼ To shoot the series of daisies (below) a flash unit was placed on either side of the daisy at 45° and pointing inwards. The tungsten lamp was used as a working light and was turned off during the exposures. A dark card was placed against the green background to provide a less distracting although not quite natural setting. *Eric Crichton*

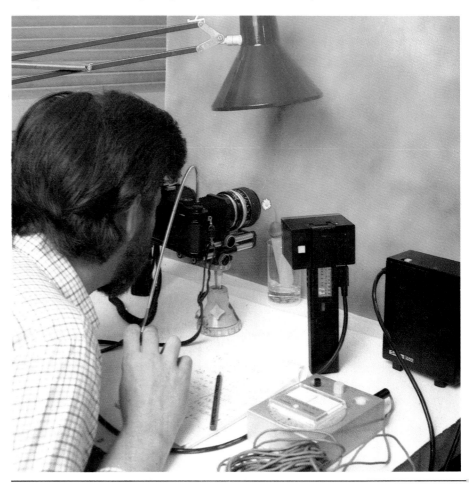

55mm lens plus 50mm extension
magnification: x1 on film

55mm lens plus 80mm extension
magnification: x1·4

55mm lens plus 110mm extension
magnification: x2

55mm lens plus 125mm extension
magnification: x2·27

55mm macro plus 125mm extension
magnification: x4

changes the magnification ratio. With most makes of bellows you can either focus by moving the camera, or the lens or both. Some bellows have an additional lower rail that fits on the tripod. With this, the whole camera and bellows can be moved bodily with very fine adjustment.

Vibration and mounting: at high magnifications vibration becomes very apparent. A good solid tripod is essential, preferably one where the camera can be suspended below it for close-to-the-ground work. Small clamps and mini tripods are not good enough. Use a cable release all the time, and avoid using motor-drives and autowinders.

Viewing and focusing: for work over 1:1 reproduction, a plain ground-glass screen or a clear screen fitted with a cross hair focusing is desirable. If the screen is fixed use the ground-glass part and ignore the centre microprism.

Depth of field is obviously very limited at reproductions greater than 1:1, and must be checked by using the stopped down preview button. Although with bellows this is often not possible as the camera is at working aperture anyway. Using the smallest aperture practically possible is essential.

Optical problems: if the edges of a picture appear unsharp with a normal lens used on bellows, stopping down may not be the complete answer. The most frequent problem with conventional lenses on bellows is that the centre focuses accurately but the edge detail is unacceptable. The solution is to use a lens reversing ring.

Buying bellows

There are several points to remember when buying a set of bellows.

● They are not really designed for hand holding—apart from being vulnerable to damage, they cannot be gripped like a long lens, and have focusing and locking knobs to operate.

● With many bellows you cannot use the automatic aperture setting mechanism. With some systems, a double cable release may be used to overcome lack of automatic aperture closing-down, one plunger first operating a mechanism at the bellows front to shut the aperture down and the other releasing the shutter immediately afterwards.

▶ Electronic flash was bounced to light this 2·5cm flower-head. Bellows were used to get a life-size image on film. *Eric Crichton*

▼ Two flash units were used to light these four-day old salmon alevins with yolk sacs. *Heather Angel*

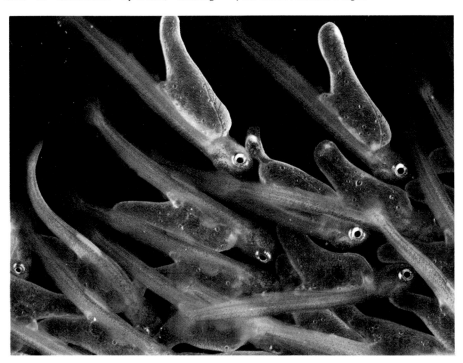

RANGE OF MAGNIFICATIONS AND EXPOSURE FACTORS

The tables below show the range of magnifications that can be achieved using different lenses on a normal set of bellows, and the additional exposure necessary as the magnification increases.

You will notice that if you extend a lens by as much as its focal length again on the bellows—that is, add 50mm of extension to a 50mm lens you get life size, 1:1; if you add double you get 2x magnification; add four times your focal length and you get 4x magnification of the subject on film.

Lens	Bellows extension in mm/magnification					
	35mm	50mm	85mm	100mm	135mm	200mm
35mm wide angle	**1:1**	1·43:1	2·14:1	2·85:1	3·86:1	5·7:1
50mm standard	1:1·43	**1:1**	1·7:1	2:1	2·7:1	4:1
85mm telephoto	1:2·3	1:1·7	**1:1**	1·18:1	1·6:1	2·35:1
100mm macro	1:2·86	1:2	1:1·18	**1:1**	1·35:1	2:1
135mm telephoto	1:3·85	1:2·7	1:1·6	1:1·35	**1:1**	1·48:1
200mm telephoto	1:5·7	1:4	1:2·35	1:2	1:1·48	**1:1**

Magnification and exposure factors for cameras without TTL metering systems

These apply regardless of the lens focal length, and depend only on the magnification.

Magnification	Plus	Marked f stop
1:1·4	1 Stop	now 1·4x f number
1:1	2 stops	now 2x f number
1·4:1	3 stops	now 2·8x f number
2:1	4 stops	now 4x f number

Macro lenses

The close-up equipment covered so far all involves the addition of some form of accessory for close focusing. The accessory is added either to the front of the camera lens or to the rear to increase the distance between the lens and the camera. Another method of achieving close-ups is to use a lens specially corrected to focus at closer distances than usual.

Most lenses are designed to perform at their best in the centre of the picture area. Focusing closer by using some form of extension exaggerates fall-off in edge definition as the lens is being used for a different purpose to that intended when the minimum focusing distance was set at, for example, 0·5m. However macro lenses are specially designed for close-up work and give their best performance when used under close-up conditions.

True macro lenses are only suitable for close-up photography. However, there are a number of lenses of varying focal lengths with both distant and macro facilities. You 'change gear' by operating a control ring which shifts internal lens units. In the macro mode these lenses are specifically designed for close focusing; they perform extremely well when used in conjunction with extension tubes and bellows.

Most macro lenses, whether fixed focal length or zoom, have a widest aperture

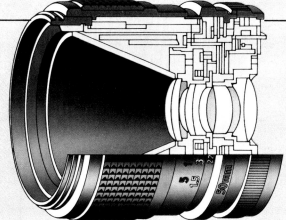

◀ Most 50mm macro lenses give 1:2 image ratios. Maximum apertures are relatively small to uphold quality, and special lens corrections permit close focusing distances.

▶ The mountain devil flower is native to Australia. The 1:2 image is enlarged here about eight times. *Eric Crichton*

of f3·5 or f4 although there are a few faster ones available.

True macro lenses

There are only a few true macro lenses. What makes them special is that they give a life-size image or greater, but they cannot be used to focus on a distant subject. True macro lenses are expensive even though the construction is generally simple. They are normally from 20-35mm focal length.

Other macro lenses

Most so-called macro lenses are really only a compromise between true macro and ordinary lenses. They are corrected to give an equally well-defined image at the centre and edge of the lens field, and at the same time can be used to

focus at varying distances up to infinity. They usually perform as well as a non-macro lens when focused on a distant subject.

This type of macro lens has a built-in helical mount to increase the distance between the back of the lens and the film in the camera. It is thus possible to focus close to a subject, and the design allows a crisp, good-quality picture.

Standard macro lenses: there are hardly any macro lenses with a short focal length, but several in the 50-60mm focal length range. Most of these lenses focus as close as 15cm in one movement to give a half life-size image. Several offer true 1:1 macro. But for most, extension tubes are needed to increase magnification. One or two extension tubes include optical

▼ The many macro options available will accommodate most budgets and requirements. Macro zooms, whether wide angle or telephoto, are extremely versatile. An extension tube can give greater image sizes with a macro lens.

Extension tubes incorporating optical correction give good image quality at life-size (available for most cameras).

True macro lenses produce larger than life images. It may be necessary to buy a special adapter to connect the lens to the camera. There are few true macros available and little choice in focal length.

70–210mm macro zoom

35–105mm macro zoom

optical extension tubes

50mm standard macro.

105mm macro lens

true macro lens

correction but most are simple tubes to increase the lens to film distance. Macro lenses perform better than a normal lens on extension tubes.

Telephoto macro lenses: there are plenty of macro lenses in the 90mm to 135mm focal length range, and one or two around 200mm and 300mm.

Zoom macro lenses: a few give a life-size image. There are two basic types. The first only focuses close to give maximum reproduction size at a specific focal length.

The other type of macro zoom can be switched to close focusing at any focal length you choose. This then offers all the advantages of varied working distances—telephoto setting allows space for lighting and keeps you away from the subject, whereas choosing a wider angle setting includes more of the subject from the same viewpoint. To change to macro the focusing ring is turned as far as it will go or a special release button is pressed to allow

▲ On some macro zoom lenses a release button allows the focusing ring to be turned further to enable the photographer to focus closer than is normal at a particular focal length.

▲ On the Vivitar 70–210mm zoom a maximum image size of 1:2·2 is attainable focusing at 29cm from the subject. Macro focusing is only possible with the lens set on 210mm.

further rotation. Both methods are similar in effect to additional bellows extension, allowing you to focus closer than normal with a particular lens.

Choosing a macro lens

A standard 50mm or 55mm lens is usually provided with a 35mm SLR camera. Buying a similar focal length macro would be an expensive doubling up of equipment. When buying a camera you may have a choice and prefer a 50mm or 55mm macro lens. This will give you a standard lens with close focusing ability—the only drawback is small maximum aperture and cost. It makes sense to opt for a focal length that extends your range of lenses

—you don't want a piece of equipment in your gadget bag which lacks versatility. For this reason true macro lenses are probably too specialized for all but the most dedicated.

A standard focal length macro is ideal for taking pictures of natural history subjects such as plants and fair-sized animals and insects, and also for copying work and other general close-ups. If you want to switch quickly to shooting a more distant subject, the lenses all focus to infinity.

There are plenty of macro zooms to choose from in wide angle and telephoto categories and at a wide variety of prices. You can use a zoom lens to cover many different photographic

situations. If the lens happens to offer close focusing too, then you really are getting good value. Always bear in mind that zooms, with or without macro focusing, rarely perform as well at the edges of the field as a fixed focal length lens does.

Nevertheless, macro zooms should theoretically perform better than non-macro lenses. However, as you get closer to the subject, and the lens extension increases, you are effectively reducing the maximum aperture. Some

▶ On the original slide this peacock butterfly was magnified to about half life size and is shown here around four times life size.

MACRO LENSES IN ACTION

55mm macro lens

With a 55mm macro lens small subjects can fill the frame.

The built-in extension tube allows a half life-size image.

105mm macro lens

A 105mm macro can fill the frame at greater working distances.

A half life-size image is possible with a telephoto macro.

70–210mm macro zoom lens

The zoom lens cannot focus close to fill the frame at 105mm.

Switching to macro focusing on the zoom permits a 1:2·2 image size.

▲ Both 55mm and 105mm macro lenses give good quality at half life size. The longer focal length allows greater subject distances keeping you away from a timid subject and providing space for lights. The zoom lens can give a 1:2·2 image, and although quality is not as good as the results from the macro lens a macro zoom is a versatile option. The quality is acceptable and the lens can be used for a wide range of subjects.
Courtesy of Worldwide Butterfly Farm, Sherborne. Eric Crichton

WORKING DISTANCES WITH MACRO LENSES
Distances shown are for the various focal lengths to focus a subject at half life size. The distances are given as a guide and may vary with lenses from different manufacturers.

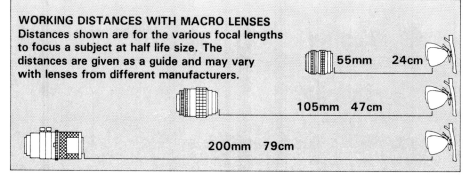

55mm 24cm

105mm 47cm

200mm 79cm

lenses give a scale showing the widest aperture you can use at a given focusing distance.

Remember, too, that if you decide to buy an extension tube to increase magnification you are stretching the optical design of the lens. The macro lens still performs better with an extension tube than any other lens would.

Using macro lenses

Most of the principles outlined for using bellows and extension tubes also apply to macro lenses. The difference is that image quality is better with a specially designed lens.

Focusing at close range must be absolutely accurate even if you are using a small aperture which gives fairly good depth of field. For example, at a magnification of 2:1 with the lens set at f16, depth of field is only 8mm. Using an even smaller aperture increases depth of field but only at the expense of image definition.

By increasing the distance between the back of the lens and the camera body, you instantly cut down the amount of light reaching the film. So you may well find yourself using a very slow shutter speed (even with fast film). Combine this with shallow depth of field and it becomes quite obvious that a tripod is essential or photographs will not be sharp as they could be.

To be successful, close-ups must be adequately lit. Use white card to reflect light, or if necessary use fill-in flash or bounced flash. Extreme close-ups may need more controlled lighting. (This is discussed next.)

The subject you choose to photograph can be almost anything—with magnification interesting details which may not be visible to the eye become apparent. At such close quarters it is not possible to change the image in any way—the photograph simply reproduces exactly what is in front of the lens, so it is very important to focus and calculate exposure carefully.

172

◀ This arrow poison frog was photographed using a 55mm Micro-Nikkor lens. Bright even illumination was provided by a Bowens twin-headed macro light flash. Macro lenses are convenient to use and, more important, quality is better than non-macro lenses on extension tubes or bellows. *Heather Angel*

▶ Using a 55mm macro lens allowed Eric Crichton to produce a half life-size image on film without having to use extra extension in the form of tubes or bellows. A single flash head lit this drum-stick flower from above, and here it is reproduced three times life size. Light from the flash falls off dramatically at large magnifications like this.

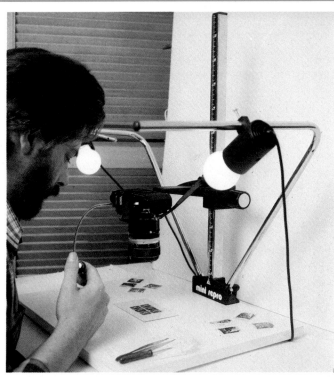

▲ A simple permanent set-up can ensure consistent results. This copying system is ideal for photographing flat subjects at large magnifications, and the lights are angled to provide even illumination. The stand is rigid enough to allow a long exposure (1/15 sec for the postage stamp). If copy quality is absolutely critical, a flat-field macro lens gives better results. *Eric Crichton*

Lighting for close-ups

A very distorted, abstract image of a human figure is still instantly recognizable in a photograph. The same does not apply with close-up detailed views of unfamiliar subjects, however, and so we need far more information to see what the subject is. So lighting for close-ups must be controlled and balanced to show as much detail as possible.

Outdoors, the natural light of a dull day is usually sufficiently directional to give good modelling and detail, but it is often not bright enough for the limited apertures which are used for close-ups, making additional lighting necessary. Indoors, a proper lighting set-up is essential for close-ups.

In either situation, the problems are similar. First of all, the light source must be small enough to be used close to the subject. It must not produce too much heat at close distances, or damage living subjects. It should preferably be compatible with any surrounding light. If the subject is mobile or the camera and subject both move, the light must either move with them or cover enough area to allow for movement. And the camera must not cast its own shadow on the picture area.

● Use flash on its own or to fill-in daylight shots. Don't mix photofloods with flash – use tungsten film with photofloods or a filter to correct the colour temperature.

Electronic flashguns

Electronic flash is the ideal light source for close-ups. It usually has a very short duration which stops most movement. Moreover, electronic flash is small, can be attached to camera or lens, and matches daylight in colour. It does not harm the subject, does not get hot, and the only disadvantage it has is lack of modelling light—that is, the absence of any light to focus by in dim conditions—and the inability to see the exact effect of the flash.

The very large professional flash units are not ideal for close-up work, although the size of their reflectors may produce a softer result. If you are able to use something like the Vivitar bounce card attachment or one of the other soft-light attachments for flash systems, very even and shadowless illumination can be achieved. Even a fairly small reflector—say, 5 x 3cm—is relatively large in relation to a subject 30cm away. The perfect flashgun for close-up illumination is a computer or automatic exposure type, with a close distance limit of 30cm and short

flash durations—between 1/1000 and 1/30,000. Most inexpensive battery-operated computer flashguns are like this. Try to buy one which has variable apertures for any given film speed. In close-up work effective apertures such as f32 are not unknown.

Ring flash

With many complex subjects (especially those with cavities) the use of an ordinary flashgun leads to heavy dark shadows obscuring some of the vital details which close-ups need. Ring flash units provide a circle of flash tube all round the lens front, thus throwing light evenly and casting no directional shadows. Their power is usually specially adapted for macro work, and cannot be used at normal distances. Exposure is not computed by the flashgun—it must be calculated as for manual flashguns.

Ring flash produces very flat results without much pictorial quality. Any reflections will show up, too, so most ring flashes are used with polarizing filters which cut out reflection.

Some typical uses for ring flash units include specialist subjects such as medical, surgical and biological photography.

▲ A ring flash fits on to the camera lens—a number of sizes and fittings are available—and runs from batteries or mains electricity. Light quality is flat and virtually shadow-free with circular highlights.

Manual flashguns

One of the problems which you may find with a manual flashgun is that with normal 100 ASA film and a lens closing down to f22, you are still

limited to a distance of 90cm. As most flashguns are not too generous in light output compared with their stated power, you can make this about 75cm for the sort of detail you need on a close-up. But normally you want the gun much closer—between 30–60cm. One method is to use the Inverse Square Law, which still applies quite well down to 60cm and slightly under, whereby, if you halve the distance you quadruple the amount of light falling on the film.

If you are working with extension tubes or bellows, you can take your exposure increase factor—say, 4x or 2 stops, working at 1:1 (life-size)—and transfer this directly to the flash distance. In this case you would still set f22 on the macro lens, but you would halve the distance between flash and subject to about 35cm. This will make the flash effectively four times brighter, and compensate precisely for the 2-stop light loss through the lens at 1:1 ratio. Similarly, if your extension tube calculations gave you a 2·25x factor, or 1⅓ stops increase, you would move the flash to about 45cm away. Exact positioning would not be worth worrying about given the accuracy of flash guide numbers generally and the behaviour of light sources at close distances. A couple of extra frames taken with the flash at slightly different distances would provide bracketed exposures. Make a note of the various exposures for future reference.

Brackets and hoods

A straight flash bracket that fits the camera tripod bush can hold a flash aimed forwards and inwards, for close-ups. Some brackets with pistol grips have swivel and angle heads, and allow a flash to be aimed in and down. You can make your own bracket, using a DIY flash shoe and tripod screw.

Some lens hoods carry flash shoes. The most obvious example is the Ambico Shade + which is a bellows lens hood with a flash shoe, capable of holding a lightweight gun for close-ups fixed to its front frame. However, this can put the gun too near the subject. Special adapters are available which fit the front of a lens, or fit the camera, and hold either one or two flashes angled inwards to illuminate close-ups. The Bowens close-up flash is a box which goes round the lens and has four separate flash tubes, like four flashguns arranged round the lens, so that any combination can be fired to produce directional lighting.

Cordless synchronization

In close-up work it can often be a great advantage to avoid trailing synchronization cables from camera to flashgun (one flashgun must be attached to the camera for sychronization). If a small flash is mounted on the camera or near it, flashguns being used as backlights or skim lights can be triggered using a slave cell (a 'magic eye' that is activated by a flash of light). But problems may arise with slave cells which are not sensitive to the extremely short durations of close-up computer flash; check before buying.

◀ A small slave cell is an ideal way to use two flash guns without the need for trailing cables. One flash connects to the camera X socket while the other is triggered by the slave. The slave sensor must be placed so that light from the main flash falls on to it.

▼ In a working set-up many different lighting techniques can be carried out with two flash guns and a slave cell. Using table-top tripods, or G-clamps fixed to the table edge (hot shoe tripod adapters are necessary) give a convenient means of support.

Using flash

To adapt a computer flash for close-up work, tape a piece of 4× neutral density filter (Kodak Wratten 96, ND 0·6) over its 'computer eye'. This causes the flash to put out four times as much light as normal, enabling you to use a 2-stop smaller aperture, and also halve its minimum working distance. So a gun which states that it must not be used closer than 30cm can now be used at 15cm. Stop down your camera lens to two stops smaller than indicated on the computer calculator of the gun if you use a 4× filter over the meter eye. The next problem is positioning the flashgun. If set on top of the camera, it is aimed at an area probably immediately above that being photographed in a close-up. Use a small angle bracket—the sort intended to aim the flash up at the ceiling for bounce flash—and aim downwards. The bracket fits between the camera shoe and the flash. Some flashguns have four-way bounce flash heads, and sometimes these can be aimed down for close-ups, but the meter eye will be aiming incorrectly. It is often possible to hold a small flash by hand and to aim it at the subject, especially if the camera is on a tripod. The advantage of computer flashguns

is that there are no complex guide number calculations to make when working out the aperture—the computer controls the flash output just as well at short distances as it does further away. This makes hand-holding practicable, as slight variations in distance will not upset exposure. You must be careful, though, to avoid putting fingers in the way of the meter eye.

Direct flash

With direct flash, you can vary the angle and position of the flash (perhaps using a pocket torch as a guide to setting up) to get a variety of lighting effects to suit different subjects.

Frontal lighting: the flash head is held as close to the lens rim as possible; this is only suitable for subjects which are non-reflective and rely mainly on colour, rather than shape or texture, for impact.

Side lighting—45°: hold the flash aiming in from the side or top; useful for many subjects that are basically round with heavy texture, or rough surfaces.

Skim lighting: flash held so that light grazes the surface of a flat, finely textured subject, bringing out detail of the texture much more strongly than usual; requires a modelling light to assess the

effect; can only be done with direct light sources, not diffused or bounced lighting; may give heavy shadows on side opposite to flash, which can be adjusted with a soft reflector.

Rim lighting: flash coming in from behind subject at about 45°, and partially backlighting through the subject, as well as grazing part of the surface facing the camera; most effective with three-dimensional objects.

Silhouette lighting: using a white card held behind the subject, the card is illuminated at 45° and the subject allowed to remain dark.

Transmitted light: with translucent subjects, the flash can be positioned directly behind with its synchro cables carefully masked. Exposure is by trial and error.

● In the case of all lighting effects apart from direct and 45°, allow one stop over the aperture indicated by the flash calculator dial for the ASA speed in use. If two flash units are used (45° main light, rim light from back) always base the exposure on the main frontal one. Each flash computer will work independently. To supplement dim daylight, use half the metered camera exposure and half-power flash (set for one stop wider than in use).

▼ **Frontal lighting:** holding the flash close to the lens is a simple but effective technique which anyone with even the most basic equipment can carry out. *R. Glover*

Side lighting: a single flash held at the side or above the subject at an angle of about 45° is ideal to emphasize shape and texture. This method is especially suitable for three-dimensional subjects.
Helmut Gritscher used a plain dark background to emphasize the shape and colour of the bloom.

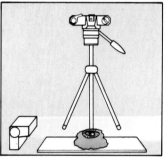

Skim lighting: a fairly flat specimen with fine surface texture is an ideal subject for skim or graze lighting — light just grazes the surface. White card or a diffused light source on the opposite side of the subject can be used to fill heavy shadows. *Heather Angel* used this technique for the fossil.

Rim lighting: this technique is best for lighting translucent subjects, in particular those with fine surface hairs. The light is positioned at about 45° behind the subject so that some light passes through and some light grazes the edge, giving a distinct line. *Chris Alan Wilton* used two flashes for this shot.

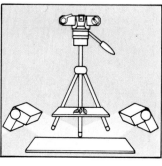

Silhouette lighting: to emphasize the shape of a subject – rather than colour or texture, silhouette lighting is ideal. A white card is supported behind the subject and lit evenly by flashes held at 45° to the card. Opaque items remain black but translucent subjects transmit some light. *Eric Crichton*

Transmitted lighting: a translucent item responds well to this technique. The flash is set up behind the subject so that internal structures are highlighted. Keep cables hidden. As the background is unlit it will be dark and undistracting. Dense parts of the subject remain dark. *Graeme Harris*

Special lighting

A subject will often be hard to support, or will be lost against a background so that it is hard to pick out. In the latter case you can use strong light and position a 'barn door' of cardboard to throw a shadow on the background area but not the subject. In the studio or indoors, picking out a subject on a plain background can be harder but the results will usually be better.

Supporting subjects on glass ensures that no visible pins, wires or other means of holding them are included in the picture. Normally, it is best to shoot at an angle to the glass, not at 90°—with straight-on photographs you may need to black out the camera body with matt tape to avoid reflection appearing in the glass (there is also the possibility of the photographer appearing). The subject can be rested on the glass, which must be scrupulously clean and free from dust.

Shadowless lighting can be achieved by raising the glass a short distance above the background (coloured card, for example) and aiming the light so that its shadow falls outside the picture area.

Dark ground illumination is achieved with translucent subjects by positioning the glass just above black velvet and aiming the lights or flashguns so that they illuminate it from the rear, picking it out against a solid black field.

Copy lighting for photographing flat subjects such as stamps, should normally be arranged with two equally matched flash units or photofloods either side of the subject at about 45°.

Tent lighting is very useful for small subjects with reflective surfaces such as jewellery. A tent is constructed of translucent white film (diffusion film, tracing film for draughtsmen, or muslin) with a hole for the camera to see through. Two or three flash units or photofloods are positioned to illumin-

ate all the surface of the tent. Inside, illumination is remarkably even. Exposure will usually need to be established by experimenting.

Reflectors and dark card

With small subjects it can be better to alter light quality by positioning reflective or black cards near the area being photographed. Particularly with ornaments, silverware, glass and similar subjects, the use of white and black cards enable the photographer to position reflections exactly on the subject so that they delineate its lines correctly. With non-reflective subjects, shadow areas can be lightened or darkened as required by using either white or black paper or cards. Portable aluminium foil reflectors or a roll of kitchen foil are particularly useful for draping round close-up subjects to throw extra light back in.

The other use of any card or sheet is to shield the subject from direct sun—

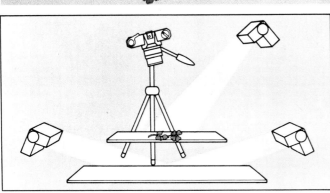

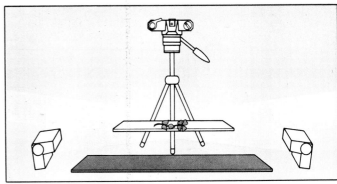

On glass: a shadow-free white background results if the subject is set on a sheet of glass suspended above a sheet of white card or paper. The background is lit separately from the subject. Be careful to avoid reflections of the camera, lights or yourself on the surface of the glass. *Eric Crichton*

Dark ground illumination: this method is suitable for translucent subjects, in particular those with fine spines or hairs. The specimen is positioned on glass just above a piece of black matt cloth. Illuminate the subject from below, taking care not to shine light into the camera lens. *Heather Angel*

often a photograph will look better with diffused light. A small card will cut out direct rays but still allow plenty of surrounding light (perhaps from reflectors) to be thrown on to the subject.
● Polystyrene ceiling tiles make very good reflectors as they reflect a 'pure' white. They are also light, readily available and inexpensive.

Lights and viewfinders
Sometimes you may find yourself using bright lights which are positioned behind the camera. With auto-exposure SLR cameras be careful to avoid influence of the metering system by light entering the eyepiece, as at close-up working distances the light being read through the lens on its extension bellows can be very dim. Viewing is helped by a good eyecup, and a blind of some kind should be used for exposure if the camera is being used in the automatic mode.

Calculating f stops with tubes or bellows and flash

If you use close-up lenses, then the f stops marked on the lens remain correct at close distances. So do the f stops on most close-up zoom lenses. But if you fit extension tubes or bellows to an SLR camera, the marked f stops no longer apply as you extend the lens away from the camera. With TTL metering you do not need to worry about this but with flash you must know how to set the correct aperture.

A simple way of finding how much to adjust the aperture is:

$$\text{factor to change f number by} = \frac{\text{length of lens in use}}{\text{focal length of lens in use} + \text{extension in use}}$$

Thus, if you use 50mm of extension bellows on a 50mm lens, the amount to change the f stop by would be: $\frac{50}{50+50} = \cdot 5$ or $\frac{1}{2}$.

So instead of f16 you would need f16 × ·5; that is, f8.

This is one formula where you actually divide the f number physically. There are other ways of calculating the exposure but this is the easiest as you can always measure the length of the extension between camera and lens (other formulae depend on the magnification).

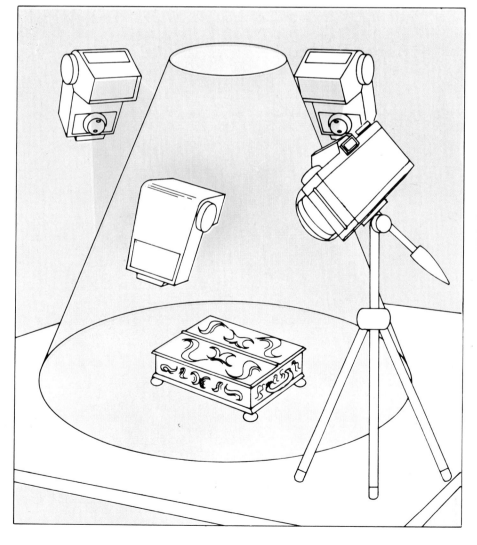

▲ Highly reflective surfaces such as polished metal are difficult to photograph well. *Graeme Harris* used a 'tent' to avoid confusing highlights and reflections and to provide bright diffused lighting.

◄ Photographic tents can be bought but most people make their own. You need to construct a frame (use black non-reflective wire) to support white muslin or tracing paper. The size depends on the types of subject you photograph, but for close-up techniques the tent can be on a small scale. Cut a small opening to accommodate the camera lens and position two or three flash units outside the tent to light the whole surface. The light inside is soft and even.

Filters for black and white film

Filters can add magic and sparkle to your photographs. Fluffy clouds stand out above landscapes; snow scenes retain depth and daylight can even be made to resemble moonlight.

The most common black and white film used is panchromatic or 'pan' type. Pan film is sensitive to light across the whole colour spectrum, but its reaction to individual colours is different from that of the human eye. We are more sensitive to yellow light than to blue and red, but black and white pan film reacts more strongly to blue and violet. As a result, filters are needed to deal with situations in which the unnatural response of the film would cause the resulting photograph to reproduce the tones falsely.

The function of a filter is to change the light reaching the film in some specific way and to produce an image that is more accurate, interesting or dramatic. Filters are easy to use and even easier to misuse. The subtle use of filters can lift a photograph out of the ordinary, but no filter can make up for errors of composition or exposure.

Modern filters are made from optical quality glass or acrylic plastic. These are either mounted in a metal ring which screws on to the front of the lens, or made to fit a universal holder. A cheaper way to get occasional filter effects is to use gelatin squares and mount them over your lens. They don't have the same durability as the more expensive filters but they are useful where these are unavailable in the required size for a particular lens. Filters are made in different sizes, so always take your lens with you when buying them to make sure they fit.

Types of filter

Filters for black and white photography can be divided into three categories: correction filters, contrast filters and special-purpose filters. The difference between them is that a correction filter restores tone whereas a contrast filter emphasizes and even exaggerates tone.

A classic case for using a filter is when photographing a picture which includes a cloud-studded sky. Black and white film will record the clouds as white. But, because of the hypersensitivity of this type of film to blue light, the blue sky will also register as white and the final negative will print as if there was no sky at all, only a blank white area. In order to rescue the tonal difference between cloud and sky, a yellow filter is needed to hold back the blue. Holding back the light will obviously affect the exposure and this must be taken into consideration when deciding on the f stop or aperture.

Filter factors

All filters interfere with light entering a camera. This interference is minimal in the case of some filters but others reduce quite considerably the amount of light that reaches the film and so need an exposure increase. The amount of extra exposure needed depends on the particular filter and is known as the filter factor. Contrast filters being darker have a larger filter factor than correction filters (see chart overleaf).

Most filters are marked with a factor which is expressed by a whole number followed by an X. A filter with a factor of 1X requires no additional exposure but a 2X filter requires an extra f stop, while a 4X filter needs an increase of 2 f stops. An alternative method is to express the required correction with a minus number. A filter marked -1 requires a one-stop adjustment, -2 two stops and so on.

Filter factors for any given filter can

▼ An image, as it appears to the eye in colour, is translated into black and white (far right). The tones of various colours can be controlled by using filters. A coloured filter lightens colours of a similar hue and darkens complementary colours.

▲ Effect of green filter

vary with different light sources. The factor given on the filter is usually calculated for daylight, so carefully check the literature supplied with any filter before using under artificial light.
● Cameras with through-the-lens meter systems do not require any adjustment as the reading on the meter will automatically take into account the reduced light, except with some deep orange and red filters.

Correction filters

The sky isn't the only outdoor subject that can suffer through the blue bias of pan film. Portraits in daylight tend to

result in pale, insipid skin tones. The solution is a pale green, or yellow/green filter to darken both the red skin tone and the blue tone of the sky. It also lightens foliage.

Artificial light poses a different problem for black and white photography. Tungsten or halogen lighting has a reddish cast that needs to be corrected by a pale blue filter if truthful tonal rendition is desired. This is especially important for portraits where flesh tones can appear too pale. A blue filter, used in artificial light, also prevents red lips from appearing too light and blue eyes too dark.

▲ Effect of a red filter
▼ Effect of a blue filter

▼ Without a filter these particular shades of blue and red appear as similar tones. A darker shade of green would also appear as the

same tone. A green filter corrects tanned skin tones; red makes skin tones very pale; blue lightens towel and background.

Contrast filters

Darker coloured filters have similar effects to the paler correction filters on pan film, but to an exaggerated degree. They can be used to accentuate tonal differences between colours that appear equally bright to the eye, or to introduce additional overall contrast.

The sky is a particularly suitable subject for contrast filters. A deep yellow filter darkens a blue sky and brings out the clouds even more vividly than a pale yellow corrective filter. An orange or red filter will produce higher contrast, with blue sky appearing as grey or even black with the latter. Though these colours darken greens, grass and trees contain so much yellow that they do not suffer. Using a green filter lightens foliage but has only a slight effect on sky tones.

Used with care, black and white contrast filters can add bite to an otherwise flat photograph, juggle tone rendition to give specific subjects more impact and to add drama.

▲ **A deep yellow filter** is less dramatic; it darkens the sky to appear as the eye sees it.

▼ **Without a filter** the sky appears unnaturally pale and completely lacking in detail.

▲ **A deep red filter** dramatizes the sky as it increases the contrast between the sky and the clouds.

Correction filters

Filter	Effect on b/w film	Uses
Pale yellow X1½	Lightens yellow, darkens blue, slight haze penetration.	Slightly darkens sky tones in landscapes. Clearer pictures on hazy day.
Yellow X1½	Lightens yellow, darkens blue, lightens green slightly.	Increased contrast between clouds and blue sky.
Yellow/green X2	Lightens yellow and green, darkens blue and diminishes red.	Landscapes, outdoor portraits as it corrects skin tones, and beach scenes.
Green X3	Lightens green, darkens red and blue. Slightly darkens orange.	Photographs containing a lot of green, such as a lawn, and also for outdoor portraits as it corrects skin tones and lightens background foliage against a darker sky. Makes tans look darker.
Pale blue X1	Lightens blue and blue/green colours slightly. Darkens red.	Portraits in artificial light. It removes the reddish tones from the lighting and corrects skin tones. Be careful if subject is wearing red lipstick as it will turn darker.

Contrast filters

Filter	Effect on b/w film	Uses
Deep yellow X2½	Lightens yellow and orange, darkens blue.	Adds contrast between clouds and a blue sky. Full correction to what the eye sees.
Orange X5	Lightens orange and red, yellow slightly, but darkens blue and green. Good haze penetration.	Landscapes, architecture. Brings out detail of grain and texture in hardwoods.
Light red X4	Lightens red and orange, darkens blue and green. Penetrates haze and mist.	Increases contrast and penetrates haze. Good for misty landscapes, furniture, buildings. Differentiates between grass and red in a mixed subject by darkening green and lightening red: roses are a good example.
Deep red X10	Lightens orange and red, darkens blue almost to black; also green. Penetrates mist and fog.	Maximum contrast for landscapes with sky very predominant. Good for sunsets, dramatic cloud formations, copying blueprints. Photographs on foggy days.
Blue X5	Lightens blue, turquoise, violet, darkens red and yellow; green slightly.	Emphasizes hazy effect. Can make for mysterious pictures in misty conditions.
Green X6	Lightens green and yellow/green slightly, darkens red and orange; some blues.	Lightens foliage on trees. Good for pictures in forests and gives more detail in leaves and other green subjects.

Filter factors

Fractions in aperture changes are rounded to the nearest whole number. The filter factor numbers are those marked on the filter mount.

Factor	1¼	1½	1¾	2	2⅓	3	4	5	6	7	8	12	16
Aperture change in f stops	-½		-1			-2			-3			-4	

183

Filters for colour film

Filters for colour give the photographer some measure of control over the final quality of his picture. He can cut through haze, or make colours more realistic by adjusting for excess blue or red light at certain times of day. Filters are amongst the cheapest accessories you can buy and will last for years if you look after them.

Colourless filters

Possibly the most useful filters of all are those which can be used with either black and white or colour film.

Ultra-violet filters absorb UV radiation and therefore effectively reduce haze. On black and white film this adds detail to distant mountains, for example, and on colour film it reduces the haze common in landscape photographs. This filter has little visual effect beyond holding back unwanted ultra-violet light. So it can be left on the lens to protect it from dirt and scratches.

Skylight filters are similar to UV filters. They are widely used and perform several functions. They absorb some ultra-violet light, a major cause of haze and excessive bluishness. But, unlike UV filters, they are slightly pink and come in different densities. Like UV filters, they can be left on the lens all the time.

Neutral density filters don't affect either colour balance or contrast but simply reduce the light entering the lens. They are useful when a camera loaded with fast film is suddenly used to photograph a brightly lit scene, or if shooting at full aperture to give shallow depth of field and the available shutter speed isn't fast enough to prevent overexposure.

Polarizing filters also act as neutral density filters, reducing the light entering the lens by as much as $1\frac{1}{2}$ to 2 stops, but they do much more than this. They help eliminate glare (reflected light) from surfaces such as windows and water, and the blueness one associates with distant views. The filter also darkens a blue sky if used at right-angles to the sun. Rotate the filter while looking through it until you get the effect you want.

Creative effects

Beyond the purely technical considerations governing their use, filters can be employed to achieve specific creative

▶ **The sea in the background is made distinct from the sky by using a skylight filter to reduce haze.**

◀ A polarizing filter, used at right angles to the sun, increases the blueness of the sky. A distant horizon has greater contrast and appears more distinct. The sky and background (below), photographed without a filter, appear lighter.

▶ A neutral density filter effectively reduces the light entering the camera. It does not affect the colour or contrast but simply has the effect of down-rating the film speed. This in turn gives a smaller depth of field which means a subject can be made distinct against a more out-of-focus background (see right and below).

◀ Coloured filters for black and white photography can be used on colour film. The effects are extremely dramatic and although not natural, do have visual appeal. The red filter produces a fiery sky while the blue filter gives a cold moonlit effect. The branches are silhouetted against the strong colours of the sky.

▼ The angle of the sun is such that the polarizing filter has no effect on the sky (top left). But the sunlight creates highlights on the water and a polarizing filter is needed to reduce the reflections. A UV and skylight filter would not have any effect on the reflections as they only reduce haze and ultra-violet light.

◄ A polarizing filter reduces the light reflected from glass, making it possible to photograph the driver through the window. The polarizing filter has the same effect on all non-metallic surfaces. This makes it possible to photograph into water, for example, to get a detail of the bottom of a clear stream or fish and plants in the water.

effects. Such use is entirely at the discretion of the photographer and is not subject to hard and fast rules.

Filter ranges include specially designed colour filters to produce pastel or sepia tones with colour film, but any colour filter can be used in conjunction with colour film for a greater variety of effects and moods as shown later in this chapter.

Fluorescent lighting

Tube lighting usually renders natural colour tones incorrectly. With most fluorescent tubes colours tend to be tinged with green. It is difficult to overcome this as different types of tube vary in their colour. As a general guide, with 'daylight' tubes (bluish) use daylight type film; with all other tubes use tungsten type film. Filters are available to correct certain combinations of tube lighting. But for best results, avoid this lighting.

Colour temperature

The eye adjusts almost instantaneously to record nearly all light as white, even candlelight. But film cannot make the same adjustment. Colour films are balanced for light of a specific colour temperature, usually daylight or a particular type of tungsten light. If used under different conditions the colour can be affected by the change in colour temperature. Radiating light sources, such as the sun or an electric bulb, produce light of various colours depending on the temperature at which the source is glowing. (If an object is heated it will glow red, more heat will turn it white and, eventually, increased heat will turn it blue.) It is this combination of colour and temperature which holds the key to understanding filters (see the section on filters to use with black and white film). The colour temperature is measured in degrees Kelvin (K)

◄ Fluorescent lighting produces a colour cast on colour films. The resulting photographs usually have a greenish tinge. For warm white fluorescent lighting use an FL-D filter to correct the colour cast for more natural looking results.

► Different combinations of fluorescent lighting produce different colour casts. If using daylight type film and the light source is daylight type fluorescent use an FL-Day filter to correct the colour.

which grades the light from candlelight to a blue sky. Daylight film (5500 K) responds naturally when exposed in midday sun. But there are certain situations that produce unwanted shifts. For instance, candlelight (with a low colour temperature) produces a warm reddish cast. An intense blue sky or a snow scene (which has a higher colour temperature) will produce a blue cast. So colour temperatures work contrary to our notions of warm and cold colours.

If you know the colour temperature of a light source you can anticipate the effect it will have on daylight or tungsten film. A filter can then be used to correct the colour temperature so that the film will reproduce the scene naturally—that is, without a red or blue cast.

Which filter to use

There are various types of colour filters, including colour correction filters and the colourless type such as haze or ultra-violet and skylight filters, which are suitable for black and white as well as colour film.

While you are experimenting with filters and how to use them, always keep a record of the photographs you take—the type of film, shutter speed and aperture, the filter, and the time of day. This helps you to repeat successes and avoid failures.

Colour correction filters

Colour correction filters include colour conversion, light balancing and colour compensating (CC) filters. The categories are based, for convenience, on the way filters are marketed. If you cannot distinguish between the categories it doesn't really matter: there is a certain amount of overlap anyway. (CC filters are dealt with in a separate article.)

The main thing to bear in mind is
• Orange/amber filters reduce colour temperature.
• Blue filters increase the colour temperature.

Conversion filters are designed to adapt specific types of colour film to light sources of a different, but known, colour temperature. Daylight colour film is balanced for midday sunlight of

▼ Coloured filters adjust differences in colour temperatures. Colourless filters reduce haze.

Gelatin filters

The advantage of using a gelatin filter is that it is much cheaper than glass and can be cut to the required size; if no mount is available it can simply be taped to a cardboard frame. The range of gelatin filters is extremely wide.

Caring for gelatin filters
• Avoid getting fingerprints on gelatin filters.
• Handle the filter by its edge only.
• Put the filter between sheets of paper when cutting and handling it.
• To clean a filter, use a soft brush to remove dust and grit. Wipe filter gently with clean, soft, lintless cloth.

▼ Gelatin filters can be used with universal mounts to fit most lenses; alternatively cut the filter to the required size.

Colour conversion filter Film		Colour temperature
Daylight 5500°K	Tungsten 3200°K	
	85	20,000
		10,000
		8,000
		7,000
None	85B	6,000
		5,500
		4,800
80D	85C	4,200
80C		3,800 3,700
80B	85	3,400
80A	None	3,200
		2,800
		2,000 1,800

5500°K to 6000°K (electronic and blue flash are also of this temperature). Colour film is also available in tungsten balanced versions for 3200°K light sources, such as studio lighting. Examples of useful conversion filters include a blue (80A) filter for use with daylight film under tungsten light (3200°K) and an amber (85B) filter for use with tungsten balanced film in daylight; but others are made to deal with a variety of conversion problems. **Light balancing filters:** colour film is specifically balanced to give a neutral response when exposed to light of a matching colour temperature. Light of a higher or lower temperature will cause a shift in the colour balance of the film. The two most common examples of this occur when subjects are in a shaded area, lit only by the reflected blue light of a north sky (in the case of the northern hemisphere), rather than directly by the sun, or when photographed by the light of early morning or evening sunshine. To eliminate the excessive blue cast of north light a pale yellowish filter is used to lower the colour temperature, while a bluish filter will correct the yellow bias of a rising or setting sun. Light balancing filters are graduated by subtle changes of colour and a complete set includes 10 or more yellow (81 series) and blue (82) filters. Strictly speaking, an expensive colour temperature meter and complex calculations are necessary to determine accurately the exact correction required for particular circumstances. However, as a general guide, the most useful balancing filters include the 81A and 81B for use with daylight colour films on cloudy or rainy days; and the 82A for morning and evening light.

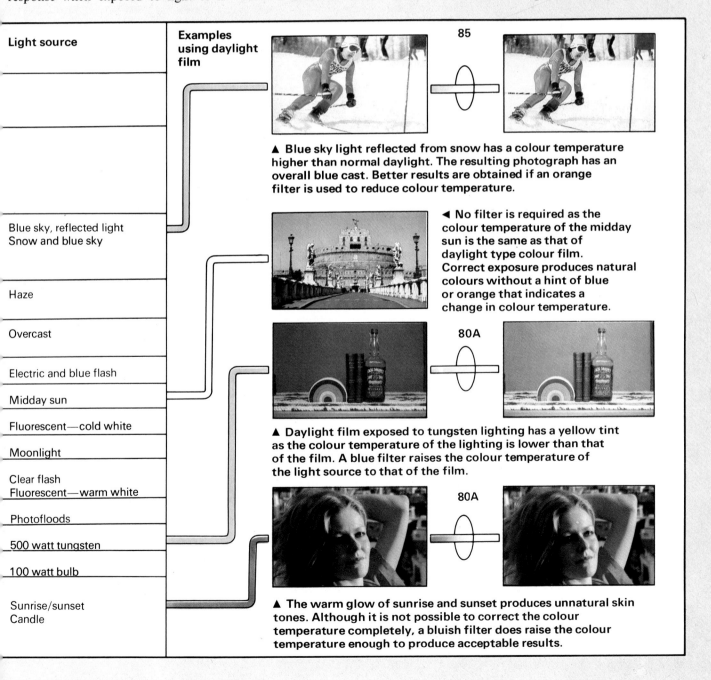

Light source

Examples using daylight film

Blue sky, reflected light
Snow and blue sky

Haze

Overcast

Electric and blue flash

Midday sun

Fluorescent—cold white

Moonlight

Clear flash
Fluorescent—warm white

Photofloods

500 watt tungsten

100 watt bulb

Sunrise/sunset
Candle

85

▲ Blue sky light reflected from snow has a colour temperature higher than normal daylight. The resulting photograph has an overall blue cast. Better results are obtained if an orange filter is used to reduce colour temperature.

◄ No filter is required as the colour temperature of the midday sun is the same as that of daylight type colour film. Correct exposure produces natural colours without a hint of blue or orange that indicates a change in colour temperature.

80A

▲ Daylight film exposed to tungsten lighting has a yellow tint as the colour temperature of the lighting is lower than that of the film. A blue filter raises the colour temperature of the light source to that of the film.

80A

▲ The warm glow of sunrise and sunset produces unnatural skin tones. Although it is not possible to correct the colour temperature completely, a bluish filter does raise the colour temperature enough to produce acceptable results.

Effects with special filters

Recently photographers have started using many more special effects in their photographs, and there has been a boom in the manufacturing of unusual but simple attachments to produce all sorts of images. Any amateur can, without spending much, match the creative armoury which once cost the professional a large sum. Starbursts, colourful rainbows, rotating prisms, superimposed images, and soft dream effects, are all available to the amateur. The big change has come, in the case of 35mm SLRs, with the multi-purpose filter holder. These attachments screw or push on to the lens, and gelatin, plastic or glass squares are slotted in.

Mounted filters At one time, each round attachment was a glass disc individually mounted in a metal rim, and only one could be screwed on to a lens at any one time. Separately mounted filters are still available, though the very expensive ones, which are used to produce special effects, have been superseded by the multi-purpose filter holder systems.

Step-up/down rings adapt round mounted filters to lenses with a different thread size. This makes it possible to fit filters from independent manufacturers on to most lenses.

How a filter holder works

Unlike round mounted filters, square filters can be placed in their holder at any angle, and the holder can usually be rotated without unscrewing it from the lens rim. The square filters can also be slid up and down freely. Two filters can be sandwiched in one holder or, in the case of the Cokin holder, two slots are provided so that more than one can be used at a time.

In front of this holder, which would be very exposed if left on its own, a lens hood is fitted to shield the filter and lens from direct sun which might cause flare patches or poor contrast in the final picture.

A holder and hood are often combined but detachable. Makes include Hoya (technical filter holder), Cokin (filter systems, holder and hood).

Filter effects

There are several types of special filter available, all creating different effects. **Starbursts** are line ruled filters. They are made by scratching fine lines on a glass or plastic filter, which then produce stars or bursts of light from any point source, such as a street light. Deeper scratches produce stronger effects, and so do more frequent scratches. Very deep rulings may spoil sharpness and closely covered filters, heavily ruled, diffuse the image and give odd colours to the light bursts. Types available include cross-screen (90°), starbursts (60°), and vario-cross (two filters, each parallel ruled, which can be rotated for different angles). There are usually two strengths in any one type of filter. They are generally made in circular mounts and can be rotated. Light burst filters for the Cokin system use irregular scratches instead of line ruling.

Diffraction filters are made by ruling lines far closer together, so finely that the eye cannot tell they are lines. This produces coloured rainbows instead of light bursts, using diffraction to split the light into its colour spectrum elements. Diffraction filters are available in various forms with many effects ranging from a simple line of colour from a light source to a whole array of coloured blobs appearing

▲ A filter holder holds gelatin, glass or plastic squares flat and in position in front of the camera lens. The filter is simply sandwiched between the two sections of the holder. A lens hood can be used in conjunction with a filter holder.

▶ Diffraction filters split light into its colour spectrum elements. They are best used on scenes that have small light points against a dark background.
Paul Constancio

LENS HOODS
metal
rubber

Step-up/
step-down
rings

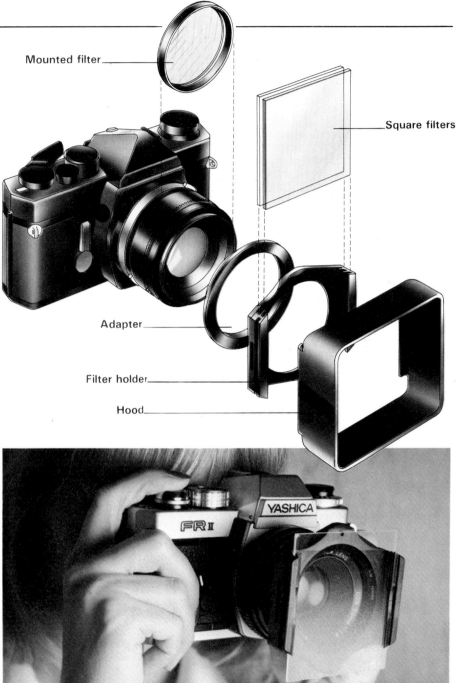

Mounted filter

Square filters

Adapter

Filter holder

Hood

▲ Step-up/down rings adapt round filters to lenses with a different thread size, for example a 52mm filter can be adapted to a 49mm lens or vice versa. Lens hoods can be of metal or rubber and either screw on or snap on to the lens. They can be used even when a filter is attached.

▶ The Cokin universal filter holder can be used with lenses which have a screw thread of 49mm to 58mm. An adapter fits the holder to the lens. The holder takes round and square filters and more than one filter can be used at a time.

▼ 1 A split-field lens has a close-up lens in one half and the other is clear.
2 A soft focus filter diffuses light and creates a soft image.
3 Starburst filters are etched with lines which create patterns on light sources.
4 A centre focus lens is a close-up lens with a hole in the middle.

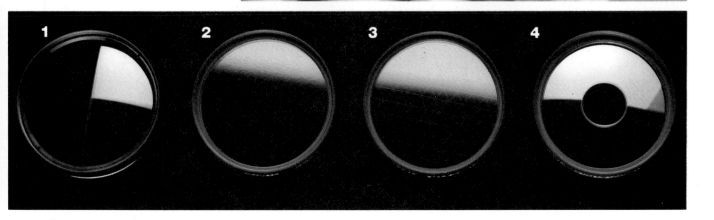

1   2   3   4

Starburst filters give light sources star shapes. The number of points depend on the pattern of lines on the filter. They can be 4, 6, 8 or multi-burst and each one has its particular use. Two very different uses are shown here.

▶ A multi-burst filter gives the only light source a radiating effect—if there were more light sources the effect would be distracting rather than creative.
Jill Richards

▼ Each light source is broken into 8 points and this regular pattern enhances the lines of lights as they converge on the central image.

▲ A diffraction filter gives the rays of light shining in through the window a touch of colour. The effect is much softer and more natural than diffraction of small strong light sources.
Peter Goodliffe

◀ Far left: without a filter colours appear naturally. Left: adding a fog filter makes the scene become misty and generally more atmospheric without looking contrived.
Lisa le Guay

round a source. The heavier the effect, the more diffusion and unsharpness is introduced. Filters mounted for the camera are normally produced using plastic diffraction sheets mounted on glass. Loose plastic sheets can be bought far more cheaply—these are very fragile but perfectly acceptable for experimenting.

Fog filters do just what they say—they make the picture look as if it has been taken through fog or mist. Unlike real fog, they do not have more effect on distant parts of the picture than near ones, but the effect is still realistic. Fog filters are misty-white to look at, but almost clear to look through, because they have the effect of scattering light passing through them. In darkness, they have no opacity and are, in theory, quite clear. Only when you let light fall on them is there any light to scatter inside them. They do not affect picture sharpness. There are four strengths: pastel, fog no.1, no.2, no.3. The most useful ones are the first three. Fog filters are available in mounted discs and acrylic squares.

Centre focus lenses, also called 'spot' lenses, consist of a dioptric lens (usually +3) with a hole through the middle, so that the edges of the photograph are focused at about 30cm while the main central image is at infinity (dioptric lenses reduce the focusing distance). These lenses are deliberately incapable of making the edge sharp. The result is a sharp central image with blurred edges—suitable for eliminating distracting city backgrounds, for example. These lenses are made in circular mounts.

Sandgrain filters are made by sandblasting or etching the outer edges of a plain glass filter. The outside of the image can then be made not only to blur, but also to fade to grey.

◄ A soft focus filter gives an overall diffused quality to the picture.

► A centre focus filter keeps the image in focus at the centre but the surroundings and the background are put out of focus. This is particularly useful for losing distracting backgrounds when photographing portraits in cluttered surroundings.

► (Below) A misty is made by spreading vaseline on a clear glass filter, such as a UV filter, which then softens the image.

▼ A split-field lens with a close-up lens on one half focuses on the foreground while the other half allows the lens to focus normally at infinity for a distant subject.

To make a 'misty'

Mistys are made by smearing petroleum jelly on the edges of a clear sheet of plastic in a pattern which surrounds the subject but does not interfere with it. The diffusion is very strong but can be controlled and made to follow the lines of the image. This can be done on a plain glass filter—for example, a UV filter—but with less control. It is best to use a clear plastic sheet inserted in the front of a lens hood. Never, of course, attempt smearing material on the lens itself.

Soft focus filters, also called diffusers, have fine lines etched on the filter which softens the edges of the picture but leaves the centre sharp. Filters for an overall soft focus effect are also available. These filters are particularly suitable for portraits as skin blemishes become less obvious.

Split-field lenses are made by cutting a close-up lens in half, which results in a split field. This allows one half of the lens to focus on a close distance while the other half is on a distant subject. The filter can be rotated to move the division round, and in square moulded form can slide up and down in the holder to adjust the division ratio. Split-field lenses are made to achieve a sharp image, unlike centre focus lenses. The camera lens must be used quite wide open to prevent sharp distinction between the two planes of focus appearing in the middle of the picture.

Special effects using colour filters can add interest to an otherwise dull scene. To be successful these filters should be used with discretion; scenes low in colour or contrast, for example, lend themselves to added colour. The colour can be added in different ways depending on the particular colour and type of filter being used.

These filters can be used in combination with the special effects filters discussed previously. Shoot a roll of film with the various filters and keep a record so that you can repeat successes.

This is also particularly useful if you do not have through-the-lens metering, in which case exposure must be increased according to the filter factor. Whatever filter you use don't overdo it. A starburst in every one of your holiday photographs will ruin the whole effect; orange tints on all landscapes become boring, as do endless photographs that look as though flooded with moonlight. Be discerning in the use of filters—use them where they are visually creative and not just for the sake of being different.

Split colour filters have one half of one colour and the other of a different colour. They can also be divided into three colours. The idea of these is to add dramatic colours in strong divisions to ordinary subjects. They can be difficult to use successfully. The made-up filters, in normal mounts, have colours which are carefully balanced in density so that one does not affect the exposure more than the other. You can also make your own by buying filter acetates or gelatin and taping them together to fit into a filter holder.

▲ A combination of filters was used for this shot. A soft focus filter diffuses the overall image and a split colour filter, one half red and the other half blue, adds dramatic colour.

A graduated filter has one side clear and the other coloured. A split colour filter combines two different colours.

Graduated filters are clear on one half, with a diffused dividing line in the middle, turning to a neutral grey or a coloured half. They are also known as 'graduates' or 'chromos'. They are used where one half of a scene—normally the sky—is too bright, and positioned so that the coloured half covers the bright area and the clear half allows the darker part of the scene to come through at full brightness. They can be used to correct, as when using a grey filter to darken a bright sky; to enhance, as when using a blue filter to make a dull white sky look blue; and to produce effects, as when turning a sky red or the sea green, or imitating a sunset. They are available as round mounted filters (Hoya, Cromofilter, Lee, Vivitar Halfchrome) and as square acrylic ones (Cokin).

▲ A graduated filter adds a warm tint to this misty scene. Without the filter the picture would have been almost without colour, with the reflected image simply being a repeat of the subject.
Martin Riedl

◀ The same scene shot with various filters produces different results. A starburst filter breaks the light source into eight points. A split colour filter, used in conjunction with the starburst filter retains the star-shaped light source and adds blue and red to the sky.
David Morey

197

Pastels and sepia effects can be achieved by using coloured filters. These filters are lightly coloured and allow the subject colours to show through that of the filter. They can be used very effectively in conjunction with soft focus filters, or diffusers. Another successful way to use them is to combine a sepia filter with a 'misty'. The effect of this is to soften the outer edges of the picture and can be very atmospheric.

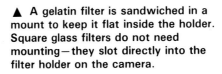

▲ A gelatin filter is sandwiched in a mount to keep it flat inside the holder. Square glass filters do not need mounting—they slot directly into the filter holder on the camera.

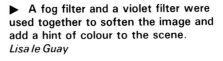

▶ A fog filter and a violet filter were used together to soften the image and add a hint of colour to the scene.
Lisa le Guay

▲ A coastal scene photographed without a filter produces normal colour tones.

▲ A pink filter completely changes the colour and mood of the scene to a monochrome image.

▲ A sepia filter reduces some of the colour in the scene to create a slightly sombre picture.

Pure colour filters are produced in very strong colours such as blue, purple, orange or red. They can be used with colour film to give an overall hue with high contrast. Red, blue or yellow filters expose only one emulsion layer and may give a stark effect; secondary colours like purple are richer. Even with a dense filter, bright light sources may 'burn through' to produce white on the film with adequate exposure.

▼ Colour filters can be round or square and some have a clear centre spot for a special effect.

▲ A graduated filter was used to reduce the brightness of the sky, giving it a stormy appearance. This reduction in brightness prevented the foreground from being under-exposed.
Chris Alan Wilton

◀ A dark blue filter gives a moody, monochromatic picture.

◀ A green filter with a clear centre spot leaves the central image its natural colour while the surroundings take on the colour of the filter.
Eric Hayman

▲ A colour filter gives the sky a greenish colour. The tint decreases in intensity towards the light source.

Special filters and attachments

The image on a film is formed by a lens which has been designed very carefully to produce an exact picture of the scene it is focused on. But it is possible to form a coherent clear image on the film which does not resemble the original scene. Extra optical attachments which change the path of the light rays coming through the lens, but still bring them into focus can repeat, split, blur, colour, bend or fracture the image in many ways. There are various gadgets which can be used to create unfamiliar perspectives on the world seen by the camera. Distortion is possible, just as it is with fairground mirrors.

Many of the devices which are normally sold as filters for lens mountings or to slot into filter systems fall into this category of optical effects rather than filters (see centre focus lenses, page 194). However, they are often referred to as 'special effects filters' because the word has come to be used to describe anything which fits in front of a lens. These filters can be used in combinations—for example, a colour filter can be used with a multi-image filter.

Multi-image filters

These are thick optical glass discs cut as prismatic facets which split the image into repeated, overlapping images. Many different types are available. The simplest ones repeat the image three times, side by side; more popular ones give a sharp central normal image surrounded by three, four, five, or six repeat images which are less crisp and contrasty than the central image.

Repeater or echo prisms use three or six facets cut very close together to give a series of parallel images tailing away from the main subject.

Colour prisms have each facet coloured differently, so that overlapping coloured versions of the main picture are produced. These are expensive, but you can make a temporary colour prism by colouring a plain prism with a felt tip pen.

By putting a much thicker prism at an angle in front of the lens, you can produce an elongated or colour-fringed image – the effect is similar to looking through cut glass at a light, without clearly repeated images. This can be done by holding some normal multi-image prisms at an angle or by buying a special colour fringe prism such as the one available in the Cokin system. Any laboratory prism, if you can get hold of one, can be used to experiment with.

 ▲ A filter with three parallel facets (left) repeats the image three times. The filter can be rotated on the lens to change the direction of the repeated images.

◀ A filter with three facets (above) repeats the images at random. *Derek Bayes*

 ▶ Six parallel facets on one half of a filter (above) gives an added effect of movement. *Julian Calder*

▼ A filter with five facets around a central one (above) gives a circular repeat.

▲ A filter with five facets (left) was used together with a colour filter to produce this photograph of a hot air balloon.

Bi-colour filters

This is a special type of filter, which can be rotated to change its colour or density, and is designed to be used in combination with a polarizing filter. A bi-colour filter looks like a normal single-colour filter such as a yellow or red one, but when you fit a polarizing filter over it and turn the polarizing filter, the colour filter changes—from yellow to red, for example, or from red to blue. Some start off as light red and gradually deepen to a full red. Others have pale tints only. Used on their own, they give a scene an overall colour except where there is polarized light—as in the sky, or in reflections—where they will produce whatever their 'opposite' colour happens to be.

Astigmatic lenses

Pictures with one way distortion, in which everything seems to be blurred in one direction, as if swept over with a brush, can be produced by using cylindrical (astigmatic) supplementary lenses. These are usually only available from opticians as spectacle lenses, but the effect is interesting enough to try to obtain one of these to experiment with.

Kaleidoscope attachments

As an alternative to using a prism to make multiple images on the film you can use mirrors. These usually surround a central normal image, roughly circular, with a whole series of inverted peripheral images rotating round the scene. An example of one made for 35mm SLRs is the Cenei Vario Spiegel-Vorsatz from Germany, which is obtainable in most countries. Kaleidoscope attachments are widely used, in

▲ A kaleidoscope attachment consists of a series of angled mirrors which reflect a number of images around the centre of the picture area. The attachment crops the picture so that it appears as a circle.

◀ An optician's astigmatic lens held in front of the standard camera lens gives the image an impressionistic quality. *Lisa Le Guay*

Using a flexible plastic mirror

▲ A flexible mirror is supported in front of the subject and the photographer shoots the reflection in the mirror.

▲ The mirror distorts the image in much the same way as fairground mirrors do. The degree

of distortion depends on how much the mirror is bent—in extremes a multi-image is possible.

bigger versions, on television, and are usually more expensive than multi-image prisms and filters.

Mirrors

Mirrors have other uses in photography, apart from in kaleidoscope attachments. A 90° attachment is available to allow the photographer to shoot at right angles to the direction the camera is aimed in. This device consists of a mirror mounted in a small black box similar to a lens hood. The mirror is angled at 45° to the lens front and is usually surface-silvered to give sharper results. This makes it fragile, and the surface of the mirror must not be handled. These attachments are designed to be used with standard and telephoto lenses. They do not work with wide angle lenses as the mirror housing would be included in the picture.

A flexible mirror, such as the plastic mirror designed for home decoration, can be used to distort an image. A sheet about 45cm square is needed to allow enough working distance in front of the camera. It helps to have some way of clamping the mirror to keep it in position. The mirror reflects just like a proper glass mirror but can be bent to produce distorted images. It is essential to stop the lens down to f16 or f22 to get really sharp results.

Using special filters

Using special effects filters can be creative, but a whole collection of multi-images can be boring, and it should not be assumed that these accessories can transform a boring picture into the prize-winning slide or print. Be selective and look through the lens with the filter in position to see exactly what your picture is going to be like—and if it is not visually stimulating as an image don't waste the film.

Right-angled attachment

A mirror attachment makes it possible to take candid shots of subjects at 90° to the camera.

How to use basic flash

Flash lights a dark room, lets you photograph objects outdoors at night and even lightens shadows on sunlit subjects. A good flash gun is simple to use effectively if you follow a few basic rules. Unlike electric light or studio lamps, flash is balanced for use with daylight type film. You can take a picture outdoors, come inside, and immediately use the flash with the same roll of film.

Flash cubes

The simplest type of flash is the descendant of the flash bulb, a miniature cube. It is sold in multiple units such as bar flash, Flipflash and the familiar cube used on 110, 126 and instant picture cameras. These multiple flash cubes are fine for occasional pictures indoors but they are expensive to use frequently. Their small size also limits their light output.

Electronic flash

A more versatile development is the electronic flash gun, which passes an electrical charge through a glass tube filled with an inert gas. Power is supplied by ordinary dry batteries, an accumulator or mains current. As well as alkaline batteries, some units use the rechargeable NiCad type. They are more expensive but can be used over and over again and charged off the mains.

110 cameras

Several 110 cameras have a hot-shoe to take a simple electronic flash. These are effective for subjects between 2m and 4m from the camera, but the flash becomes softer and dimmer the further you are from the subject. The instructions which come with the camera will tell you the ideal distance for taking flash pictures.

Range of equipment

The cheapest guns have few frills and are unlikely to be effective beyond about 4m. But they are adequate for small rooms and shots of friends and family. Most have a built-in accumulator, but

1 The sunpak Auto Zoom 3000 has five settings from full power to 1/32. Useful for close-ups and fill-in flash.

2 Quite expensive for its type, the Metz 34BCT2 is well made and gives an even flash. An optional wide angle diffuser is marketed.

3 The Agfatronic 201B is simple and effective.

4 The Vivitar 283 can be bought as a basic unit or with system accessories. Energy-saving thyristor circuitry conserves the batteries.

5 For the advanced flash user the Braun F900 has a separate, rechargeable battery pack. The NiCad pack can be left permanently on charge when not in use.

more expensive equipment can use an external power pack connected by a lead to the flash head. The fairly small current from the batteries is stored in a capacitor until a sufficient charge has accumulated to fire the gas-filled tube.
Built-in electronic flash: some cameras have built-in electronic flash linked to the camera shutter mechanism for automatically controlled flash exposures.

Automatic computer flash

A little more money will buy an automatic computerized gun, which simplifies calculation and makes flash easier to use. A photo-electric sensor in the unit controls its light output and cuts off the flash when enough light has been reflected from the subject. This guarantees correct exposure, reduces the duration of a flash, and may give significant power savings and a shorter recycling time between flashes with some models.

All but the cheapest computer guns have two, three or even four power settings corresponding to specific apertures on your camera. So setting the aperture you need for the photograph gives fully automatic flash within specified distances.

The advantage of an automatic unit is that, providing you keep within the specified distances, you can move closer or further away from the subject without adjusting the aperture.

Some guns even have remote sensors which fit in the camera's accessory shoe and allow computer control when the flash is used off the camera.

Extras: many of the automatic units now on the market have extra features: flash heads that can rotate in every direction while fixed to the hot-shoe, for bouncing off walls or ceilings; energy-saving thyristor circuitry; coloured filters; diffusers to cope with different focal length lenses; reflectors for bounce flash; mains adaptor leads; and L-brackets to attach a hand flash to the side of the camera.

The usefulness of these items depends on your requirements. But, if you have a wide angle lens, it is worthwhile to look for a gun with an optional wide angle diffuser, since most guns only cover an angle slightly greater than that of a standard lens.

At the top of the market come the professional quality flash guns. They are expensive, but both power and quality take a big leap forward. Optional extras become standard equipment, although such items as separate battery packs are heavy to carry around.

◄ This advanced flash has a whole host of optional extras. A clip-on adapter can hold diffusers for wide angle or telephoto lenses as well as colour filters for special effect. The bounce board above the flash gun acts as a portable ceiling. The pistol grip and camera bracket make the whole outfit easier to hold.

▼ A bracket to connect camera and flash is useful on a camera with a waist-level viewfinder. The automatic computerized sensor shows up clearly on this flash gun — just above the photographer's hand.

► Some flash guns now have colour filters for special effects.

▼ Coloured segments on the calculator dial correspond with automatic settings on the flash unit.

Calculating exposure

Whichever type of flash you use the factor governing correct exposure is the flash-to-subject distance.

Flash cubes: with flash cubes and other types of disposable flash the distance at which you take a flash picture is usually printed on the flash pack, or in the camera instructions. In most cases, it is between about 1m and 3m, depending on the type of flash, the particular camera you are using and the speed of the film.

Electronic units: with electronic units, the method of calculating exposure depends on whether the unit is automatic or manual.

Manual flashguns: the light output of a flashgun is indicated by a Guide Number—the higher the Guide Number, the more powerful the flash. Dividing the Guide Number by the subject-to-flash distance gives the correct f number to set on the lens for a correct exposure.

With modern units this type of calculation is not usually necessary as they have calculator dials or scales on the back. All the photographer has to do is set the ASA speed rating of the film in the camera on the calculator dial. The dial then shows the aperture settings for each flash-to-subject distance.

A simple way to work out the distance, if your camera has a coupled range-finder, is to focus on the subject and read off the distance from the lens. Alternatively you can use a metal retractable tape measure. A manual unit always gives a constant full power output. If you decide to move closer or further away from your subject, the flash-to-subject distance obviously changes and so the exposure has to be re-calculated from the dial. In this way, the aperture is used to regulate the amount of light reaching the film, so you may have to compromise on depth of field to get a big enough aperture.

▲ The Braun 200B is a good all-round flashgun. It is non-computerized, slips into the pocket and takes ordinary batteries. A table on the back gives correct camera settings.

▼ A typical hot shoe. The central contact triggers the flash to synchronize with the shutter when the speed is set on X.

▲ Calculator dials can be laid out as a sliding scale (above) or as a circular dial (above right). Both of these are computer controlled unless the manual setting is selected. The gun above also has a switch to tell the computer whether wide-angle or normal flash is in use.

▶ Using the calculator: on the circular dial (a more common type) set your film speed (ASA), then find the measured subject/flash distance on the feet/metres scale. Choose the colour (red, yellow, green or blue) nearest to this distance and set the switch on the front of the flash (bottom right) to the appropriate colour. In this case, green gives you f8 for a subject 7 to 8 metres away with the flash on full power. So set f8 on the camera and shutter speed (X) to synchronize.

▲ To use flash off-camera requires a longer lead, available from camera shops. On this computerized gun, a Vivitar, the sensor unplugs and mounts on the camera's hot shoe. Hold the flash at arm's length.

▼ Some cameras do not have a hot shoe, but they will have an X socket to take a sync lead from the flash gun. The gun can be hand-held, fitted to an accessory shoe on the camera, or to an L-bracket.

Shutter speed

The burst of light from an electronic flash lasts for 1/1000 sec. or less so there is no particular advantage in using fast or slow shutter speeds. The only vital consideration when choosing the shutter speed is that the flash is synchronized to fire while the shutter is fully open. The maximum speed at which focal plane shutters synchronize with flash is usually 1/60 or 1/125 depending on the type you have. If you use a faster shutter speed only part of the frame is exposed. There is no problem with slow speeds. Cameras with between-lens shutters synchronize with flash at all speeds—important when using flash to fill in shadows on a brightly lit, moving subject.

Testing your flash

It is wise to have your flash tested from time to time as the actual power output of a gun is often lower than the figure marked on the equipment. Loss of flash intensity will put all your calculations out and gives under-exposed pictures. Even one stop under the claimed output means that the gun is only producing half the light it should.

If your flash pictures seem to be wrongly exposed first check the batteries—they may be weak, causing the unit to throw out less light than it should. If you still have problems, take the equipment to a retailer or reputable camera repair shop and have it tested on a flash meter. Alternatively, put a roll of film through the camera and test the flash by taking shots at different exposures. Keep a record of the apertures used and study the results for under- or over-exposure. Once the extent of under- or over-exposure is known you can compensate for it. Adjust the ASA dial on the flash calculator to an appropriately slower film speed—1 stop under-exposure on 400 ASA film means that the calculator should be set at 200 ASA.

Indoor hints

Never point the flash directly at a highly reflective surface such as a window or mirror. If the subject includes such a surface, ensure that the light strikes it at an angle and doesn't reflect straight back at the camera.

When photographing groups, it is important for everyone to be approximately the same distance from the flash. If they are not, the closest people will be over-exposed, while those further away will be under-exposed. At parties this is not always possible, but make sure no one is in the immediate foreground.

Using flash

Because of its extremely brief duration, flash is ideal for freezing rapid motion. But, because it is so fast, there is no way of seeing the effect until the film is printed.

Direct: on-camera

Simply pointing the flash directly at the subject with the gun mounted on the camera may be the most convenient method, but the effect is usually harsh and flat. It is the only course open to you with a camera which uses cubes and other multiple miniature units, but an extender that fits between cube and camera body will prevent your subject having 'red eye'—the effect you get when the flash is too close to the lens.

Direct: off-camera

Setting up the flash away from the camera eliminates the flat appearance common to many flash-lit pictures.
Introducing some shadow into your pictures heightens impact and is a good basic technique for portraits although the pictures still look hard with strong reflections.

Bounce flash

To remove the hardness caused by a direct light source, bounce the flash off a ceiling, wall or piece of white card, or use the accessory bounce attachment available with some flash guns.

Exposure for bounce flash

1 Work out the total distance the light has to travel—camera-to-bounce-surface plus bounce-surface-to-subject.
2 Set this on your flash calculator dial and read off the f stop.
3 For a white surface, open the lens two f stops wider and for a tinted or grey surface, three.
Remember that the flash must be powerful enough to give adequate light at two or three times the distance which your subject is at. Always take a direct shot as well if in doubt.
Light diffuses as it reflects off a surface and, depending on the colour and texture of the surface you're bouncing off, different amounts of light will be absorbed. The amount you need to open up the lens is really a matter of trial and error. White surfaces reflect more light than coloured ones, and smooth textures more than rough. A great variety of lighting effects and angles can be achieved so don't be afraid to experiment. You can soften the flash effect even further by taping a white handkerchief or a stocking over the gun.

Fill-in flash

Flash isn't only limited to situations where the available light is too dim for photography. It will fill in, or lighten, daytime shadows, even in bright sunny conditions. The idea is to lighten the shadows by directing the flash towards them, not to overpower the daylight with a mighty flash. So set the camera as normal for the available light, and the flash to under-expose the subject by a stop or so. The easiest way to regulate the intensity of the flash—to balance it with the existing light—is to alter the flash to subject distance. You can do this by taking the flash off the camera and getting someone else to hold it, but you will need a long flash lead. Some of the more expensive and complicated flash guns have settings for half power and less—useful for fill-in and close ups. Be careful, though, to use 1/60 or 1/125 unless you have a between lens shutter.

Direct on-camera: Hard shadows and harsh colours deaden the picture.

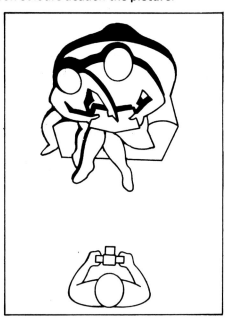

Direct off-camera: Shadows are still hard but give some shape to the faces.

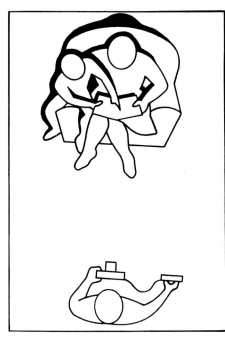

Bounce flash: Bouncing the flash off a wall or ceiling softens the lighting. But note how the colours in the picture—clothes, faces, and armchair—have been influenced by the pale cream of the walls. Here it has helped to 'warm' the colours, but imagine the effect of blue or green walls. If you aren't sure about the effect on the finished photograph use some white card or a white sheet as a bouncing surface. Alternatively, add to the effect using a coloured filter.

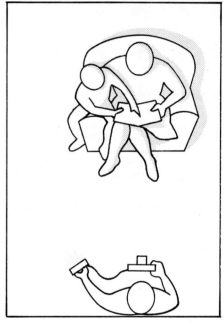

Fill-in flash: Compare the picture below with the one at right which uses only daylight.

Better flash lighting

1 A bounce panel used with Vivitar 283 provides a portable ceiling.
2 Powerful 'hammer' style guns like Toshiba ES30G are available with bounce heads and flash brackets.
3 Sunpak MX134 is one of the few manual bounce guns.
4 Wotan B12 is a small fixed head manual flash.
5 Toshiba 312 is a cheap manual fixed head flash.
6 The Starblitz Twin has two flash tubes. As with many units, colour filters are available.
7 Hanimex TB655 has a rotating head and turns itself off when not in use.

Most amateur electronic flash units are designed to be clipped into a camera hot shoe. The flash is therefore in a fixed position close to the lens, and points directly at the subject. The effect of direct flash (see earlier) produces harsh, flat lighting with heavy shadows on, and behind the subject and perhaps bleached-out highlights. With the flash so close to the lens red-eye effects often occur. The effect is totally unnatural, it is immediately apparent that flash has been used and, particularly in portraiture, it gives unflattering results. Any way in which the light can be diffused dramatically improves the results: shadows are softer and the overall lighting more even. To diffuse light it must be spread out. This can be done either by bouncing it or by dispersing it at source.

Bounce head flash guns

A number of flash guns with bounce heads are available and they provide the means for more interesting lighting effects. Bounce heads make it possible to tilt the flash tube upwards, independently of that part of the gun which connects to the camera, and enables you to reflect the light from the ceiling, for example.

Lighting with bounced flash generally makes portraits more flattering and a view of a room is more evenly and naturally lit without heavy distracting shadows.

Choosing a flash gun

There are very few manual guns with bounce heads so your choice is limited to automatic flash which does cost a little more. Automatic flash guns give one or more aperture settings. The film speed is set on the calculator dial on the flash gun and an indicator of some sort shows the aperture (or choice of apertures). The calculator also shows to what distance the flash gun gives correct exposure at the given aperture. The automatic facility cuts off the flash as soon as the subject has received the right exposure.

This sets you free from complicated exposure calculations and, as long as the flash is correctly set up, you are practically guaranteed a correct exposure every time. This is even more useful when you start varying your flash techniques. However, you may be able to use an ordinary manual gun wired to the camera via an extension sync cable allowing you to direct the flash up towards the ceiling.

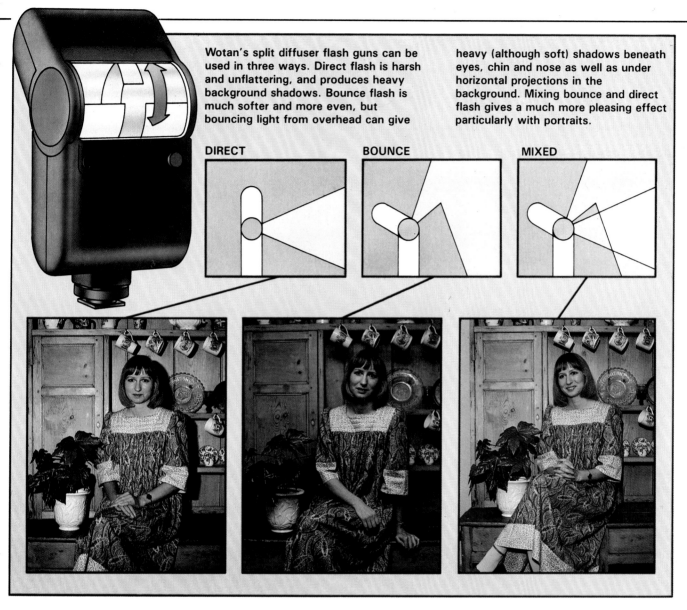

Wotan's split diffuser flash guns can be used in three ways. Direct flash is harsh and unflattering, and produces heavy background shadows. Bounce flash is much softer and more even, but bouncing light from overhead can give heavy (although soft) shadows beneath eyes, chin and nose as well as under horizontal projections in the background. Mixing bounce and direct flash gives a much more pleasing effect particularly with portraits.

DIRECT   **BOUNCE**   **MIXED**

A good alternative is to invest in an angle bracket which allows the entire flash gun to be angled so that light bounces from a chosen surface. Remember to measure the total distance the light has to travel (camera to ceiling to subject for example) and use this information to calculate the correct aperture. Make sure that the light is reflected from the bounce surface at the correct angle to fall on to the subject. If the angle is wrong the results will be poor.

A flash with a guide number (GN) of **20 to 24 (metres at 100 ASA)** is powerful enough for bounce flash in a normal sized room. It is also powerful enough for many other types of photography, although spending a little more on GN30 to GN40 allows more versatility in different situations.

All the automatic flash guns can be used totally manually if you want to do so. In this case you have to calculate the appropriate aperture based on total flash to subject distance.

Some bounce head auto guns have a flash confirmation light or 'distance checker' as an added bonus. This indicates that the exposure is correct. Firing the test button in advance of making an exposure saves you wasting a frame if the lamp does not light up—it indicates that you should move the flash closer to the bounce surface, or perhaps select a wider aperture setting.

Practical aspects

Ceilings are usually light in colour and at a suitable height for reflecting bounced flash. But there may be times when the ceiling is just too high for the

▼ Hanimex TS855 has a bounce head which can be used for direct flash or for bounce flash. Using the small auxiliary flash tube with the main tube in the bounce position, mixes bounce and direct flash for better lighting.

effect you want or for the power of the flash. You can still use the bounce head but substitute a large white card for the ceiling and hold it closer to the flash head. This may cause problems if you don't have someone assisting, although you can work single-handed with a gun which has a built-in bounce panel.

An alternative is to bounce the light from the side rather than overhead. This gives a totally different side-lit effect. You can use a variety of surfaces, whether a wall or a large piece of cartridge paper which someone is holding for you. For this you will need a flash gun with a head which rotates from side to side.

The sensor on an auto flash gun reacts to the overall light it reads. This can lead to over- or under-exposure depending on the circumstances.

● If the background is very light and the subject is close to it, the sensor will under-expose the subject. In this case set the camera one stop larger than that indicated on the flash unit.

The subject will then be correctly exposed even though the background may be slightly over-exposed. The reverse is also possible—if the background is very dark the subject may be over-exposed. Decrease the aperture one stop to that indicated on the flash gun calculator dial.

Portraits need soft lighting if they are to be flattering. If the flash is bounced overhead don't work too close to the subject. If the bounced light comes down directly above the subject, hard shadows around the eyes will show.

● Regardless of whether you are bouncing the flash from overhead or from the side bear in mind that the closer the reflecting surface is to the subject the more contrasty the lighting will be.

● Backgrounds in portraits can be distracting. Stark white backgrounds aren't ideal, nor are patterned backgrounds. To make a background less distracting move the subject as far from it as possible. A white background will then become grey because less light reaches it and a patterned one will be out of focus.

● The colour of the reflecting surface will influence the colour of a portrait just like using a colour filter. This hardly matters when working with black and white but in colour, red and green surfaces could lead to unnatural tones in the resulting photographs.

● If you are using a wide angle lens its coverage may be more than that of the flash gun. If you bounce the light then

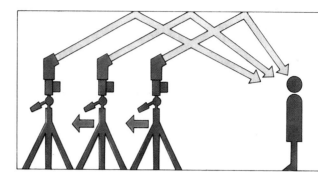

◀ When bouncing flash from a ceiling the effect can be changed by moving the flash nearer to or further from the subject, or by varying the bounce head angle; make sure that the light does not miss the subject.

Light from fixed head flash guns can be softened in several ways. 1 Most flash guns can be fitted to an angle bracket for bounce flash—a sync cable extension is required. 2 Sof-Touch diffusers fit over most flash units to soften light output. 3 Some of the Braun range have built-in soft reflectors. 4 An Air Diffuser (colour filters are provided) fits over many flash heads.

the light is sufficiently scattered not to make this a problem. An alternative is to fit a wide angle diffuser over the flash head.

Off-camera flash

Removing the flash from the camera opens up a new world to the photographer. You don't need a special flash gun; all you need is a long synchronization lead to plug into the camera X socket.

Buying a 1m or 2m extension cable allows you to remove the flash from the camera and point it at the ceiling, walls or card to bounce the light at any angle and distance relative to camera and subject. It's best to have the camera on a tripod to leave your hands free. If you use a pneumatic cable release (or the camera's delayed action mechanism) you can even move away from the camera (to hold the reflecting

▼ These Philips flash guns have built-in slave cells, but many other guns can be used with a separate slave cell which makes it possible to use several flashes, all perfectly synchronized with the shutter. Lighting can become far more versatile, and trailing cables around the set-up are avoided. Separate stands and hot shoe adapters are needed for each extra flash in use.

card perhaps). By taking the flash gun away from the camera the exposure will be affected: the sensor on the flash gun will read the light reflected back at it and this is not necessarily the same as that reflected to the camera. For the right exposure switch the flash gun to manual and calculate the aperture on the total distance between the flash unit and the subject.

Using two flash guns

If you have two flash guns they can be used simultaneously. A slave cell is used to fire the second flash gun—one gun must be connected to the camera for synchronization. The slave cell is connected to the second flash gun and is positioned so that light from the flash connected to the camera reaches the cell. When the shutter is fixed light from the main flash falls on the cell. The cell gathers this light energy and converts it into a tiny electrical impulse. This fires the second flash virtually instantaneously. With this system there is no need to have wires and cables trailing around the floor. Obviously the second flash gun needs to be supported on a tripod or with a G-clamp. (You can use any number of flash guns as long as each additional flash gun has a slave cell.)

In effect you have a mini-studio system

and can use your lights for far more varied effects than is possible with just one flash. You can use one flash as the main light and the other to fill in heavy shadows or, alternatively, move one flash behind the subject to act as a backlight. In addition you can soften the flash (or flashes) by bouncing it.

Softer direct flash

To save yourself the trouble of working out correct apertures and whether the flash is bouncing at the correct angle you may prefer to use something simpler. Some flash guns have soft reflectors rather than shiny chrome ones and this helps disperse and therefore soften the light. The results are not as soft as for bounced flash.

If you are happy with the fixed-head gun you already own you can soften the light by taping a tissue or handkerchief over the flash head. Soft diffusers are available to clip over the flash. As light passes through the diffuser it is dispersed to give a more pleasant effect.

However you diffuse the light at source the intensity is reduced. An automatic gun will adjust the duration of the flash accordingly, but with a manual flash gun you must open the aperture by about one stop—though do experiment first.

Tungsten lighting

Long before electronic flash was invented tungsten lighting systems were used in many studios. They are versatile, easy to add to and, compared with studio flash systems, tend to be reasonably priced. If you have ever experienced the unpredictable lighting caused by using flash without modelling lights, an economical tungsten system may be the answer. As you move the lights or use different reflectors and diffusers you can immediately see the effects they produce.

'Tungsten lamps' are so called because the basic construction is a thin filament of tungsten contained in a glass envelope—domestic light bulbs are of this type.

Photofloods. There are several types of tungsten lamp, the most common choice for the amateur being a 500W photoflood. The lamp contains a thin filament such as is found in much lower voltage bulbs. When connected to a domestic mains supply the filament glows extremely brightly. These lamps have a limited life.

Photographic lamps. It would be inconvenient for the hard-working professional to change his lamps every few hours and for extended use 'photographic' lamps are preferred: these have standard 500W filaments to provide a longer working life.

Tungsten halogen. A third type of lamp, known as tungsten halogen, is often found in spotlights. The specially designed glass envelope is shaped differently and is smaller than a photoflood or photographic lamp with the same output. The glass envelope contains a halogen gas, such as iodine, which maintains consistent light quality throughout the long life of the lamp because blackening of the inside of the bulb is reduced to a minimum.

Colour effects of tungsten lighting

The quality of tungsten light is much 'warmer' or redder in tone than daylight or flash, and you must therefore use specially balanced tungsten film. An alternative is to use a special correction filter over the camera lens (or in front of the lights, but this tends to be rather expensive).

The only colour negative film balanced

soft reflector

matt reflector

umbrella reflector

chrome reflector

boom arm with counterweight

lighting stand

white reflector

A large number of reflectors and supports are available for use with tungsten lamps allowing the photographer to build up a comprehensive and versatile lighting system.

214

for tungsten lighting is Vericolor Type L (available in 120 roll film). Kodacolor 400 has subdued sensitivity to red and blue light and acceptable prints may be obtained with tungsten lamps. Tungsten slide film, such as Kodachrome, is balanced for use with photographic lamps and you must use filter 81A over the camera lens when using photofloods. Filter 80B allows use of daylight balanced film with photofloods while filter 80A on the lens permits correct balance with photographic lamps.

Reflectors

Inserting a photoflood into a domestic lamp holder is not recommended because the bulbs become hot after a very short time. In addition this will not allow you to control the light spread and you would be restricted to a bright harsh patch of light to illuminate the subject.

The more lamps and different types of reflector you have, the more versatile the lighting effects can be. But to be practical you can achieve a wide number of effects with just two lamps and two or three different types of reflector.

Soft reflector. To produce diffused, soft-edged shadows, direct light is prevented from reaching the subject by positioning a metal reflective guard over the bulb.

Floods. Placing a deep bowl-shaped polished reflector around the lamp (without a metal guard covering the bulb) provides bright widespread light much harsher in quality than that from a soft reflector. The smaller and deeper the reflector the narrower is the light beam.

Reflector boards. There is no reason why you shouldn't make your own reflector boards. White card or cartridge paper are suitable for bouncing light to give a soft effect, while silvered paper or crinkled aluminium foil stuck to

rigid card gives more sparkle—a slightly less diffused effect. You could make a whole range of sizes to suit different subjects. Angle the light at the reflector so that it falls on to the subject to provide the desired effect.

Umbrellas. Studio umbrellas are more commonly used with flash because it is a cool light source, but if you are careful not to over-heat the 'brollies' they can be a more convenient, easily portable version of reflector boards.

Screens. Proprietary diffusion screens are available but, here again, you can improvise. Tracing paper or translucent plastic stretched over a rigid frame are suitable materials for diffusing light from tungsten lamps. Remember to keep the screen at least 50 cm away from the bulb or it may melt or scorch. Using a screen in this way softens the light according to the distance between screen and subject— the closer the screen to the subject the softer the light quality produced.

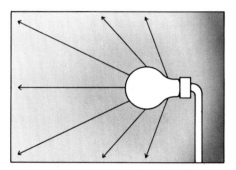

▲ A tungsten lamp without a reflector cannot be used for controlled lighting. Light spreads in all directions is harsh and gives heavy, distinct shadows.

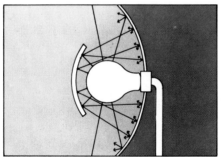

▲ A soft reflector with a baffle over the bulb prevents any direct light from reaching the subject. Lighting is diffused and shadows are soft-edged.

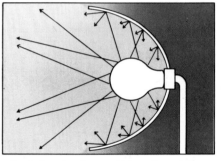

▲ A bowl reflector lights the subject directly and forms distinct, hard-edged shadows. Different diameters and surfaces vary the light effect.

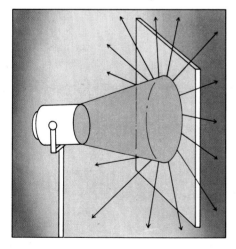

▲ By using a large white card you can make your own soft reflector. Light is reflected from the card and is diffused. This is ideal fill-in lighting.

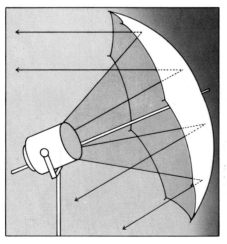

▲ Aiming the lamp and reflector at the interior surface of an umbrella reflector also diffuses light and gives soft and even lighting.

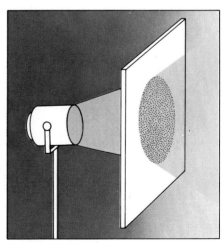

▲ Placing a diffusion screen in front of the lamp causes scattering of light as it passes through the translucent material and softens the effect.

Spotlights

These fall into a separate category basically because no large reflector is used (it has a small internal one) as this would defeat the object. Just as it sounds, a spotlight produces a narrow beam of light, harsh in quality with distinct shadows, and which you can easily control to light a limited area. Often the beam can be varied in width by focusing the lamp through a fresnel lens in the front of the unit.

A small degree of softening can be produced by clipping a metal grid over the spotlight. There is often a connecting point for filter holders so that coloured spots can be shone on to subject or background and the most sophisticated 'effects spots' allow patterns to be projected on to the background.

Supports

You will need to hold the lamp and reflector off the ground, adjust the height, and angle the light. A number of supports are available. They can be raised and lowered at will, and some have castors allowing the lamps to be repositioned quickly. All stands are available with special lamp holders.

Positioning adapters allow lamp and lamp holder to be clipped to any convenient support such as a table leg or even to a lamp support so you can position the lights wherever you wish.

Using the lamps

Make sure that you have sufficient power points from which to run all your lamps. Most lights will need a considerable length of cable to allow you to move the lights around your 'studio'. A socket bar with three or four plug sockets assembled together with a supply cable plugged into the mains provides a central run-off point. Take care not to trip over the cables—keep them out of the way as much as possible.

● A lighting control socket consisting of square-pin sockets (up to 500W each) can be used to vary light intensity at the flick of a switch. Each socket has an independent on/off switch and full- or half-power settings. But do not shoot on colour film with the lights at half power or a red cast will result—this is only suitable for black and white photography.

● When the lamp is warm the filament is fragile. Only move the lamps if necessary and do so gently or the bulb may blow. Castors give smoother, less traumatic, mobility.

● All tungsten lamps produce heat along with light. This is uncomfortable for a portrait subject and does not do your reflectors much good either. Turn off the lamps periodically to allow them to cool—this is particularly important if you are using a snoot or diffusing screen. Do not, however, turn the power on and off repeatedly and at short intervals. Be careful not to block cooling vents and keep your studio well ventilated for your own comfort.

The main advantages of tungsten light is that financial outlay for a complete system is less than for an equivalent studio flash system. You can see the lighting effect at a glance whereas modelling lights, if the flash system has them, may not equal the power of the flash. Nor do you need to use a special meter as with flash—your camera's meter or a separate hand-held one can be used.

However, one of the biggest disadvantages is the amount of heat produced and the uncomfortable constant glare of the lamps. This may make a human subject fidgety and perhaps dry out still-life specimens. The lamps give less intense light than flash and, in addition, burn power all the time they are switched on.

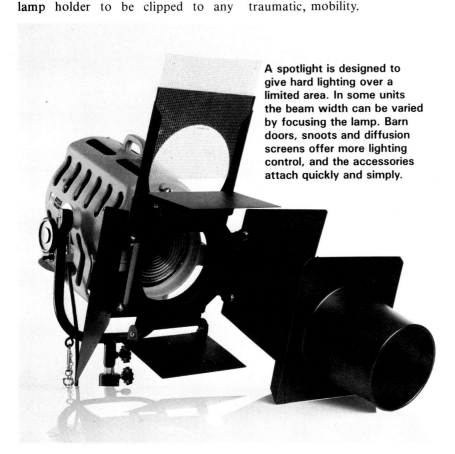

A spotlight is designed to give hard lighting over a limited area. In some units the beam width can be varied by focusing the lamp. Barn doors, snoots and diffusion screens offer more lighting control, and the accessories attach quickly and simply.

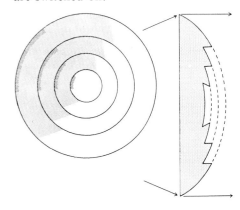

▲ **The design of a Fresnel lens is particularly suitable for use in a spotlight. It converges the light beam and disperses heat from the lamp.**

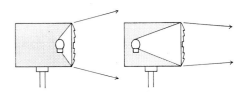

▲ **A focusing spotlight lamp allows variation in diameter of the light beam. The broad beam setting (left) gives the hardest shadows.**

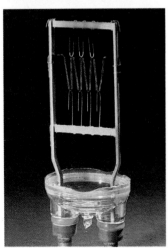

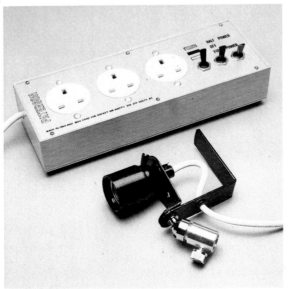

▲ A lighting control unit adds a touch of versatility to your system—it is suitable for black and white work. You must use suitable lamp holders for your tungsten lamps.

Above left: tungsten lamps are similar in construction to domestic bulbs, but tungsten halogen lamps are longer and narrower.

◀ A high power spotlight element.

▲ You do not necessarily need a complicated tungsten lighting set-up to photograph still-life successfully. A soft reflector, tracing paper and a fill-in card are extremely effective.

Be safe

● Check that all plugs are correctly wired and adequately fused. Worn or frayed cables and cracked plugs are dangerous.

● Never plug several lamps into an adapter.

● Make periodic checks to connections, especially where cables enter the lamp holder. The constant heat produced by tungsten lamps may make insulation brittle.

● If you run more lamps from your electrical circuit than it was designed for, the cables will overheat and there is a great risk of fire.

● If fuses blow there is obviously a reason for it. Do not replace a blown fuse with one of a higher amperage. If you cannot find the reason for the fuse blowing seek professional advice.

● Never handle electrical appliances with wet hands.

Studio flash lighting

Studio flash units are much more powerful than the small electronic flash you might use on your camera hot shoe. They normally have built–in modelling lights to help you control lighting effects, run from mains electricity, are used on lighting stands and often have interchangeable reflectors and other accessories. More sophisiticated models have a variable power switch enabling the photographer to reduce light output—this might be in full power, three quarters, half and quarter power steps for example.

All these features are ideal for studio photography, although many systems can be packed away into a carrying case allowing the photographer to undertake location work.

Advantages

There are several advantages in using studio flash rather than tungsten lighting. The short duration of the flash, perhaps 1/1000, can eliminate subject movement and camera shake.

Flash is also a cool light source, making it suitable for lighting fragile subjects without drying them out; portrait subjects do not suffer long periods of 'grilling' as with tungsten lights, and the studio remains fairly cool and comfortable to work in. The modelling lights do generate heat, but not to the same extent as a number of tungsten lamps.

The high light output of studio flash permits use of small lens apertures, perhaps f22 and, with the extensive depth of field this provides, you are almost assured of sharp photographs.

The colour of the light from the flash tube is similar to that of midday sunlight so ordinary daylight balanced colour film can be used, unlike with tungsten light. No matter how old the tube may become, or how great the mains voltage variation, the colour temperature and the light output remain constant (tungsten lamps eventually discolour). Flash tubes give thousands of flashes and should last for several years rather than several hours.

Modelling lights. These are small lamps which let you see in advance the effect which will be produced by the flash when you take the picture. You can therefore note any ugly shadows, or position a hair light, for example, to give the best effect.

They are fairly low wattage bulbs, and do not therefore burn an excessive amount of electricity. Units with variable power switches can be used to vary the modelling light intensity so

that the photographer can accurately assess the lighting effect.

The exact position of the modelling bulbs and their strength varies according to the make of the unit, but generally speaking they should be as close to the flash tube as possible so that the light distribution and direction mirrors the effect from the flash tube. They should be bright enough to make focusing easy in a blacked–out room, and to let you see the effect of the lighting even when working at reduced power. They must not, however, be so bright as to have an effect on the film during exposure.

Recharging. The electrical make–up of studio flash is designed to take high voltage current from the mains rather than from low voltage batteries which power small portable flash guns. They therefore recharge rapidly even though they are so powerful. A small camera–mounted flash with a guide number (see beginning of chapter) of 16 (metres) might take as much as nine seconds to recycle after taking a picture even with fresh batteries. A studio flash with a guide number of 47 (metres) would probably recycle in between one and two seconds.

Supports. The stands available vary greatly from portable models to heavy studio stands mounted on castors. It is important that they are adjustable in

height to allow the flash to be positioned at a low level or a high one, or somewhere in between, to suit the subject. They must be stable enough to support the flash head even when using a large bulky reflector.

Reflectors. Most manufacturers supply a wide range of diffusers and reflectors permitting a large number of lighting effects—at least equal to those provided by tungsten light reflectors. The principles for each type of reflector and attachment are much the same as for tungsten lighting (see earlier).

Umbrella reflectors are extremely popular, particularly for portraits. To use these, the flash head is turned away from the subject and pointed towards th interior surface of the umbrella. The lighting is then even and diffused. Umbrellas are often used when working with colour material since the differences in the colours of the subject can be allowed to supply the contrast rather than the lighting.

There is a large number to choose from, such as white nylon, white matt, silver (for slightly less diffused light) and gold (to improve skin tones in colour). Many are reversible, providing two reflective surfaces on one umbrella. With a little ingenuity and an old rain umbrella you could probably make your own reflector by stretching white material over the spokes.

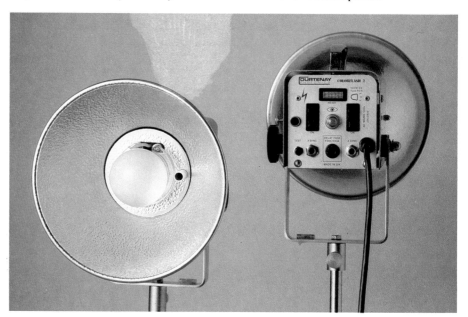

▲ A modelling lamp is used to show the effect of a flash lighting set–up. The flash tube surrounds the base of the lamp, and the bowl reflector controls quality and direction of the flash. The control panel on the back of this flash head contains modelling light and flash on/off switches, flash charge indicator, built–in slave cell, flash test button, fuse holder, and two X sync sockets— one for connection to the camera and the other for a flash meter.

OURTENAY COLORFLASH 2 SYSTEM

This particular flash system is a popular choice for many because it combines versatility with a reasonable price.

1 Diffusers are available with different surfaces to vary the effect. The flash is directed through the diffuser on to the subject to soften light.

2 An adaptor spigot enables accessories to be mounted on a lighting stand.

3 Many reflectors are available including white matt (illustrated) and silver.

4 Flash head with small reflector.

5 Silver brolly (white and gold are also available, both square and circular).

6 Three section stand.

7 Snoot.

8 Barn doors.

Types of studio flash

The present trend, especially for amateurs and professionals using small studios, is towards the one–piece unit in which the power pack and small built–in reflector holding the flash tube and modelling lamp are combined in one compact package. This has many advantages over the older professional type in which a large heavy power pack is separated from the reflector by a long cable. The one–piece unit is easy to transport and move about the studio, and is generally much cheaper.

The main manufacturers of studio flash supply a range of one-piece units varying in power from small lightweight ones with a guide number of perhaps 34 with 125 ASA film, to ones designed for use in large studios with a guide number of 98 or more. Units more powerful than this need a separate power pack since the weight is too great to support on a stand.

Using more than one flash

When using several units one of them must be connected directly to the camera via a long flash synchronization lead, but the others are normally

▲ Flash lighting can be extremely versatile. An umbrella gives soft diffused lighting, a white or silver reflector can be used to fill in heavy shadows, and mounting a flash head on to a boom arm enables an accent light to be quickly repositioned. Attaching a snoot to the flash head produces a circular patch of harsh direct light to highlight the model's hair.

▶ The model is comfortable during a photography session because flash is cool (lighting was as shown above).

triggered by means of photocells (slave units, see page 213). These might be built-in, or separate ones are available which plug into the top of the flash casing or into the back with a short length of cable. Provided the slave cells are positioned to receive light from one or other of the flash units, when the camera shutter fires the first flash all the others trigger simultaneously, with no delay. The only cables found on the studio floor are those connecting the units to the mains. This reduces clutter and the danger of tripping over wires.

Flash meters

You cannot use a normal hand–held or TTL meter to determine flash exposure because the flash duration is far too short to allow sufficient time for the meter to respond. It is also difficult to calculate exposures using guide numbers when using a number of flash units because they will all be at different distances from the subject.

Using a flash meter is the most efficient method of working out correct exposures. The meter is used to measure the strength of light falling on to the subject (incident) rather than reflected from it. It looks something like a conventional hand–held meter but is connected to one of the flash units by a long lead.

The photographer holds the meter as close to the subject as possible, pointing it towards the camera lens. A button is pressed on the meter, and as long as the slave cells are correctly angled all the units in use flash together. The pulse of light causes the meter needle to move across a scale, or lights up a light emitting diode (LED). This information allows the photographer to read off the exact aperture at which to set the lens—it is usually accurate to within a quarter of a stop.

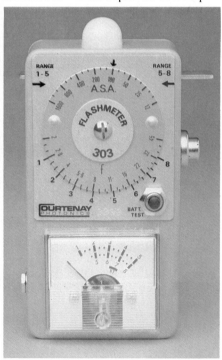

▲ A flash meter ensures correct ex–posures; a conventional meter cannot be used. There are two ranges for high and low power flash, and the reading is transferred to the meter aperture scale to determine correct exposure.

Choosing studio flash units

It is a common mistake to buy units which are too powerful for the size of studio used, so that they are always used at reduced power.

A minimum of two units should be purchased, but three will form a far more versatile system, allowing you to use one flash to light the background with two on the subject, for example.

At least one umbrella reflector will be needed. Two bowl reflectors of different sizes, a soft reflector, and a set of barn doors and snoot will form a complete and versatile system. A flash meter is a must.

Choosing a unit with variable power

▲ A flash meter is usually used close to the subject with the white dome (similar to an invercone on a hand–held meter) pointed towards the camera. Be sure you have selected the correct flash synchronization speed on the camera.

switching, even if only from full power to half power, will allow you to bring lights closer to the subject, or to use a wider aperture to limit depth of field. In a small room you can position several units equidistant from the subject, but switch down the power on one or more to vary the intensity of light—this gives greater control over the lighting effect.

Autowinders

An autowinder is a motorized unit designed to advance film automatically after each frame is exposed, and is a relatively recent phenomenon. To have motor-driven film transport built into the camera would need a major re-design, but because of the increasing use of electronics to control the various basic components it is a simple matter to provide contacts on the camera to connect to an external motor. The obvious place is the camera's base plate which provides direct access to the shutter and film transport mechanisms.

Motordrive units (which are dealt with in detail in a separate section) have been available for some time for a few high-priced cameras which are specially designed to withstand constant rapid shooting and film advance. By simplifying these and taking advantage of the more robust mechanisms in modern cameras, electro-mechanical winders are possible even with moderately priced cameras.

Although theoretically autowinders are simply for winding on film, most modern units are capable of continuous sequence, shooting up to two frames a second. The more sophisticated models rewind an exposed film back into its cassette.

Power

Autowinders consist of a low-voltage electric motor powered by small batteries—1·5 volt AA or AAA pen-light cells. The number of batteries required varies with the winder model and its features, but the average is about six. Manganese alkaline batteries are recommended because they last longer than ordinary batteries.

Construction

Batteries and motor are usually housed in a single unit, designed to follow the contours of the camera with which it is compatible. The winder top plate has electrical contacts for mating with

▶ Many different format cameras accept autowinders but you must buy a compatible unit to ensure correct operation. The Auto Winder-II fits the Topcon RM300. The winder has a built-in grip to ease manipulation of the combined assembly. Some grips also have a shutter release button at the top of the handle to make use even easier. The tiny Pentax 110 format SLR can be fitted with an equally small winder for single frame advance. The aperture priority Minolta XG2 accepts a flush design autowinder which fits some of the other Minolta X series 35mm SLR cameras.

▼ A special cradle eases battery insertion.

▼ An on/off and film rewind button are usually provided.

▶ Holding the assembly vertically is often easier if the winder has a grip.

▶ All autowinders give single frame film advance, but the great majority can also shoot frames in succession to provide a continuous exposure rate of up to two frames per second provided the release button is held down. This capability can be used to photograph moving subjects to form a sequence of frames, following the movement of the subject. The sequence can be used as a record and is also useful for teaching purposes. *Eric Crichton*

those on the camera base, together with a drive to engage the film take-up spool in the camera as well as a means for screwing the unit into the camera tripod socket.

The weight varies between models, but it is usually around 200–300 grammes without batteries. The extra weight is added to the base of the camera, thereby lowering the centre of gravity which makes a camera/winder combination stable and easy to manage. Although there is more weight to carry, the combined assembly is still portable.

Some winders have a built-in handle which makes the winder/camera assembly easier to hold and use—often these have an auxiliary shutter release. All winders have a tripod bush. Other features include an on/off switch and a warning light which glows when the motor is on or running. There is generally a separate control for selecting single frame advance or continuous running, and a release for film rewind so that the winder need not be removed from the camera to change film. Some models also have a battery test facility.

Autowinders are not cheap, and are even more costly when purchased separately from the camera. However they are at least half the price of a motor-drive unit, and are available for many of the popular 35mm SLR cameras. One major disadvantage is that the autowinder must match the camera—they are not freely interchangeable between makes.

Built-in winders

The Konica FS−1 is a 35mm SLR with a built-in autowinder; as soon as a film cassette is loaded and the camera back closed the film advances to the first frame.

After each photograph the film advances automatically and sequence photography is possible.

Agfa-Gevaert and Vivitar have several 110 pocket cameras with tiny built-in winders. The Agfa cameras accept top

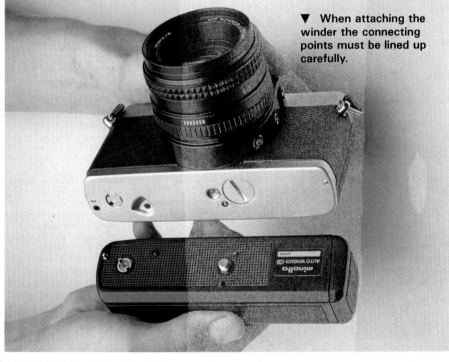

▼ When attaching the winder the connecting points must be lined up carefully.

▲ Using an autowinder allows you to capture a whole series of 'fleeting moments' which you might well miss by winding on manually. *John Garrett*

◄ ▼ As the shutter priority automatic Konica FS-1 has an autowinder built in for automatic film loading and advance, no film wind-on lever is required. This looks rather strange at first. The Agfa 901 is one of the few 110 cameras with an integral film winder.

flash allowing several flash pictures to be taken in quick succession.

Exposures

Using an autowinder is simple with an automatic camera, whether aperture or shutter priority. You simply set the aperture or shutter speed (according to the type of automatic camera in use) and the metering system automatically compensates for changing light levels. With a manual camera a little more care must be taken to ensure that you do not waste a whole roll of film if the sun unexpectedly disappears behind a cloud and you are operating the camera remotely. When using a manual camera you must make periodic checks to ensure that the aperture/shutter speed combination selected is appropriate.

Using a winder

● Do not over use your autowinder. Not all subjects will benefit from its use, and unnecessary sequences waste film and money without producing worthwhile results.
● Keep the batteries fresh or you may run out of power part-way through an interesting photography session.
● Make sure batteries are correctly inserted.
● Remember to switch winder power off when not required.
● Keep coupling points on winder unit and camera base plate clean and dust-free to ensure good electrical contact.

Practical aspects

Using an autowinder relieves the photographer of the need to wind on manually after each exposure. Apart from the obvious convenience this gives a number of distinct advantages.
● It can take the photographer several seconds to release the shutter, engage the lever wind, advance the film and again sight and compose the subject—with the camera held vertically it could take twice as long. Using an autowinder enables another picture to be taken rapidly should the subject move, or perhaps blink.
● In extreme close-up work, when the camera is mounted on a microscope or telescope, or has a long telephoto lens fitted, the disturbance caused by exerting pressure on the shutter release may cause a disaster. Camera shake may result, the composition may be altered, or the region of sharp focus may be changed. Vibration caused by an

electro-mechanical winder is considerably less than that of the hand. Using an autowinder demands less time for vibration to die down before another picture can be taken.

● For self-portraits when the shutter is being fired via a lengthy cable or other type of release, the photographer would normally return to the camera to advance the film. Using an autowinder eliminates the need for this as well as the possibility of being out of position on return.

● In nature photography birds and animals are often more disturbed by human presence than by noise—they soon become accustomed to the gentle whir of the winder, and may even show curiosity, possibly with some comical results. Watching from a distance, the photographer can fire the shutter at the appropriate moment by using a cable or pneumatic release, or some form of remote control accessory, and continue to take pictures without disturbing the subject. If the winder is a little too noisy a sound-absorbing case or cover may help.

Sequence shooting

Pressing and holding down the shutter release allows most autowinders to operate continuously. The normal maximum shooting rate applies only in good light when fast shutter speeds can be used. Obviously if the shutter speed required for the aperture in use is longer than half a second, shooting at two frames a second would be impossible.

Sequence photography ensures the maximum number of pictures are taken in a short period of time (useful for rare opportunities of action shots which are difficult to repeat). Sequences of pictures can be built up when a

single frame may not capture the vital moment. Typical examples are a horse jumping over a fence, a dog stretching lazily, or perhaps geese taking off and landing.

Accessories

All accessories which extend the capacity of an autowinder are expensive. Three examples are given, but in general they are only of interest to those who could make full use of the specific applications. Some autowinders can be fitted with an intervalometer or dosimeter, although this usually applies only to the more expensive models.

Intervalometer: this provides an automatic delay between each frame, typically variable between one frame per second to several hours or even days. The camera is set up and focused on the subject. When the first exposure has been made manually the photographer can leave the equipment to continue taking single frames at the pre-set intervals.

Dosimeter: this controls the maximum number of pictures in a single sequence. The precise number varies with the individual unit, but is often from four to 30 frames in regular steps. If it is used in conjunction with the intervalometer a sequence of pictures recording changes too slow to be perceived by the human eye at the time can be recorded (for example, flower growth). The photographer does not even need to be present after the initial pressure on the shutter release.

Data backs: although not specifically for use with an autowinder, data backs can help the photographer to document his sequence pictures. More sophisticated SLR cameras have a removable back which can be replaced

by a data back which reflects a set of figures on to the film during exposure. There are normally three sets of figures which can be adjusted by three dials on the unit. The figures often correspond to day, month and year, but you can adapt the sequence to suit your own requirements. Some compact non-reflex 35mm cameras have a date imprinting facility built in—for example the Canon Datelux and Minolta Hi-Matic SD.

▼ Some photographers use an autowinder for some of their most successful animal pictures. Timid birds can be frightened by a nearby photographer. Pre-focus the camera, and hide, using an air release to trigger the shutter.

Motor-drives

Like autowinders already mentioned, motor-drive units automatically advance film after each frame is exposed. They are, however, more versatile than autowinders, are generally capable of much faster sequence shooting rates—often up to five frames per second (fps), sometimes faster—and most offer a range of fps settings. Many can be used in conjunction with a bulk capacity film back and perhaps with sophisticated remote control devices.

They can cost twice as much as autowinders, but this pays for their more rugged construction and faster winding rates. Motor-drives can only be used with cameras robust enough to withstand the demands of rapid shooting and winding.

Motor-drives play an important role in 35mm and larger format roll film camera systems, not only for motorized film transport and fast sequences, but also for unmanned or programmed photography, and as such are used frequently by professional photographers.

Power

Motor-drives with modest continuous shooting rates (such as 2·5 fps) often run from six or eight 1·5 volt AA penlight batteries, while others with faster rates may need 10. Conventional zinc carbon batteries will transport between 50 and 80 36-exposure 35mm films, while a set of manganese alkaline batteries can last twice as long.

Although many incorporate a motor and battery compartment in the same unit, other more versatile motor-drives have a choice of battery holders which are completely separate from the motor section, and often have a built-in shutter release. The following types are available:

● A conventional battery holder, usually comprising a flat pack which lies flush with the motor unit.

● A similar design battery pack made to hold rechargeable nickel cadmium (NiCad) batteries. NiCad batteries are of a slightly lower voltage than the penlight cells (1·35 volts rather than 1·5) and are more expensive. But if regularly used and recharged from the mains they can last for several years thereby paying for themselves.

● A battery pack which can be removed

▶ **A motor-drive is ideal for capturing a picture sequence of rapid action. This set of pictures shows a dramatic sequence which happened too fast to be recorded without use of a motor-drive.** *Steve Powell*

from the motor-drive and clipped over your belt connected by a long (perhaps 10 metre) cable to allow remote operation.

● A battery grip consisting of a long tubular battery holder which attaches at right angles to the motor unit baseplate and allows the grip to be firmly held in one hand while focusing and adjusting controls with the other.

Always remember to remove batteries in an item like this which is not in constant use.

Some motor-drives can also be operated from AC mains electricity with a special power pack.

Construction

Many motor-drives have a handle or grip shaped to fit the right hand, usually with its own shutter release button. (If such an auxiliary release is provided, the camera's own release may well be inoperational when the motor-drive is in use.) The contoured handle helps support the camera firmly, especially when using long telephotos or heavy zoom lenses.

The motor-drive generally connects to couplings in the camera baseplate, secured by a screw into the tripod bush. A tripod socket is provided on the underside of battery packs. The camera couplings sometimes have a dust cover which must be removed before attaching the motor-drive.

Weight without batteries is often in the region of 300g, and most units add about 30mm to the height of the camera.

All motor-drives can be used for single frame film advance (like an autowinder) as well as for sequences, and a means of selecting either is provided. One or two also have a dial allowing the photographer to select a high, medium or low picture shooting rate. Most units have an on/off switch to prevent battery drain when not in use; some automatically switch off when the unit is disconnected. A built-in rewind button is always included so that you can rewind and change film without removing the motor-drive from the camera.

Other features may include a frame

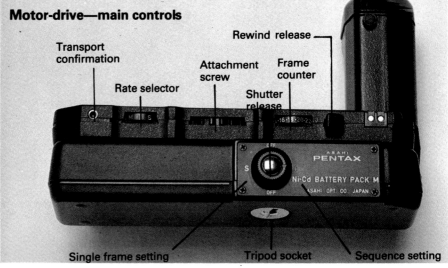

Motor-drive—main controls

Transport confirmation
Rate selector
Attachment screw
Rewind release
Frame counter
Shutter release
Single frame setting
Tripod socket
Sequence setting

Motor-drive power sources

Battery grip

Power pack (mains)

Motor-drive unit

NiCad battery pack

You can often choose from a variety of motor-drive power packs according to your particular needs.

counter which you can preset manually to the number of frames on the loaded film, or perhaps set to expose and wind a certain number of frames. The motor stops when zero is reached. There may well be an LED (light emitting diode) which glows when the motor is on or running, and some units have a battery check.

As with autowinders, it is generally impossible to use a different make of motor-drive to your camera.

Exposures

When used with an automatic exposure camera the motor-drive's electrical contacts connect with the camera's metering circuits. Exposure adjustments are therefore automatically made should the lighting conditions change during a rapid motor-drive sequence. With a manual camera you have to set the aperture and shutter speed before commencing a sequence.

The slower the shutter speed in use, the fewer pictures can be taken in one short period. (As a guide to average frames per second with particular shutter speeds see the table). The maximum shooting/winding rate at fast shutter speeds depends entirely on the capability of the motor-drive.

Practical aspects

Motor-drives offer all the advantages of autowinders:
● automatic, motorized film advance
● rapid picture-taking
● minimal vibration (especially important when using slow shutter speeds and in close-up photographs).

You can use a motor-drive to take wildlife photographs—using a long or remote control release from a 'hide'. Its main function, however, is to shoot picture sequences of fast motion, and to

allow you to capture the one critical moment during a period of activity. If you were winding on manually these moments would doubtless be lost.

But even a fast motor-drive does not capture every fraction of a second on film. If you are shooting with a shutter speed of 1/125 at 5 fps, you are only making exposures for a total of a ¼ second, and ¾ second is lost. So select carefully suitable subjects for motor-drive, and consider whether you've more chance of catching a climax by single frame shooting.

Sequence shooting

Press and hold down the motor-drive's shutter release, following the direction of a moving subject, until you have recorded as much as you want of the action. Immediately you remove your

finger from the release, the motor stops running. At fast rates, perhaps 4 fps, you may at first take one or two more frames than you intended if your reactions aren't fast enough to remove your finger in time. At such speeds it can take only a few seconds to use up a 36-exposure film, so make your sequences selectively.

To ensure the fastest rate of which the motor-drive is capable choose a sufficiently fast film and shutter speed for the lighting conditions and speed of motion. If the movement is across your field of vision pre-focus on the spot at which you think the subject will first appear in the viewfinder. For subjects moving towards you practise the art of changing focus as you expose each frame. Adjust the aperture ring to bracket exposures rapidly.

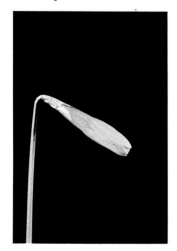

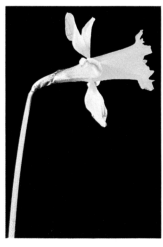

▲ With a long power cord between battery pack and camera (with motor-drive) you can take single frame or continuous picture sequences without having to return to the camera to wind on film. Choices of cable length are available (often 3 or 10 metres).

◄ A flower may take hours to open. A time-lapse sequence is usually made with a motor-drive and an intervalometer, without the photographer having to be present.

Bulk back

250 back
rear cover

250 back

250 film
magazine

Spare bulk
film spool

Bulk
magazine
in chamber

▲ A bulk back and 250-shot magazine
enables you to take long sequences
without constantly having to reload the
camera with fresh cassettes of film.

▶ A bulk film back adds greatly
to the size and weight of the camera.

Accessories

The use of available accessories enables the photographer to get the most from his motor-drive.

As with some autowinders, an intervalometer can be used to provide an automatic delay between each frame. The camera and motor-drive are set up and pre-focused, and after the first manual exposure, subsequent frames are exposed and wound automatically (useful for unmanned, time-lapse photographs). A dosimeter can be set to expose a pre-determined number of frames in any one sequence, and can be used alone or with an intervalometer.

Considering that at 4fps you would use 36 exposures in nine seconds, a 250 or even 750 bulk film back is essential for sports photography, for example, when the time spent in rewinding and reloading film could result in the loss of a valuable picture. You will need a minimum of two bulk film magazines, and a bulk film loader. The film winds from a full magazine into an empty one, which is removed when full of exposed film,

and does not therefore need rewinding. The bulk back can also be used for a long time-lapse sequence when repeated attendance to change films is impossible or impractical. You will also need a large film spiral and tank if you intend to do your own film processing.

Motor-drive or autowinder?

If both autowinder and motor-drive units are available for your camera and you are undecided which to buy there are three basic considerations:

Price: as motor-drives are always more expensive than autowinders, the price factor alone may force your decision.

Purpose: if you are looking only for motorized film transport, with the occasional modest sequence, choose an autowinder. If you are interested in action photography and need high winding rates to capture fast-changing sequences, a motor-drive is the only answer. For occasional fast sequences you may prefer to hire a motor-drive.

Versatility: a motor-drive can offer high speed photography. If you want to

use a bulk back, remote control and a range of accessories, a motor-drive is more versatile than an autowinder.

Don't buy an autowinder if you need a motor-drive: you will have wasted your money, and will be left with superfluous accessory.

WINDING RATES
This table is a guide to the maximum number of frames per second you can expect with different shutter speeds.

Set shutter speed	Maximum frames per second
1/2	1·5
1/4	2
1/8	2·5
1/15	3
1/30	3·5
1/60	4

The higher fps rates only apply to motor-drives capable of operating at such speeds. With slow shutter speeds the camera should of course be used on a tripod.

The improvised studio

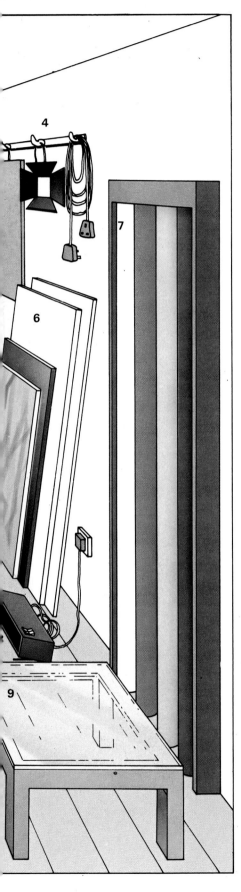

Although daylight will do most of the time there is the occasion when you may want to photograph a still-life, a portrait or do some glamour photography. By working indoors and using artificial light you have complete freedom to work how and when you like—rather than relying on daylight and the vagaries of the weather. Using artificial light and excluding daylight completely gives you total control of lighting effects. For details of tungsten lighting see page 214; for studio flash see page 218.

The word 'studio' often conjures up visions of a grand room equipped with an expensive battery of lights, cameras and background materials. You may be surprised therefore to find a professional photographer taking portraits, still-life sets and antiques in a studio no larger than a fair-sized living room.

Size of studio

You can improvise a temporary studio in almost any room, even if you live in a small flat. If you are lucky enough to have a spare room then it can perhaps be set aside as a permanent studio.

The only rooms not suitable are those smaller than about 2½ x 3½ metres and those with ceilings lower than 2½ metres. In a small room you are forced to have the lights and camera too close to the subject, and the subject too close to the background. The results are cramped, harshly lit photographs with unwanted shadows on subject and background. At the smallest you could get away with a room 4 metres long by 2½ metres wide, but the ideal width is 3 metres to allow room for backgrounds and lights on either side. The 4 metre length allows you to use a

135mm lens on a 35mm camera for example. This gives good perspective with head and shoulder portraits and allows room to position the background and lights to best advantage.

Blacking out the studio

Daylight streaming through a window swamps the studio lights, whether tungsten or flash, so the studio needs to be blacked out with opaque material fixed over the windows. It is best to use a system which allows you quickly to place and remove the black-out material, and the choices are either a special vinyl material, preferably stretched over a rigid frame slightly larger than the window frame, black roller blinds, or any other flexible opaque material.

Colour of studio

To control light to the utmost the studio should be decorated in neutral colours, such as black or dark grey. White flats (large sheets of white reflective material mounted on a rigid frame, or perhaps huge sheets of polystyrene) can then be used to reflect light on to the subject. Many photographers prefer a white studio, however, because they have a greater choice of reflective surfaces from which to bounce light—perhaps to imitate soft, overcast daylight.

If you are using a room temporarily as a studio and the walls are colourful, rig up sufficient white sheets or flats to prevent unwanted colour casts on your subject.

The floor should be uncarpeted and clear of clutter. The best floor coverings are flat with a pile-free surface, such as vinyl or wood. If you

The ideal permanent studio is located in a fair sized room with pale, neutral walls and a flat pile-free floor.
1 Removable black-out material 2 Wall mounted background paper (other support systems are possible) 3 Collapsible trestle table for still-life subjects 4 Rack for storing large lighting accessories 5 Studio flash unit 6 Various sizes of fill-in cards 7 Background paper (available in other widths) 8 Hot and cold fan heater 9 Glass topped table for close-up work and special lighting techniques 10 Adjustable height stool 11 Camera with cable release (have as many optional lenses to suit your needs as you can afford) 12 Sturdy tripod with pan and tilt head 13 Bean bag cushion 14 Wheeled trolley for storing small

props and accessories 15 Table tripod 16 Glass for still-life sets and mirror for special effects 17 Adjustable height lighting stand 18 Reversible umbrella reflector.

Avoid having a network of cables stretched dangerously across the floor. Install sufficient power points for convenience and safety. Choose a flash or tungsten lighting system to suit your means as well as a range of diffusers and reflectors to permit varied lighting techniques. Don't throw away old pieces of felt, cork, or slate, and keep your eyes open for inexpensive lengths of material—all these items can be used to set the scene for a successful photograph and add an original and professional touch. Good photographers are innovative.

can't move the carpets be careful not to tread on the background paper or it will crease and tear because of the soft flexibility of the carpet's pile.

Backgrounds: special photographic background paper is free from creases and texture, and has high colour saturation. You do not need a whole spectrum of colours—black, white and one or two pastel and bold colours are

adequate. Background paper tends to be expensive—persuade a friend to split the cost of a 3m wide roll with you and cut the roll across its width.

You can equally successfully use carefully ironed lengths of plain-coloured material (bought as off-cuts at the local market) or painted sheets of hardboard. Plain velvet curtains also lend themselves beautifully as backgrounds.

Studio equipment

You do not need to buy expensive professional equipment; success relies mostly on innovation. Basically you need items to put the structure of the picture together—to hold the background, lights and camera in the right positions.

Supports: lightweight aluminium tubing with push-fit plastic joints,

hinges and feet, is available from agricultural wholesalers. You may prefer a heavier system with steel tubing and screw clamps including camera mounts and lighting adapters, or for small lamps you may be able to use microphone stands—although special lighting stands are comparatively inexpensive. Good quality Bakelite lamp holders are perfectly good to

◀ A temporary studio can be quickly set up without disrupting the house. Move enough furniture to provide clear floor space around you and the subject, and leave room for the background. Equipment can be as simple or complex as you wish to make it.

▶ When using props to help you with a difficult subject, such as an infant, make sure to choose something which complements both mood and composition. *John Garrett* chose a colourful toy.

▼ This portrait was taken in the improvised studio illustrated (left) using two flash guns with built-in slave units. A piece of stocking over the lens gave a soft focus effect.

use with photofloods—they must be wired to the mains with heat-resistant silicon-rubber cable.

Two lighting stands can be used to hold a roll on which your background paper is supported. A U-shaped trough is also available to hold background rolls on a single stand. The same type of lighting stands are, of course, used to support tungsten and electronic flash units, and you can buy adapters for hand-held flash guns.

Buy a sturdy tripod for your camera. This allows you to stand away from the camera which often makes a human subject more at ease. Use a cable release to fire the shutter.

Props: a small, wheeled trolley with drawers and shelves can be used to house handy bits and pieces, such as double-sided tape, a stapling gun to secure backgrounds, drawing pins, cans of spray paint, bulldog clips and G-clamps as well as a supply of film, a set of filters, lenses and several small camera accessories.

Two or three adjustable height stools are useful for model and photographer. A stool on wheels allows the photographer to change position easily. You will also need a small table (preferably a collapsible trestle type for easy dismantling) and a large sheet of glass for still-life. If you photograph children a few toys and bean bag cushions are a boon, and keep various sizes of white fill-in cards on hand.

A large mirror can be used as a prop or to add a 'hair light' if there is insufficient room behind the subject to place a lamp. The mirror must be positioned carefully to reflect back one of the main lights on to the subject's hair without the mirror showing in the shot.

Power

For ease of working a studio must have enough power points to allow a number of lamps to be positioned to create the best effect. A cable stretched across the room or four plugs in one adapter are dangerous.

Tungsten lights: if you intend to use a number of tungsten lights remember that 2000W halogen lamps, 1000W spot lights and 500W photofloods quickly add up to the full capacity of a fuse in a plug, and a tungsten system, especially if you use other electrical appliances such as a fan heater, may require a separate 30 amp ring main. Apart from being dangerous, ignoring this may be against conditions of tenancy, lease or electricity supply.

Electronic flash: this consumes less power for effective light output, and of course battery operated guns make no demands on your domestic supply. If you use studio flash with modelling lights, or add modelling lights to small

units, this will burn more power but the modelling lights are usually no more than 275W each.

Tungsten lights generate heat, and a busy session soon warms up a small studio. But when using flash you should have some form of heating to keep you and your model warm. If the lights are used only periodically you should maintain minimum temperature of around 10°C, to avoid rust or, even worse, condensation inside electrical units. A portable fan heater which blows cold as well as hot air will be helpful for summer and winter photography sessions. Never use a paraffin or gas heater in an enclosed room with poor ventilation facilities.

▲ This still-life was set up to produce a master negative for a colour analyser, using the grey scale as a reference point. To provide reliable information for analysis the card was lit in the same way as the subject.

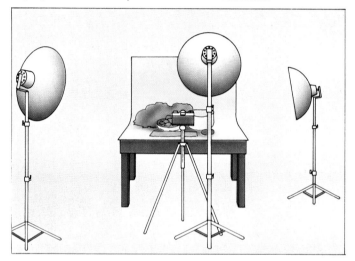

▲ Bright, even illumination was provided by three tungsten lamps. A large bowl reflector to the right of the subject provided modelling, and two large soft reflectors produced diffused frontal and side fill-in illumination.

▲ A dark background and a dark-haired model were *Michael Busselle's* natural choice to create a mysterious mood. To maintain the atmosphere a simple lighting technique was used to give soft illumination.

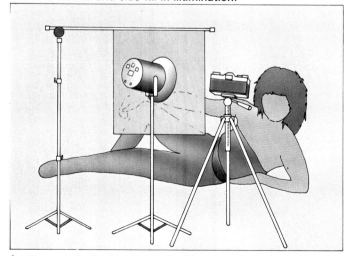

▲ One studio flash unit fitted with a standard chrome bowl reflector was positioned close to the camera and angled slightly downwards. A piece of tracing paper over the flash head softened light from the flash.

Daylight

Daylight can be used, especially if the room has a large north-facing window (south in the southern hemisphere) or a diffused skylight and if the décor is light and neutral. To make the best use of daylight you need two or three large reflector flats on stands, or white cartridge paper or crumpled kitchen foil pasted to stiff card. These are used to direct fill-in light.

● If you are using black and white film mixing light—daylight and tungsten for example—is possible. If you want to mix daylight with tungsten using colour film you must cover the windows with special sheets of orange-brown filter plastic to balance the two types of light and use tungsten balanced film.

If you don't want to go to the trouble of setting up a studio, whether temporary or permanent, choose a room with sufficient clear wall area and enough room for you to move around.

▲ (Left) Late evening sunlight gives a pleasantly warm effect, but such directional light sources produce heavy shadows. The side of the face next to the window is well lit, but the other side is cast into heavy distracting shadow. (Right) To improve portraits using daylight from a window some form of fill-in is necessary to provide shadow detail and to balance the lighting effect. Both needs have been met and the warm quality of the scene is maintained with a simple technique.

▶ If you use daylight in your studio then you can fill shadows by reflecting light back on to the subject. Ask an assistant to hold a large white card, or support it on a suitable stand.

You may have the sort of living room that lacks clutter and which makes a good studio set without shifting furniture or having to make other special arrangements.

Projectors, screens and viewing aids

A projector allows you to view your slides in detail and enlarged many times, and for a group of people to view the slides at the same time, making it possible for the whole family to join in and relive holiday experiences. To be successful a slide show needs interesting pictures correctly exposed—don't be tempted to show the duds, set them aside as there is nothing more boring than sitting through lengthy descriptions of what the picture should have been. Get your facts right so that you know where or what each picture is—viewers are bound to ask the odd question and if you can make the information interesting, so much the better.

How projectors work

All slide projectors are basically similar. Like photographic enlargers, they consist of an arrangement similar to a camera with the film (now developed) lined up with a lens. A light source is positioned behind the film so that instead of light coming in through the lens to make a picture, it shines through it to recreate that picture on a screen. It is a direct reversal of the light path of a simple camera.

Because there is no sensitive material involved, projector lenses do not need any kind of exposure control, such as shutters or aperture stops, but they do need to be able to focus, so that the screen can be at any chosen distance to get different sizes of the projected picture. Projector lenses are therefore mounted in plain tubes, often with a helical thread which screws in and out of the projector for focusing.

The film carrier could in theory be the same as on a camera, taking a roll of slides, but handling filmstrips is very inconvenient if you want to select the best images, or pick slides from different batches. Filmstrips are also very vulnerable. To overcome this, card or plastic mounts are used to hold each frame individually with enough room to pick up the slide without touching the image area. For 35mm, these measure 50x50mm. Projectors must, as a result, have a transport mechanism which can remove one mounted slide from the lens rear and then insert another.

Some projectors have a built-in editing tray. This is a small illuminated rectangle where one slide at a time can be checked before insertion into the magazine. Others have a small illuminated panel in the hand control for this. The GAF projector has a secondary optical system which lets you write on the slide mount so that the writing, perhaps the slide's subject title, is displayed on a small screen at the rear of the projector and can be read out by the projectionist. Some hand controls also include a light pointer.

1 Rondette 1500S is semi-automatic with manual focusing. Takes straight magazines with 36 or 45 slides and rotary magazines with 120 slides.
2 Rondette 1500RF is a more sophisticated version with forward and reverse remote control facilities and remote focusing. Takes straight and rotary magazines.
3 Gnome Sprite is a very basic projector with push and pull slide changes. It has a standard 85mm lens and includes a heat absorbing filter.

4 Paximat 850 has a detachable control unit which includes a light panel for previewing slides when sorting and arranging them. The control includes a built-in light pointer. The projector can be set to project slides automatically at intervals between 5 and 45 seconds.

5 Kodak Carousel S-AV 1000 takes rotary magazines with 80 slides. Accessories include forward and reverse remote control and remote focusing, and a timing device which allows slides to be projected at intervals between 4 and 40 seconds.

The light in a projector must be perfectly even and bright. It is projected from behind the slide so that the illumination on the screen extends right into the corners giving a brilliant image, with high contrast and colours, and without hot spots. This demands the use of a condenser system to collect and direct the light accurately. To get adequate brightness for comfortable viewing a bulb ranging from 12v 100w to 240v 300w may be used, the brightest normal ones being 24v 250w, and the standard fitting 24v 150w.

The intense heat created by the very small tungsten halogen low voltage bulbs, run by a transformer in the projector, must be cut down by a special infra-red absorbing glass filter, or else slides would curl up and plastic mounts melt. To keep the whole system cool, a motorized fan is fitted, blowing air over the bulb and slide area, and this motor is also used in many current projectors to operate a mechanical system for changing slides. The most expensive aspect of projecting is often replacing the bulbs, which normally last 50 hours, but may go after half that time of running. Some projectors have a dimmer switch for low-level output from the bulb. This is not just to compensate for thin transparencies —it increases the life of the bulb to 500 hours.

Further necessary features on nearly all 35mm projectors include some sort of angle adjustments and levelling screws, so that books don't have to be piled

Types of 35mm projector

Type	Slide-change	Focusing	Light source	Lenses
Basic	Single slide manual in push-and-pull carrier or filmstrips	Limited	240v 150w 100w 50w	Fixed 85mm 100mm
Semi auto magazine	Slides in magazines of 30, 36, 50, changed by single action	Full range manual	24v 150w	Fixed or changeable
Autochange remote control	Slides in magazine of 30–50 changed by remote hand control button	Full range manual	24v 150w	Changeable 85mm f2·8 standard
Autochange and focus	As above, but extra button on hand set adjusts focus	Manual or remote	24v 150w	Changeable 85mm f2·8 standard
Autofocus	Remote slide change but focus set automatically each time slide changes	Manual or fully auto	24v 150w	Changeable 85mm f2·8 standard
Autofocus rotary	As above but accepts rotary magazines	Manual or fully auto	24v 150w	Changeable 85mm f2·8 standard

These specifications are quoted for clearly identifiable types of projector to which most popular makes adhere.

4

5

Kodak CAROUSEL S-AV 1000

under the front to raise the height of the image on the screen.

The danger of using a pile of books is that, if the projector is at too steep an angle, the auto-shift mechanism may jam. Don't prop the projector higher than the built-in feet allow. There is also provision for removing and changing the lens, so that if you are projecting in a very small space a wide angle type can be used, and for large lecture halls a long throw lens.

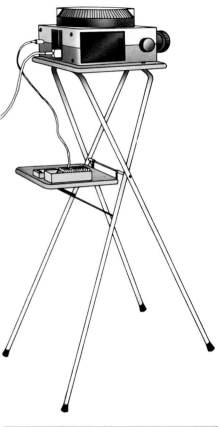

▶ A projector stand gives a comfortable working height. It raises the projector sufficiently to project over people's heads. A shelf below the projector platform is useful for holding spare magazines and storage trays.

▼ Rondette 110 (left) for 110 format slides takes a slide belt with 40, 80 and 120 slides. The Fantimat 110 has a rotary magazine which holds 60 slides. Both have remote control facilities.

Lenses

Projectors for 35mm slides are normally fitted with an 85mm f2·8 standard lens (the aperture may vary from one manufacturer to another), usually costing very little but of reasonable quality, mounted in a plastic rim. A better lens option can give sharper projected pictures from top quality slides; these are usually 90mm f2·5 in metal mounts, costing substantially more than the standard lens. For large rooms, a 135mm or 150mm lens can be used, and for small rooms, a 60mm or 50mm lens. Many projectors can be bought fitted with a 70–120mm f3·2 zoom lens which is capable of working in almost any size room and costs little more than the standard lens (a small extra on the price of the projector).

Other projectors

Projectors are not confined to 35mm slides. There are some makes for projecting 110 slides, which share the features of the 35mm ranges—from basic to autofocus rotary magazine models, including prestige projectors from Leitz and Agfa. They generally resemble scaled-down 35mm models. For larger format users, there are some projectors available for 6x6cm, 6x7cm and 6x4·5cm; for example, Planet and

Rollei. These too can have full autochange and remote focus options, but in this case are very expensive and look like large versions of 35mm models. There are a few projectors available that handle 6x6cm transparencies as well as the smaller 35mm ones.

Projector stands

A good projector stand is useful, as they are normally much higher than coffee tables or other household furniture used as stands. They match up to the centre of a standard 100cm screen, meaning you do not need to buy a screen with 'keystone' correction. You can also buy a stand with an adjustable angle on the projector platform plus a second platform in the middle to hold your spare slides or magazines.

Accessories

The only accessory you may find useful for projection is a light pointer—some projectors have these built in to their remote hand controls. The pointer projects an arrow-shaped light focused on the screen, so you can point out parts of a picture without putting your hand across the lens to cast a shadow. A film strip attachment is available for some projectors. This allows 35mm filmstrip to be projected.

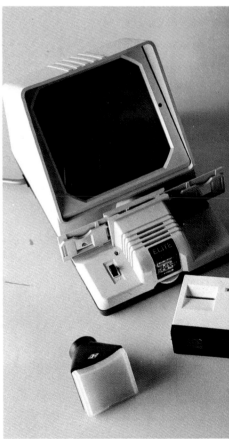

Viewing aids

There are various viewing aids available so that you can look at your slides without having to set up the projector. This is useful when you receive a batch of slides and want to have a quick look through, when viewing slides on your own or when sorting and arranging slides for a showing. You can just hold them up to the light but this does not allow for critical appraisal of the image as little detail can be seen.

▼ Editing trays for sorting slides.

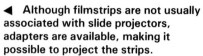

◄ Although filmstrips are not usually associated with slide projectors, adapters are available, making it possible to project the strips.

▼ The Liesegang A60 is a semi-automatic projector for 6x6cm slides. The magazines hold 30 slides. The lenses available for this projector are 150mm, 200mm and 250mm. The projector has an economy setting which increases the life of the lamp.

▲ Viewing aids for sorting and editing slides range from a simple eyepiece which is held up to the light for viewing, to battery and mains operated viewers.

An eyepiece is the cheapest and simplest aid. It acts as a magnifying glass and all you do is hold the slide up to a light source and look at the picture through the eyepiece.

An editing tray, such as a light box, consists of a glass panel with a light behind it. You put the slides on the box to view them. This is best used in conjunction with an eyepiece as you can then see quite clearly how sharp the image is.

The light box is useful for getting a quick, overall view of a number of slides at the same time.

Hand-held viewers have a glass panel with a light source behind. They work on batteries and give a reasonable picture. Slides are inserted manually, one at a time, and only one person at a time can view the slides.

Screens

Most projector screens for popular use are generally available in sizes ranging from 100cm square to 177cm square. The reason for the square format is to accommodate both horizontal and vertical 35mm slides. Most screens are on free-standing tripods with adjustable height, but some are designed to stand on tables or to be fixed to the ceiling and pulled down when needed.

Good screens have a 'keystone' correction which enables the screen itself to be tilted downwards at anything from 5° to 15°, so that when the projector is sitting on a normal height of table and aimed upwards, the screen can be made parallel to it. This keeps the picture rectangular instead of taking on a 'keystone' shape with the top broader than the bottom.

Screen surfaces determine the cost more than anything else.

Matt white allows you to project in a darkened room, and people sitting almost anywhere can see the picture properly, though it is not really very bright in overall terms.

Beaded surfaces use thousands of tiny glass beads to reflect the light back directly, so you do not need such a dark room, but people must not sit more than 40° off the axis between projector and screen.

Pearl beaded screens, which do not use glass beads but other methods of coating, are a compromise. Genuine glass beaded screens can become very brittle after a few years and are extremely hard to clean.

Silvered screens give a very high brightness but you really don't see anything unless you sit within 20° on either side of the projector.

High gain screens use a combination of silvering and glass beads to produce an incredibly bright image. They cost a great deal but some do not allow any deviation from a narrow viewing band area in line with the projector.

Back projection screens are small, about 60 x 91cm, in frames, and can be used in daylight, with the projector shining the picture through the screen so that you view it from the other side. The slides must be inserted backwards for correct viewing.

Choosing screens and lenses

To decide what lens and screen you need, first measure the room where you intend to do most projection. Use metric measurements as lenses are marked in millimetres. Measure from the point where you can plug in the projector to the best screen position.

● To calculate the screen size and a suitable lens, proceed as follows. If you would like to use a 100cm screen, you will be blowing up the slide from its 35mm width to 100cm, which is an enlargement of 28 times.

Divide your available distance by 28 and you get the focal length of lens which fills it. If the available distance is about 2·3 metres, you need an 85mm lens. This is not a totally accurate calculation—for projecting distances and screen sizes, see below.

● Note that with an 85mm lens in a living room with only 3 metres clearance, anything bigger than a 127cm screen would be a waste of money unless you bought a wide angle as well.

Screen sizes and projection distances

Screen sizes		75 x 75cm	100 x 100cm	120 x 120cm	127 x 127cm	150 x 150cm
Format	Lens	Projection distance in metres				
35mm	50mm	—	1.5	1.8	1.85	2.2
	85mm	—	2.5	2.9	3.0	3.7
	120mm	—	3.5	4.2	4.4	5.2
	150mm	—	4.4	5.2	5.5	6.5
110	45mm	2.0	2.7	3.2	3.4	—
	60mm	2.7	3.6	4.3	4.5	—
6 x 6cm	150mm	—	2.6	3.1	3.3	4.0
	200mm	—	3.5	4.2	4.4	5.2
	250mm	—	4.4	5.3	5.5	6.5

▶ The Leitz Pradovit A projector can be combined with a cabinet so that slides are projected on to the back of the screen. The cabinet does not have to be used in a darkened room.

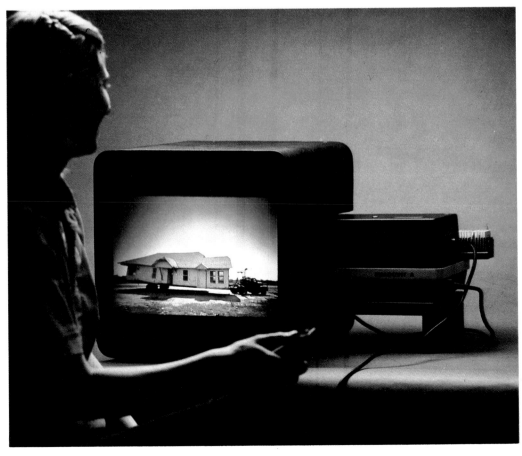

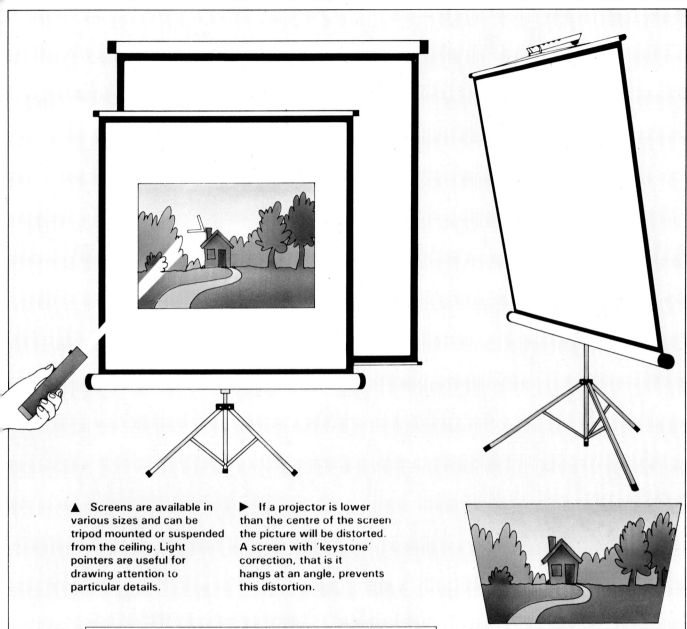

▲ Screens are available in various sizes and can be tripod mounted or suspended from the ceiling. Light pointers are useful for drawing attention to particular details.

▶ If a projector is lower than the centre of the screen the picture will be distorted. A screen with 'keystone' correction, that is it hangs at an angle, prevents this distortion.

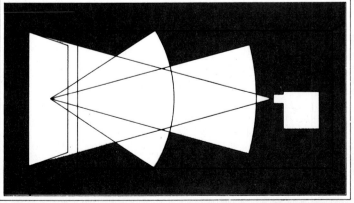

◀ The darker a room is the more brilliant the projected image appears. To see the image at its best the audience should be within a certain angle of the screen. The angle depends on the screen surface. Beaded screens have a wider angle of view than silvered screens.

Slide mounts and magazines

▲ Sorting slides is made easy with an illuminated slide sorting tray. An eyepiece allows for critical appraisal of the quality of a slide.

After commercial processing, slides are mounted in card or plastic frames. These do not offer much protection to the actual slide although they keep the slides uniform and suitable for projection. Glass mounts are preferable as they completely cover the slides, keeping them clean and free from scratches. But glass mounted slides have one disadvantage—if the glass breaks the slide will probably be ruined. Therefore never send slides in glass mounts through the post.

There are various ways of keeping and storing slides. Obviously if you intend projecting them they must be mounted in frames. As your collection of slides increases, it becomes more important to have some sort of filing system so that you can find any particular slide

you may want. It is therefore essential to caption each slide—do this as soon as the slide is processed, otherwise you may forget what the picture is. Indexing the slides depends on how large your collection is, the sort of photographs you take and the amount of detail you require. Label each magazine or number it and keep a separate record of its contents.

Slide mounts

Slides are usually returned to you from processing mounted in card or plastic mounts, and most people find these acceptable. But the slide is not firmly held and it can 'pop' from the warmth of the projector, causing it to go out of focus as the film expands and curves in the mount. With remote focus projec-

tors you have to correct the image; auto-focus projectors have a moment of unsharpness before sensors catch up and change the setting, although they sometimes fail to do this.

To overcome the problem completely, you need to sandwich the slides between glass. Glass mounts are readily available and must be handled with care: brush dust away and avoid fingerprints on the glass when mounting the slides. The result is a permanently protected slide which will not fade or 'pop' in the projector.

Newton's Rings: coloured light rings

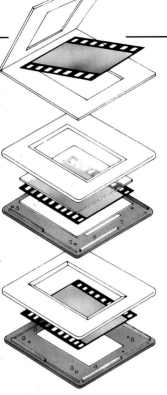

▲ Slide mounts can be card or plastic. Plastic ones are available with and without glass.

▼ Slide mounting jigs snap plastic mounts together. The larger jig has an illuminated panel to ensure accurate alignment of the transparency.

▲ Slide mounts are available in a variety of shapes and sizes. The different shapes are used to crop or mask unwanted picture area.

may appear on a projected slide. This happens when a slide is glass mounted and the glass is making partial contact. Some frames are designed to prevent this from happening.

Projecting slides

All slides are inserted into a projector with the emulsion side of the film facing the lens and the picture upside down. The emulsion side is usually dull or has some slight relief on the image while the other side, facing the light source, is shiny. If in doubt, look at the picture so that it reads correctly, facing

243

the screen, and then insert it into the projector upside down without turning it round, keeping the correct side facing you.

● To help recognize which way up the slides should be inserted, stick small circular stickers on the top right-hand corner of each slide when it is in the projection position (the bottom left-hand corner when viewed by eye). A great help in sorting slides is some sort of viewing aid. Either a light box or a hand-held viewer will do.

● If the slides are to be kept in a particular sequence, draw a diagonal line, from corner to corner, on the outer edges of the slides in the magazines. It is then easy to see if any slides are in the wrong position.

Magazines

Slides can usually be stored in their boxes as returned by the processor, but then they need to be arranged every time you want to project them. Spare magazines are available for projectors. They are a convenient way of storing any number of slides and the magazines can be put directly into the projector—so there is no need to transfer slides laboriously every time you want to project them. Depending on the sort of magazines you are using, you can use transfer trays for your slides. These allow you to invert the slides into the

Magazines for 35mm slides

Magazine type	Capacity	Storage method
DIN standard straight magazine: Agfa, Leitz, Rollei, Chinon, Kindermann, Zeiss Ikon, many others	30, 36 or 50	In magazines, usually two per stacking storage box In 'transfer trays' which are placed over magazine and inverted to load up in one action
DIN standard rotary	100 slides	In magazine
GAF Rototray	100 slides	In magazine
GAF straight magazine	36 slides	In magazine
Hanimex etc straight magazine	36 slides	In magazine
Hanimex etc rotary	120 slides	In magazine
Carousel 80	80 slides	In magazine Transfer tray

magazine quickly and easily.

Some projectors, such as Chinon, accept both the DIN standard magazines which are now almost universal and also GAF or Hanimex type straight or rotary magazines, using an adapter which allows either system to be chosen. Apart from magazines there are other storage systems.

Cellophane sleeves: if slides are not mounted, or are in card mounts and are being handled, keep them individually in cellophane sleeves to prevent them getting covered with fingerprints.

Transparent plastic sleeves are available to hold a number of slides. The sleeve can be filed either in a filing cabinet, in a box file or in an album. The sleeves are useful as they can be placed directly on a

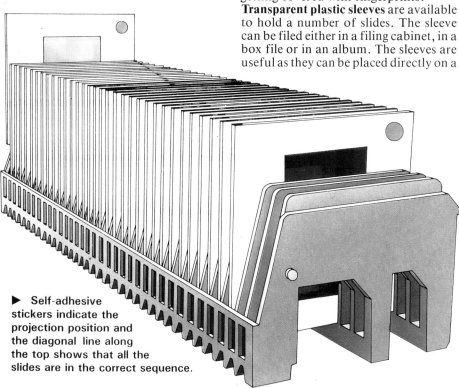

▶ Self-adhesive stickers indicate the projection position and the diagonal line along the top shows that all the slides are in the correct sequence.

light box to view a number of transparencies at once.

Are slides permanent?

Some people worry about how much they can project their slides. Tests conducted with several popular types of film based on running a set of slides for 10 hours a day through a 250w projector for three months—total projection time per slide 15 hours—revealed the following: Kodachrome slides had faded badly, but those in glass mounts were much better than the card mounted ones. Ektachrome slides had not all faded but some had. Agfa slides were hardly affected. Fuji remained unchanged. Sakura remained unchanged. Ten hours a day is a very long time, and if slides are stored in magazines with protective boxes, there should be no chance of any real colour change.

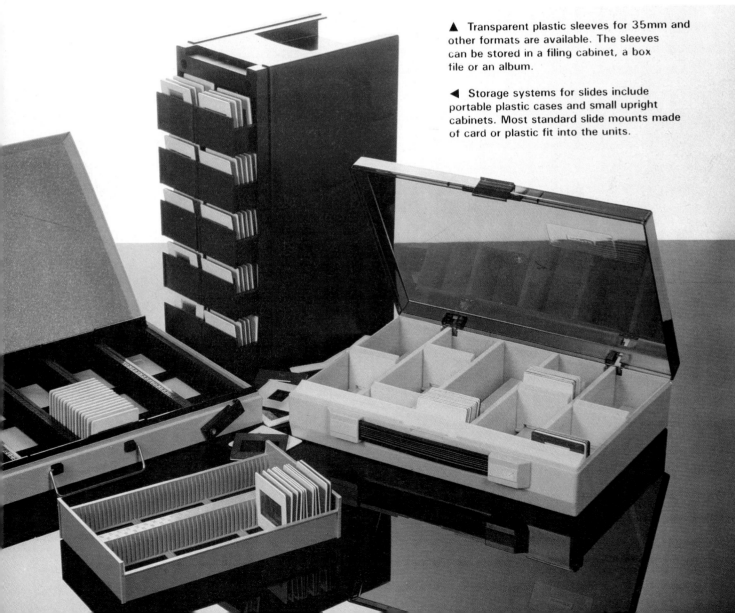

▲ Transparent plastic sleeves for 35mm and other formats are available. The sleeves can be stored in a filing cabinet, a box file or an album.

◀ Storage systems for slides include portable plastic cases and small upright cabinets. Most standard slide mounts made of card or plastic fit into the units.

Glossary

Words in *italics* appear as separate entries.

A

Aberration An optical defect in a lens that causes it to produce an unsharp or distorted image. There are several kinds of aberrations—the most common being chromatic, spherical, coma and astigmatic. Modern lenses (designed by computer) contain several lens elements which reduce aberrations to a minimum.

Achromat A lens that is corrected for two (normally green and red) of the three primary colours (blue, green and red). Although it is not completely free from chromatic aberration, this type of lens performs perfectly well in most conditions. Most lenses are achromatic as it is very expensive to correct for all three primary colours.

Additive colour A method of mixing light where virtually any colour (except the pure spectrum colours) can be produced by adding various proportions of the primary colours—blue, green and red. The additive colour mixing system was used for early colour photographs, such as autochrome and Dufacolour and is used today in colour television.

Afocal lens An optical unit which, when combined with the main camera lens, changes the focal length. A wide-angle afocal attachment reduces the overall focal length and therefore gives a wider angle of view. A 'telephoto' attachment increases the focal length and 'enlarges' a small portion of the scene.

Anamorphic lens A lens that compresses or stretches its images, normally in a horizontal plane. Cinema processes, such as Cinemascope, first use an anamorphic lens to condense a wide-angle view on to the film, and then project this on to a screen using an anamorphic lens to stretch the image.

Anastigmat A lens which is relatively free of optical aberrations, especially astigmatism.

Angle of incidence The angle at which light strikes a surface. This being measured between the perpendicular ('normal') to the surface and the direction of the light source.

Angle of reflection The angle at which light travels after it has been reflected from a surface. The angle being measured between the emerging light and the perpendicular ('normal') to the object surface. The angle of reflection equals the angle of incidence.

Angle of view This is the maximum angle 'seen' by a lens. Most so-called standard lenses (for example 50mm on a 35mm camera) have an angle of view of about 50°. Lenses of long focal length (200mm for example) have narrower angles and lenses of short focal length (eg 28mm) have wider angles of view.

Anti-halation backing A thin coating of dye, pigment, or carbon on the back of the film which helps to prevent light from reflecting back to the light-sensitive emulsion. Without the backing, all bright lights in a scene would have a strong 'halo' of light around them.

Aperture The circular opening within a camera lens system that controls the brightness of the image striking the film. Most apertures are variable—the size of the film opening being indicated by the f number. (See *Relative aperture.)*

Aperture priority A term usually applied to an in-camera automatic exposure system where the aperture is first selected by the photographer and the camera automatically sets the appropriate shutter speed (for the scene, brightness and film being used). Most aperture priority systems are connected to an electronic shutter and the camera-selected speed is usually indicated in the viewfinder.

Apochromat A lens corrected for all three primary colours (blue, green and red) and completely free of chromatic aberration. These lenses are very expensive and only necessary for special applications, such as when colour photographs are copied by the large 'process' cameras used by printers.

Artificial light This term usually refers to light that has specifically been set-up by the photographer. This commonly consists of floodlights, photographic lamps, or flash light (electronic or bulb).

ASA American Standards Association. The sensitivity (speed with which it reacts to light) of a film can be measured by the ASA standard or by other standards systems, such as DIN. The ASA film speed scale is arithmetical—a film of 200 ASA is twice as fast as a 100 ASA film and half the speed of a 400 ASA film.

Astigmatism An aberration of lenses and of the human eye. It is the inability of the lens system to focus, simultaneously, lines in the same plane but at right angles to each other. Only one of these two lines appears correctly focused at any one time.

Automatic diaphragm Most modern SLR cameras have lenses which are wide open for viewing, stop down automatically to the pre-selected aperture during the exposure and then re-open to full aperture for viewing. This automatic-diaphragm system ensures bright, full-aperture viewing coupled with fast camera operation.

Automatic exposure A system within a camera which automatically sets the correct exposure. There are three main types:
1 Aperture priority—the photographer selects the aperture and the camera selects the correct shutter speed.
2 Shutter priority—the photographer selects the shutter speed and the camera sets the correct aperture.
3 Programmed—the camera sets an appropriate shutter speed/aperture combination according to a pre-programmed selection.
(In semi-automatic exposure systems the photographer adjusts the camera controls until 'needles match' or LEDs are lit correctly.)

Automatic focusing Cameras with built-in automatic focusing correctly set the focus of the lens for the subject which needs to be fairly central. These cameras use either an opto-electronic system (comparison of two separate light paths from the subject) or an ultra-sonic system which has a special ultrasonic/transmitter receiver. At present these systems are only available in relatively simple cameras.

Auto-winder In the strictest sense an auto-winder is a unit which can be attached to many SLRs for motorized, single frame film advance. After each exposure the auto-winder automatically advances the film to the next frame and cocks the shutter. Many units, however, are capable of modest speed picture sequences. Some cameras have an auto-winder built into the main body. See also *Motor-drive.*

Auxiliary lens Sometimes referred to as a supplementary lens, this is a simple lens or lens system that can be clipped or screwed on to the front of a camera lens to change its focal length. The most common type is the close-up lens. Typically, with a 50mm lens on a 35mm camera, a +1 auxiliary lens gives a focusing range of 43-100cm and a +3 lens gives a range of 27-34cm.

Available light A general term describing the existing light on the subject. It normally refers to levels of low illumination—for example, at night or indoors. These conditions usually require fast films, lenses of large aperture—for example, f2—and relatively long exposure times.

B

Back focus This is the distance between the back surface of the lens and the film. Wide-angle lenses designed for SLR cameras usually have a back focus that is greater than the focal length of the lens to allow the mirror to operate freely. Conversely, telephoto lenses have a back focus that is less than the focal length of the lens to minimize their size.

Barn doors A flap-like attachment which fits around the rim of a light. They are adjusted like car visors, and can be used to control light falling on the subject or to prevent light shining directly into the camera lens.

Barrel distortion A lens aberration that causes lines at the edge of the image to bow—a photographed rectangle appears like a barrel with the sides bulging outwards. This effect is particularly noticeable with extreme wide-angle lenses such as fisheye lenses.

Bayonet mount A type of fitting on lenses, extension tubes, and other attachments which enables them to be quickly and easily mounted on the camera body. The usual procedure is to line-up a mark on the attachment with one on the camera, join the two, and turn the attachment (usually counter-clockwise) through about 60°. Removal of the attachment is just as simple. There are several types of bayonet mount in use, only some of which are interchangeable through the use of adapters.

B camera setting A shutter set to B remains open as long as the shutter release is depressed. To avoid camera shake it is advisable to use a cable release when making long exposures using the B setting. The origin of B comes from the term brief exposure and the earlier term bulb exposure.

Bellows A concertina-like unit that fits between the camera body and the lens. A bellows unit enables the lens to focus on close subjects, and gives a large image of the subject. The magnification of the subject depends on the focal length of the lens and the extension of the bellows. For example, using a bellows unit with a 50mm lens on a 35mm camera gives a subject magnification range of about x1 (that is, lifesize) to x3.

Between-the-lens shutter A shutter that is located between the lens elements and normally next to the aperture blades. Most non-reflex 35mm cameras have a between-the-lens shutter, whereas most 35mm SLR cameras have a *focal plane shutter* built into the camera body.

Bi-concave lens A simple lens which has both of its surfaces curving inwards from the edges to the centre.

Bi-convex lens A simple lens which has both of its surfaces curving outwards from the edges to the centre.

Binocular vision Vision which is achieved by the use of two eyes as opposed to the use of one eye (monocular vision). Binocular vision is essential for 3-D photography.

Boom light A light (electronic, flash or tungsten) that is suspended at the end of a long horizontal pole and counter-balanced by a weight on the other end of the pole. A boom light is used where a light on a conventional stand would show in the picture area, for example, where a top light is needed to illuminate the hair in a portrait.

Bounce light Light (electronic flash or tungsten) that is bounced off a reflecting surface. It gives softer (more diffuse) illumination than a direct light and produces a more even lighting of the subject. There is a loss of light power because of absorption at the reflecting surface and the increased light-to-subject distance. It is best to use white surfaces since these absorb only a small amount of light and do not impart any colour to the illumination.

Bracketing To make a series of different exposures so that one correct exposure results. This technique is useful for non-average subjects (snowscapes, sunsets, very light or very dark toned objects) and where film latitude is small (colour slides). The photographer first exposes the film using the most likely camera setting, found with a light meter or by guessing. He then uses different camera settings to give more and then less exposure than the nominally correct setting. An example of a bracketing series might be 1/60th sec f8, 1/60th sec f5·6, 1/60th sec f11, *or* 1/60th sec f8, 1/30th sec f8, 1/125th sec f8.

Brightness range The brightness difference between the darkest and the lightest parts of a scene (or image). This range depends on the reflectance of the various objects in the scene and on the nature of the illumination. On a sunny day with few clouds this range may exceed 1:100, but the same scene on a dull day may have a brightness range of less than 1:20. With careful exposure and development, both these conditions can be accommodated by the film.

Bulk loader A device that holds long lengths (normally up to 30m) of 35mm film for loading by hand on to empty cassettes. Any required number of exposures to a maximum of about 36 can be loaded. Once the film has been loaded into the bulk loader in complete darkness, all other operations may be carried out in normal lighting. Note that both ends of the film within the cassette are fogged.

Bush (for tripod) This is the 'hole' in the baseplate of a camera which accepts the threaded stud from a tripod, monopod, flash bracket or other accessories. Most bushes are of a standard size, but adapters are available for other bushes.

C

Cable release A flexible cable which is attached (usually screwed-in) to the shutter release and used for relatively long exposure times (1/8 and more). The operator depresses the plunger on the cable to release the shutter, remotely. This prevents the camera from moving during the exposure.

Cadmium sulphide cell (CdS) A type of cell used in some hand-held light meters and some built-in camera meters. The resistance of the cell to a constant electrical voltage (supplied by a battery) changes as the light falling on the cell varies. The resulting current is either used to move a pointer on a scale or employed directly to alter the camera's shutter speed or aperture. CdS cells are more sensitive than selenium cells and are ideal when photographing in dim lighting conditions.

Camera movements Facilities available on most large-format cameras (10·3 x 12·7cm and larger) and some smaller ones to move the relative positions of the lens and film planes. Skilfully used, these camera movements can be employed to overcome such technical problems as limited depth of field or converging verticals—the latter occurs when the camera is pointed upwards to photograph tall buildings, for example.

Cartridge A light-tight film container designed for easy loading. Normally they are made of plastic and come in two sizes—a 126 size and a 110 size.

Cassette A metal or plastic light-tight container which holds various lengths of 35mm film. They are smaller and simpler than cartridges, and some types may be used more than once.

Catadioptic lens See *Mirror lens.*

CC filters These are 'colour correcting' or 'colour compensating' filters which may be used either in front of the camera or when printing colour film, to modify the final overall colour of the photograph. Their various strengths are indicated by numbers usually ranging from 05 to 50. Filters may be combined to give a complete range of colour correction.

CdS See *Cadmium sulphide cell.*

Chromatic aberration This is a lens fault which causes light of different

colours, but from the same object point, to focus at different image points. Lenses having a relatively large amount of chromatic aberration produce images with colour fringes; and in black and white photography this results in a loss of sharpness. Most lenses are corrected for two of the three primary colours (red, green and blue) and produce very satisfactory results. For special applications, such as in the printing industry, *apochromatic* lenses are made which correct for all three colours: these are very expensive.

Chromofilters A range of graduated colour filters which produce unusual and surrealistic results. Most of these filters consist of two colour bands which gradually merge into one another towards the centre band of the filter.

Circle of confusion All out-of-focus points of a subject appear as circles (of confusion) on the final photograph. These circles are 'seen' as acceptably sharp if their diameters are below a specified limit. This limit depends on factors such as viewer's eyesight, viewing distance, and type of subject.

Click stop The feel of an aperture ring on either a camera or enlarger lens which indicates a change in aperture setting by one full or one half stop. Sometimes this tactile change is accompanied by a quiet 'click' sound.

Close-up attachment Any attachment which enables the camera to focus closer than its normal closest distance. Such attachments include close-up lenses, bellows and extension tubes.

Coating of lens The ultra-thin layer of magnesium fluoride or other chemical, which is deposited on a lens surface and gives it a characteristic bloom or tint. This lens coating reduces flare (non-image light) within the lens and produces a brighter and more contrasty image. Many modern lenses are multi-coated with several ultra-thin layers deposited on top of each other; this process improves performance to an even higher standard.

Colour balance The overall colour cast of the film or print. Normally a film or print is balanced to give grey neutrals (such as a road or pavement) and pleasing skin tones. The colour balance preferred by the viewer is a subjective choice, and this is the reason for the variety of colour films available; each having its own colour characteristics.

Colour cast A local or overall bias in the colour of a print or transparency. Colour casts are caused mainly by poor processing and printing, the use of light sources which do not match the film sensitivity, inappropriate film storage (high temperature and humidity), and long exposure times.

Colour negative A type of film which is used primarily to give colour prints; although colour transparencies and black and white prints may also be produced. The colours of a colour negative are complementary in colour and hue to the original subject colours. For example, a light blue appears as dark yellow and a dark green appears as a light magenta. The characteristic orange appearance of all colour negatives comes from the

built-in corrector which improves overall colour fidelity.

Colour reversal A colour film or paper which produces a positive image directly from a positive original. Thus a colour reversal film gives a colour transparency directly from the original scene and a colour reversal paper, like Cibachrome or Ektachrome paper, gives a positive print directly from a transparency. Most colour reversal materials are identified by the suffix 'chrome'.

Colour temperature Different white light sources emit a different mixture of colours. Often, the colour quality of a light source is measured in terms of colour temperature. Sources rich in red light have a low colour temperature—for example, photofloods at 3400 (Kelvin)—and sources rich in blue light have a high colour temperature—for example, daylight at 5500K. Colour films have to be balanced to match the light source in use, and films are made to suit tungsten lamps (3200K) and daylight (5500K).

Coma A lens aberration which causes subject points to record as coma-shaped images. This effect is mostly found in 'fast' lenses and when large apertures (small f numbers) are used.

Complementary colours These are pairs of colours which, when mixed together, give a grey (neutral). For example, a grey is formed when yellow and blue light are mixed together; therefore, yellow is complementary to blue and vice versa. Other complementary colours include green and magenta, red and cyan.

Compound lens Any lens which contains more than one piece (element) of glass. Most camera lenses are compound lenses and have anything from three to twelve or more lens elements. Zoom lenses have the most complex designs.

Contrast The variation of image tones from the shadows of the scene, through its mid-tones, to the highlights. Contrast depends on the type of subject, scene brightness range, film, development and printing.

Conversion filter Any filter which converts one standard light source to another standard light source. For example, a Wratten 85B filter converts daylight to photoflood type illumination. This filter, when placed in front of the camera lens, enables a camera loaded with tungsten colour film to give correct colour photographs in daylight. To compensate for the light absorbed by the filter, it is necessary to give extra exposure: this is determined by the filter factor.

Coupled exposure meter An exposure meter built into a camera which is linked to either the aperture or shutter speed setting, or to both.

Coupled rangefinder A focusing device used on many viewfinder (non-SLR) cameras. The subject is framed in the viewfinder and the lens focusing ring is rotated until a second small or ghost image coincides with the main image. This secondary rangefinder image is often coloured to distinguish it from the

main viewfinder image.

Covering power The ability of a lens to fill the film format being used, with a satisfactory image. A lens designed to 'cover' the 6 x 6cm format also covers many smaller film formats such as 35mm or 110. When used for close-up work, this same 6 x 6cm lens may well cover a 10·3 x 12·7cm format. Covering power depends on the particular lens design and the degree of magnification.

Cross front Movement of the lens, either to the left or to the right. This lens (camera) movement is available on most large format (10·3 x 12·7cm and larger) cameras and on a few small format cameras. Cross movement of a lens is used when head-on photography is either impossible (eg an obscuring post) or undesirable (for example, reflection of the camera in the subject).

Cyan A blue-green colour which is complementary to red (see *Complementary colours*). It is one of the three subtractive primaries; the other two are yellow and magenta.

D

Daylight colour film A colour film which is designed to be used in daylight without or with electronic flash or blue flash-bulbs. This film type can also be used in tungsten or fluorescent lighting if a suitable filter is put in front of the lens or light source.

Definition A general term describing the clarity of an image. More precise measures of image clarity are resolution numbers, usually quoted in lines per mm, and MTF (modulation transfer function) graphs.

Density The ability of an area of a paper or film to absorb light. Areas of high density absorb a lot of light and appear black, whereas low-density areas absorb only a small amount of light and appear closer to white (theoretically having a density of zero). A density increase of 0·3 represents a doubling of light-stopping ability so a 1·3 density area absorbs twice as much light as another area of 1·0 density.

Density range The difference between the minimum density (D min) of a print or film and its maximum density (D max). Typical density ranges are 0–1·8 for black-and-white and colour papers, 0–1·2 for black-and-white and colour negatives, and 0–3·0 for colour transparencies.

Depth of field The distance between the nearest and furthest points of the subject which are acceptably sharp. Depth of field can be increased by using small apertures (large f numbers), and/or short focal-length lenses and/or by taking the photograph from further away. Use of large apertures (small f numbers), long focal-length lenses, and near subjects reduces depth of field.

Depth of field preview A facility available on many SLR cameras which stops down the lens to the shooting aperture so that the depth of field can be seen.

Depth of field scale The scale, usually surrounding the lens barrel, which gives an easily-read indication of depth of field.

Depth of focus The small allowable error in focusing which still results in an acceptably sharp image of the subject.

Diaphragm The variable-hole mechanism usually situated within the lens, which controls the brightness of the image falling on the film or paper. The size of the opening (aperture) is indicated by the f number (see *Relative aperture).*

Diaphragm shutter See *Leaf shutter.*

Diapositive A positive image which is designed to be projected or viewed by transmitted light. All transparencies are diapositives.

Differential focusing The technique of using wide apertures (small f-numbers) to reduce depth of field, and to therefore separate the focused subject from its foreground and background.

Diffraction When light rays pass close to opaque surfaces, such as the blades of a lens diaphragm, they are scattered; this phenomenon, known as diffraction, results in a loss of image clarity. Therefore, lenses which are stopped down to small apertures (f16 and smaller) begin to lose quality. Most lenses are at their best when stopped down by about three stops from their maximum aperture; at this aperture most aberrations are at a minimum and diffraction has not yet started to deteriorate the image.

Diffused image An image which has indistinct edges and appears 'soft'. Overall- or partially-diffused images can be produced in the camera by using special lenses and filters, or by shooting through various 'filmy' substances such as vaseline, sellotape, and fine stockings. Images may also be diffused during enlarging by placing a diffusing device between the enlarging lens and the paper.

Diffuse light source Any light source which produces indistinct and relatively light shadows with a soft outline. The larger and more even the light source is the more diffuse will be the resulting illumination. Any light source bounced into a large reflecting surface (for example, a white umbrella, white card, or large dish reflector) will produce diffuse illumination.

DIN Deutsche Industrie Normen. A film speed system used by Germany and some other European countries. An increase/decrease of 3 DIN units indicates a doubling/halving of film speed, that is a film of 21 DIN (100 ASA) is half the speed of a 24 DIN (200 ASA) film, and double the speed of an 18 DIN (50 ASA) film.

Diopter A measurement unit which is used to indicate the power of a lens. The diopter power of a lens is the reciprocal of the lens focal length expressed in metres, that is, diopter power = 1/F in metres. For example, a lens of 1 metre focal length is a 1 diopter lens, a 500mm lens is 2 diopters, a 250mm lens is 4 diopters. Most close-up lenses have their strength expressed in diopters, and when two or more lenses are added together their combined strength is found by adding their diopter values.

Diverging lens A lens which is concave and causes light to fan out from the optical axis. Used as components of compound lenses and in viewfinders.

Double exposure The process of exposing two separate images on one piece of film or paper. This is a relatively simple procedure when enlarging and when using most medium and large format cameras, but can be quite difficult with most 35mm cameras. Visually successful double exposures are best achieved when the photographer carefully plans the result.

E

Effective aperture This is the maximum diameter of the cone of light coming from a distant object which enters the lens and is imaged on the film. The effective aperture is a measure of the light passing power of the lens and is not directly related to either the diameter of the diaphragm or the size of the lens front element—these depend on the lens design.

Electromagnetic spectrum This refers to radiation, including atomic radiation, X-rays, ultra-violet, infra-red, radio and TV waves, and the visible spectrum. The human eye is sensitive to the visible section of the electromagnetic spectrum—which is also capable of being recorded by films.

Electronic flash A unit which produces a very bright flash of light which lasts only for a short time (usually between 1/500-1/40000 second). This electronic flash is caused by a high voltage discharge between two electrodes enclosed in a glass cylindrical bulb containing an inert gas such as argon or krypton. An electronic flash tube will last for many thousands of flashes and can be charged from the mains and/or batteries of various sizes.

Electronic shutter A shutter which uses electronic circuits, rather than mechanical gears and springs etc, to control the exposure time. Many electronic shutters are directly connected to the camera's exposure metering system.

Emulsion speed See *ASA* and *DIN.*

EV system This comprises a series of numbers (normally 1-19) which represents a range of exposures on the film. A particular EV (exposure value) number represents a series of equivalent shutter speed/aperture combinations, each speed/aperture combination giving the same amount of exposure to the film—for example, EV 13 is 1/500 f4; EV 10 is 1/500 f1·4, 1/250 f2 or 1/125 f2·8 and so on. In practice you measure the subject with a light meter which gives a required EV number for the film speed being used. The required EV can then be set on some cameras and the desired speed/ aperture combination is then selected.

Expiry date The date printed on film boxes which indicates, under average temperature and humidity conditions, when the film might produce unacceptable results. Films stored at low humidity can be used well past their expiry date.

Exposure The result of allowing light to

act on a photosensitive material. The amount of exposure depends on both the intensity of the light and the time it is allowed to fall on the sensitive material.

Exposure factor The increase in exposure, normally expressed as a multiplication factor, which is needed when using accessories such as filters, extension tubes, and bellows. For example, when using a filter with a x2 exposure factor the exposure time must be doubled or the aperture opened by one stop.

Exposure latitude The maximum variation of film or paper exposure from the 'correct' exposure which still yields acceptable results. For example, most colour negative films have an exposure latitude of −1 (one stop under) to +2 (two stops over). Exposure latitude depends on the actual film in use, processing, the subject and its lighting, and what is considered as acceptable to the photographer.

Exposure meter An instrument which measures the intensity of light falling on (incident reading) or reflected by (reflected reading) the subject. Exposure meters can be separate or built into a camera; the latter type usually gives a readout in the viewfinder and may also automatically adjust the camera settings to give correct exposure.

Extension rings (tubes) Spacer rings which fit between the camera body and the lens, and allow the camera to focus on subjects closer than the nearest marked focusing distance of the lens. A set of rings typically allows a focusing range of 56-20cm for a standard 50mm lens. These extension rings may be non-automatic or automatic; the latter type allow full-aperture focusing just prior to exposure.

F

Fast films Films that are very sensitive to light and require only a small exposure. They are ideal for photography in dimly lit places, or where fast shutter speeds (for example, 1/500) and/or small apertures (for example, f16) are desired. These fast films (400 ASA or more) are more grainy than slower films.

Fast lens A lens that has a large maximum aperture (f2 or larger) and is thus ideal for dimly lit places and when fast shutter speeds are needed. A fast lens also means that the image is very bright and therefore easier to focus. The faster the lens the more difficult it is to design and manufacture.

Fill light Any light which adds to the main (key) illumination without altering the overall character of the lighting. Usually fill lights are positioned near the camera, thereby avoiding extra shadows, and are used to increase detail in the shadows. They are ideal for back-lit portraits, studio work, and where lighting is very contrasty (such as bright cloudless days).

Film A thin flexible transparent material that is coated on one side with a light sensitive silver halide emulsion. It is sold either as rolls of variable widths and lengths, or in sheets.

Film base The material on to which the

silver halide emulsion is coated—the two main types being acetate (cellulose triacetate) and polyester (for example, Estar). The polyester type is stronger and dimensionally more stable but is more difficult to work with.

Film speed See *ASA* and *DIN.*

Filter Any material which, when placed in front of a light source or lens, absorbs some of the light coming through it. Filters are usually made of glass, plastic, or gelatin-coated plastic and in photography are mainly used to modify the light reaching the film, or in colour printing to change the colour of the light reaching the paper.

Filter factor See *Exposure factor.*

Fisheye lens A lens that has an angle of view greater than 100° and produces distorted images—lines at the edges curve inwards. Fisheye lenses have an enormous depth of field and they do not need to be focused.

Fixed focus Refers to any lens which, when attached to the camera, whether permanently fixed or not, has a lens-to-film distance that cannot be varied. The lens is thus permanently focused on one distance, normally the *hyperfocal distance.* Fixed focus lenses are usually of modest aperture (about f8) and attached to the cheaper amateur cameras.

Flare A term used to describe stray light that is not from the subject and which reaches the film. Flare has the overall effect of lowering image contrast and is most noticeable in the subject shadow areas. It is eliminated or reduced by using coated lenses (most modern lenses are multi-coated), lens hoods and by preventing lights from shining directly into the lens.

Flash See *Electronic flash* and items listed below.

Flashbulb A glass bulb filled with a flammable material (such as magensium or zirconium) and oxygen, which when ignited burns with an intense flash of light. Flashbulbs are usually triggered by a small electrical current and are synchronized to be near their peak output when the shutter is open. Flashbulbs have been largely superseded by electronic flash.

Flashcube An arrangement of four flashbulbs that are positioned on four sides of a cube—the cube being automatically rotated to the next bulb after one is fired. The bulbs are fired either by a small electrical current or by a simple percussion mechanism (Magicube).

Flash synchronization The timing of the flash to coincide with the shutter being open. For electronic flash synchronization it is necessary to use the X sync connection and a suitable shutter speed—usually 1/60 sec or slower for focal plane shutters and any speed for leaf shutters. Flashbulbs are used with M sync and a speed of 1/60 sec (preferable), or with X sync and a speed of 1/30 or slower.

Flat image An image of low contrast, which may occur because of under-exposure, under development, flare, or very diffuse (soft) lighting.

Floodlight A tungsten light (usually 250 or 500 watts) which is within a relatively large dish reflector.

f numbers The series of internationally agreed numbers which are marked on lenses and indicate the brightness of the image on the film plane—so all lenses are focused on infinity. The f number series is 1·4, 2, 2·8, 4, 5·6, 8, 11, 16, 22, 32 etc—changing to the next largest number (for example, f11 to f16) decreases the image brightness to $\frac{1}{2}$, and moving to the next smallest number doubles the image brightness.

Focal length The distance between the optical centre of the lens (not necessarily within the lens itself) and the film when the lens is focused on infinity. Focal length is related to the angle of view of the lens—wide-angle lenses have short focal lengths (for example 28mm) and narrow-angle lenses have long focal lengths (for example, 200mm).

Focal plane The plane behind the lens that produces the sharpest possible image from the lens—any plane nearer or farther from the lens produces a less sharp image. For acceptable results the film must be held in the focal plane.

Focal plane shutter A shutter that is positioned just in front of the film (focal plane). The exposure results from a slit travelling at constant speed across the film—the actual shutter speed depending on the width of the slit. As a focal plane shutter is built into the camera body, it is not necessary for lenses to incorporate shutters.

Focal point The point to which light rays coming from a point on the subject are focused by the lens.

Focusing The act of adjusting the lens-to-film distance so that the subject is sharply focused. This is achieved by rotating the lens focusing ring or by sliding the lens or film panel backwards or forwards.

Focusing screen A ground glass screen on to which the image is focused. Focusing screens may also incorporate a variety of focusing aids; a split-image rangefinder or microprism rangefinder, for example. Some cameras have screens that can be interchanged with others, according to the subject matter and the preferences of the photographer.

Format Refers to the size of image produced by a camera, or the size of paper and so on.

Frame counter The numbering system on a camera that indicates how many exposures have been made or are left on a roll of film.

Fresnel lens A 'flat' condenser lens with a number of concentric ridges that is used where a shallow thickness is necessary, such as in spotlights or combined with focusing screens to aid focusing.

Fresnel screen A transparent focusing screen that incorporates a *fresnel lens* for easier viewing.

Front element The piece of glass in a lens farthest from the film. The front element is more prone to damage than other elements and is often protected by a UV filter and a lens hood.

Full aperture metering Any through-the-lens (TTL) light metering system that operates with the lens at maximum aperture. See also *Automatic exposure* and *TTL.*

G

GPD cells A type of very small cell that is incorporated into some camera light metering systems. Gallium arsenic phosphorus photo diodes (GPD) react 1000 times faster than CdS (cadmium sulphide) cells and do not have a 'memory' (where the previous reading may affect the current light reading).

Gradation The range of tones, from white through to black, in a print or negative and how these tones relate to one another. For example, a long soft gradation indicates a large range of tones that gradually change from one to the next.

Grain The random pattern within the photographic emulsion that is made up of the final (processed) metallic silver image. The grain pattern depends on the film emulsion, plus the type and degree of development.

Grey scale A series of grey patches joined together ranging from white through light, mid and dark greys, to blacks. Usually the differences between adjoining patches are either visually equal or are of equal density increments (eg. 0, 0.3, 0.6, 0.9 etc). Grey scales are very useful for detecting contrast and colour changes.

Ground glass The focusing screens of view and reflex cameras are made of glass that is finely ground on one side—the optical image being focused on this ground glass plane. The photographer views the image from the clear side of the glass.

Guide numbers The number given to a flashbulb or an electronic flash unit that indicates its power. A guide number may be quoted in metric (metres) or imperial (feet) units and depends also on the speed of the film being used—quoted guide numbers assume that a relatively efficient reflector surrounds the flash source and is used in an average-sized room. Many modern flash units automatically calculate the correct aperture setting, otherwise the photographer simply finds the required aperture by dividing the guide number by the subject distance eg. GN = 32 (metres) for 100 ASA film and subject distance of 4 metres—therefore required aperture is 32/4 or f8.

H

Halation This is the result of light passing through the light sensitive emulsion, then through the film base, and finally being reflected back from the other side of the film and re-exposing the emulsion, but in a different place from the original exposure. Halation is largely removed in modern films by an antihalation backing which absorbs the light before it can return to re-expose the emulsion. Where very bright lights, such as street lamps, are present in a

scene, halation still occurs and produces a bright circle around the central lamp exposure.

Half frame A frame generally applied to cameras that produce negatives and slides half the size of the standard 35mm format, that is half-frame negatives (slides) are 24 x 18mm. Half-frame cameras are small and produce images of a quality intermediate between 35mm (full frame) and 110. They have lost popularity in recent years mainly because of the introduction of smaller 35mm cameras.

Hot shoe The slot on top of some cameras that accepts a flash gun and automatically connects it to the shutter synchronization mechanism, thus avoiding the need for a flash synchronizaton lead.

Hot spot A part of an image or scene that is over-lit compared to the rest of the subject, and immediately draws attention to itself. Hot spots are usually caused by badly adjusted spotlights and projectors or by reflections off shiny objects.

Hue The colour of an object is described in terms of its brightness (light or dark), saturation (purity), and hue—the hue being the colour name, for example red, blue, green.

Hyperfocal distance A lens that is focused on the hyperfocal distance produces acceptably sharp images of objects that are positioned between infinity and half the hyperfocal distance. Hyperfocal distance depends on the lens aperture, lens focal length, and the film format. For example, a 50mm lens on a 35mm camera set at f8 has a hyperfocal distance of 10m and produces sharp images of objects between infinity and 5m.

I

Image fall-off This term refers to the deterioration (fall-off) of an image in either definition or brightness, or both, towards the edges of the image produced by a lens. Image fall-off is only noticeable on lenses of poor quality or extreme design, such as very wide angle lenses.

Image intensifier An electronic device placed between the camera body and lens to amplify the brightness of the image. A x50 gain (5½ stops) is typical for an image intensifier. They are expensive and can only be used for black and white photography.

Image plane This is the plane, positioned at right angles to the lens axis, where the image from the lens is sharply focused. The image plane should be perfectly flat and coincide with the film plane.

Incandescent light Any light which is produced by the glowing of a heated filament, the most common example being the domestic light bulb, which has an electrically heated tungsten filament. Incandescent light sources emit a continuous spectrum, that is all the various colours of visible light.

Incident light The light that falls on the subject rather than that which is reflected from it. Light meter readings

that measure incident light (incident readings) are not influenced by the subject and are preferred when photographing non-average subjects, such as objects against black or white backgrounds.

Infinity In theory, this is a point that can never be reached; a measureless distance from the lens. In practice, a subject is said to be at infinity when going farther away makes no difference to the focusing of the lens. Infinity is considered to be closer for wide angle lenses than for narrow angle (long focal length) lenses.

Infra-red (IR) The portion of the electromagnetic spectrum, adjacent to red light, which is not visible to the human eye, but can be detected by instruments and special infra-red sensitive films. Part of the IR spectrum is felt by humans as heat.

Instant return mirror Any mirror on a single lens reflex camera which returns to its down (viewing) position immediately after the exposure is made. The instant return mirror gives continuous viewing (except for the actual time of exposure) of the subject through the taking lens and helps determine whether the 'best' moment has been caught on film. (An SLR camera without an instant return mirror has its mirror in the up (non-viewing) position until the film is advanced for the next exposure.)

Integral tripack This refers to the emulsion structure of modern colour films and papers which consist of three basic emulsion layers coated on top of each other. One layer is sensitive to blue light only, another to green light and the third to red light. These three layers are sufficient to analyse and then reproduce the colours of the photographed scene.

Interchangeable lens A lens which can be detached from the camera body and replaced by another lens. Each camera manufacturer has its own mounting system (screw thread or bayonet type) which means that lenses need to be compatible with the camera body. However, adaptors are available to convert one type of mount to another.

Inverse square law In photography, this law usually refers to the fall-off in illumination with increased distance from the light source. For example, if the distance between the subject and the light source is doubled the illumination is reduced to ¼ (½²) of its initial value: trebling the distance reduces the illumination to 1/9 (1/3²).

Inverted telephoto lens A type of lens design which enables a lens to be mounted farther from the film plane than a conventional lens of the same focal length. Wide angle lenses made for SLR cameras are of the inverted telephoto type so that they will not interfere with the operation of the instant return mirror. Inverted telephoto lenses are also called retrofocus lenses.

Iris diaphragm *See Diaphragm.*

Irradiation The loss of image definition

caused by the scattering of light as it goes deeper and deeper into the photographic emulsion. Irradiation is greatest when the emulsion is thick and, to a degree, the silver halide grains are large; therefore faster films show the greatest loss of definition due to irradiation.

IR setting The mark, usually in red, found on many lenses which indicates the correct focus when using black and white infra-red films. This different focus is necessary as IR radiation comes to focus farther behind the lens than visible light.

I setting A shutter speed setting found on some older cameras. This 'instantaneous' speed is usually about 1/60 sec.

J

Joule A unit of energy which is used to measure the power output of electronic flash units. One joule is equal to one watt-second. An average flash unit has a rating of around 60 joules.

K

Kelvin A temperature scale which is used to indicate the colour of a light source. Reddish sources, such as domestic light bulbs, have a low colour temperature (about 2800K); and bluish sources (eg daylight at 5500K) have higher colour temperature values. The Kelvin scale equals Celsius temperature plus 273, thus 100 degrees C equals 373K.

Key light The main light source in a lighting set-up which is usually supplemented by other less powerful lights and possibly reflectors. The key light sets the overall character of the lighting.

Kilowatt A unit of 1000 watts which is used to indicate the power of a light source, other than a flash unit. Large studio lamps are one kilowatt, or higher, in power.

L

Latitude When used in connection with films, latitude refers to the amount of under- and over-exposure permissible to achieve acceptable images. Exposure latitude depends on type of film, subject, lighting and the visual quality of the final result. Colour materials, especially slide films, generally have less latitude than black and white films.

Leaf shutter A type of lens shutter which is usually built into a lens and operates by several metal blades opening outwards to reveal the diaphragm aperture and then closing when the exposure time is completed. Leaf shutters have the advantage of being able to synchronize with flash at any speed but only have a top speed of 1/500 second.

LEDs Light emitting diodes. These are electronic devices for displaying information. They are used for a number of photographic purposes, including the indication of under- or over-exposure, or the selected aperture/shutter speed combination. LEDs are usually visible in the camera viewfinder, and are largely replacing the needles used in earlier cameras.

Lens An arrangement of shaped glass or plastic elements which produces an image of a subject.

Lens barrel The blackened tube into which the lens elements are mounted.

Lens hood (shade) A conical piece of metal, plastic or rubber which is clamped or screwed on to the front of a lens. Its purpose is to prevent bright light sources, such as the sun, which are outside the lens field of view from striking the lens directly and degrading the image by reducing contrast (flare).

Lens mount The part of a camera body which accepts an interchangeable lens. The two main types of lens mount are 'thread' and 'bayonet', the latter being quicker to operate but slightly more expensive.

Light The part of the electromagnetic spectrum to which human eyes are sensitive. See also *Electromagnetic spectrum.*

Lighting ratios This refers to the comparative intensities of the main (key) light source and the fill-in light(s). For example, a studio portrait may be lit by a main light that is four times the intensity of a fill-in light (which lightens the shadows); this represents a lighting ratio of 4:1. For outdoor photography the lighting ratio depends on the weather conditions—a cloudless day representing a high ratio, and an overcast day (where the clouds act as reflectors) a low lighting ratio.

Light meter See *Exposure meter.*

Line film A type of high-contrast film used to copy line diagrams which only gives two tones, that is black and white. However their contrast can be controlled by choice of developer and variation of development time.

Line image An image which consists only of black and white with no midtones. Line images are used where only the shape of the subject is needed, for example in posters and diagrams. They are produced in photography by the use of high-contrast films, such as line and lith films.

Lith film A film emulsion of very high contrast which is made principally for the printing industry. It is also used in a number of unconventional photographic processes such as bas-relief, solarization, and posterization.

Long focus lens Commonly used slang for 'long focal length lens', which means any lens with a greater focal length than a standard lens, for example, 85mm, 135mm and 300mm lenses on a 35mm camera. These long focal length lenses are ideal for portraiture, sports and animal photography.

Lumen A unit of light intensity which is used to measure the light falling on a subject.

Luminance The light being reflected from a subject (or source). A luminance reading is a reflected light reading.

M

Macro lens A lens which focuses on very near subjects without the aid of close-up devices such as extension tubes or close-up lenses. Most macro lenses can produce an image which is ½ life size on the film. See also *Photomacrography.*

Macrophotography Photography concerned with the production of very large images, such as are used for photo-murals and at exhibitions. Macrophotography should not be confused with Photomacrography.

Magenta One of the three subtractive primary colours on which modern colour photography is based; the other colours being yellow and cyan. Magenta is a purply colour produced by mixing equal quantities of red and blue light.

Magicube A flashcube in which the four flashbulbs are fired mechanically by a percussion cap, thus removing the need for a battery to fire the bulbs. See also *Flashcube.*

Magnification A term used to indicate the size of the image either on the film or on the final print. A magnification of x1 means the film image and the subject are the same size.

Manual iris diaphragm A type of lens aperture setting which has to be adjusted manually.

Match needle system Any device which requires the photographer to adjust camera or meter controls so that two or more needles align with one another. Match needle systems are used in a number of light meters, both within cameras and as separate instruments.

Maximum aperture The widest or largest aperture available on a lens.

Memory lock A device on a camera that holds or 'locks' the shutter speed/aperture combination already determined by the internal light meter.

Micro lens A term used by some manufacturers to describe their macro lens(es). The prefix micro should strictly only be applied to photography through a microscope (photomicrography).

Microphotography The branch of photography concerned with producing very small images, such as are used in the production of 'microchips'. Microphotography should not be confused with photomicrography (photography through a microscope).

Microprism A small glass prism which is often used in large numbers in the centre of camera focusing screens to aid focusing. When the image is out of focus the prisms refract the light and cause the image to 'shimmer'; the image becomes clear when correctly focused.

Mired A contraction of 'microreciprocal degrees'. The mired value of a light source is the colour temperature in degrees K divided into 1,000,000. The mired value is used to calculate the effect of colour temperature filters.

Mirror lens Any lens which incorporates mirrors instead of conventional glass (or plastic) lens

elements. This type of lens design is employed mainly for long focal length lenses (eg 500mm), and produces a relatively lightweight lens with a fixed aperture (about f8).

Modelling light The tungsten lamp situated within a studio electronic flash unit, which shows fairly accurately how the lighting will apear in the final photograph.

Monochrome A monochrome picture is the one which has only one colour; the term is usually applied to black and white prints or slides.

Motor-drive A motor-drive provides motorized film advance, both single frame and sequence. Motor-drive units are generally capable of much faster sequence rates (given in frames per second -fps) than auto-winders and can be used with a wider range of accessories.

M setting A flash socket found on many cameras which synchronizes the shutter to fire at the optimum moment when using flashbulbs.

MTF Modulation transfer function. A sophisticated system which can be used to measure the recording ability (definition, sharpness) of lenses, films, etc. The MTF instruments produce a series of readings which are often plotted on a graph to give an MTF curve—this needing to be interpreted by experts to have any real meaning.

Multiple exposure The process of making more than one exposure on the same piece of film, thus allowing one image to be built on top of another. Multiple exposure is easy to achieve with large studio and most medium format cameras, but can be difficult with miniature cameras (35mm, 110 etc.) because most have a double exposure prevention system whereby the film must be advanced to tension the shutter.

N

Negative A general term which is often used to describe a negative image on film, whether it be in black and white or colour. See also *Negative image.*

Negative image Any image in which the original subject tones (and/or colours) are reversed.

Negative lens Any lens which causes light entering the lens to diverge and spread away from its original direction. A negative lens cannot create a real image on its own, but is used in combination with other lens elements (positive and negative) to produce camera ('compound') lenses.

Neutral density filter A filter which, when placed in front of the camera lens, reduces the amount of light reaching the film without altering its colour. Such filters are available in various strengths.

Newton's rings A series of ring-like patterns which are found when two surfaces do not quite meet. They can occur in photography when slides are bound in glass, or when glass negative carriers are used for enlarging slides or negatives.

Nodal point Every compound lens

has two nodal points (theoretical points used in optical calculations). All light rays entering the lens appear to go through the front nodal point, and light rays leaving the lens appear to come from the rear nodal point.

Normal lens A phrase sometimes used to describe a 'standard' lens—the lens most often used, and considered by most photographers and camera manufacturers as the one which gives an image most closely resembling normal eye vision. The normal lens for 35mm cameras has a focal length of around 50mm.

O

Objective The lens or lens unit facing the object being photographed. The term is most commonly used in photomicrography (photography through a microscope).

Opacity The ability of a material to 'stop' light going through it. See also *Density*.

Open-aperture metering See *Full-aperture metering*.

Open flash The technique of opening the shutter (on B or T setting), firing the flash as many times from as many positions as desired, and then closing the shutter. Open flash can be used for large interior scenes, where the photographer can walk around while the shutter is open and add flashlight to the underlit areas.

Open up A slang term which means to use a larger aperture (for example, from f8 to f5.6). The opposite term is 'close down', that is reduce the aperture.

Optical axis The imaginary line which passes through the centre of a lens system.

Over-exposure Exposure which is much more than the 'normal' 'correct' exposure for the film or paper being used. Over-exposure can cause loss of highlight detail and reduction of image quality.

P

Panchromatic emulsion An emulsion which is sensitive to UV, and all visible light. Most black-and-white films designed for use in the camera are panchromatic.

Panning The act of swinging the camera to follow a moving object to keep the subject's position in the viewfinder approximately the same. The shutter is released during the panning movement.

Panoramic camera Any camera which produces a very wide-angle view of a subject with a minimum of optical distortion. Some of these cameras use a rotating lens and a curved film plane.

Parallax error The difference between the image seen through the viewfinder of a camera and the image seen by the lens, which results from the fact that the two view from slightly different positions. For distant subjects parallax error is negligible, but the effect increases as subject distance decreases. Parallax error only occurs when cameras have separate viewfinder and taking lenses, not with single lens reflex cameras (SLRs) where viewing is through the taking lens.

Pentaprism An optical device, used on most 35mm SLR cameras, to present the focusing screen image right way round and upright.

Permanence of photomaterials The ability of films and papers to keep their original images over a period of time. Permanence is affected by temperature, humidity, light exposure, the type of material and how it is processed.

Photo-electric cell A light-sensitive device whose electrical reading alters as the light reaching it changes. The two main types are electricity- generating cells, such as the selenium variety, and the variable resistance cells (for example, *CdS, SPD, GPD*) which alter their resistance as the light intensity changes. The latter type needs a battery to supply a constant voltage. See also *Exposure meter*.

Photoflood An over-run (subjected to a higher voltage than the bulb is designed for) which gives a bright light having a colour temperature of 3400K.

Photomacrography Close-up photography in the range of x1 to about x20 life-size on the film.

Photometer A type of light meter which compares the light from the scene (or the projected negative) with the light from a small standardized bulb. Photometers have a small acceptance angle (less than 1) and are suitable for very precise metering.

Photomicrography Photography through a microscope.

Pincushion distortion A type of optical aberration which makes scene lines near and parallel to the edges of the frame distort so that they curve inwards at their centre and outwards at the frame corners. A square object appears like a pincushion.

Polarized light Light which vibrates in only one plane as opposed to non-polarized light which vibrates in many planes.

Polarizing filter A polarizing (or pola) filter, depending on its orientation, absorbs polarized light. It can be used to reduce reflections from surfaces such as water, roads, glass, and also to darken the sky in colour photographs.

Positive image An image which has similar colour and/or tone relationships to the original scene, that is, shadows are dark, highlights are light, and colour reproduction is relatively accurate.

Positive lens Any lens which causes parallel light to converge.

Power winder A camera attachment (or built-in unit) which automatically advances the film from one frame to the next. It enables the photographer to make about three exposures every second. Motor drives are more sophisticated power winders, designed to produce more frames per second.

Preset aperture A 'semi-automatic' system of focusing a lens at full aperture and then stopping the lens down, by means of a lens ring, just before exposure.

Pressure plate The plate, usually made of metal, which holds the film both flat and in the correct position for exposure or projection.

Primary colours See *Additive colour* and *Subtractive colour synthesis*.

Projector A device for shining an enlarged image (still or moving) on to a screen.

Q

Quartz-halogen lamp See *Tungsten-halogen lamp*.

R

Rangefinder A device incorporated into some cameras which helps focus the camera lens. Correct focus is achieved by turning the lens focusing ring until the double or split image produced by the rangefinder is aligned in the viewfinder.

Rare earth glass Glass which incorporates rare earth oxides (for example, Lanthanum oxide), to improve optical quality, in its manufacture. This type of glass is used extensively in modern lenses.

Reciprocity law failure Failure of the reciprocity law (which states: exposure = image brightness at the focal plane x shutter speed) manifests itself in loss of sensitivity of the film emulsion and occurs when exposure times are either long or very short. The point of departure from the law depends on the particular film, but for most camera films it occurs outside the range 1/2-1/1000 second, when extra exposure is needed to avoid under-exposure.

Red eye The phenomena of red eyes can occur when taking colour portraits by flashlight. They are avoided by moving the flashgun further away from the camera.

Reflected light reading A lightmeter reading taken by pointing the meter at the subject. It measures the light being reflected from the subject and the actual reading is obviously influenced by the nature of the subject. See also *Incident light*.

Reflector Any surface which is used to reflect light towards the subject, and especially into shadow areas. They may be curved metal bowls surrounding the light source or simply a matt white board.

Reflex camera Any camera which views the subject by using a mirror to reflect light from a lens on to a viewing screen. The two main types are the *single lens reflex* (SLR) and the *twin lens reflex* (TLR).

Refractive index A number which indicates the power of a transparent material to bend (refract) light. The higher the refractive index, the greater the light bending.

Relative aperture This is the fractional number found by dividing the lens focal length by the diameter of the light beam entering the lens. The more commonly used f-number is the reciprocal of the relative aperture.

Resolving power The ability of a lens or film emulsion to record fine detail. Resolving power, usually quoted in line pairs per mm, gives an indication of how sharp the final photograph will appear. See also *MTF*.

Retrofocus A type of lens design which permits short focal-length lenses to be mounted further away from the focal plane than conventional lenses of the same focal length. This design allows wide-angle lenses to be used with reflex viewing systems.

Reversing rings An adapter ring which screws into the lens filter thread and permits the lens to be mounted rear-end-out on to the camera body. It is used for extreme close-up work to improve image quality.

Rim light Light placed behind the subject to give a pencil of light around the subject's outline. Rim lighting is often used to highlight hair.

Ring flash A circular-shaped electronic flash unit which is positioned around the camera lens and produces shadowless lighting of the subject. It is ideal for much medical and scientific close-up work.

Rising front A lens panel which may be moved up or down. It is often used in architectural and advertising work. A rising front is available on most large format (9 x 12cm and larger) cameras and on a few special 120 and 35mm lenses and attachments.

Roll film A film which is loaded on to a spool and protected by a backing paper. The most common roll film size is 120.

S

Saturation The purity of a colour. The purest colours are spectrum colours (100% saturation) and the least pure are greys (0% saturation).

SBC See *SPD*.

Screen A flat surface on to which an image is projected, for example a projection screen, a focusing screen, or a photomechanical screen used to break up an image so that it can be reproduced by printing processes.

Selective focus The technique of choosing a particular part of a scene to focus on. The aperture setting determines whether this selected portion of the scene alone is in focus or whether it is simply the centre of a zone or sharp focus. See also *Differential focusing*.

Selenium cell See *Exposure meter* and *Photo-electric cell*.

Self timer A delayed action mechanism which causes the shutter to fire about ten seconds after the release is depressed. This can be used so the photographer can place himself in the picture or to minimize camera shake at slower shutter speeds caused by depressing the shutter without a cable release.

Sensitivity of an emulsion The response of an emulsion to light, referring to both the spectral response (that is, which spectrum colours cause exposure) and film speed (how much light is needed to cause exposure).

Sharpness The subjective evaluation of how clearly fine detail is recorded.

Sheet film Film which is cut into flat sheets and loaded into special film holders (double dark slides) designed for large format cameras.

Short focus lens A slang term meaning short focal-length lens.

Shutter The device which controls the duration of exposure. See *Focal plane shutter* and *Leaf shutter*.

Shutter priority An automatic-exposure system whereby the photographer first selects the shutter speed and the camera then automatically sets the correct aperture.

Single lens reflex (SLR) A camera which views the subject through the 'taking' lens via a mirror. Many SLRs also incorporate a *pentaprism*.

Skylight filter A filter which absorbs UV light, reducing excessive blueness in colour films and removing some distant haze. Use of the filter does not alter camera settings that is, filter factor x1.

Slave unit A light-sensitive device which triggers other flash sources when activated by the light from the camera-connected flash. The use of slave units does away with the need for trailing leads and also allows for more remote placing of flashguns.

Slide copier Device which produces a duplicate slide. Slide copiers range from simple 'lens attachments' to sophisticated professional units.

Snoot Cone-shaped lamp attachment which concentrates the light into a small circular area.

Soft-focus lens A lens designed to give slightly unsharp images. This type of lens was used primarily for portraiture. Its results are unique and are not the same as a conventional lens defocused or fitted with a diffusion attachment.

SPD Silicon photo diode. Very sensitive photo-electric cell (photocell) used in a number of recent exposure meters, both separate and those built into cameras. Many SPD cells are 'blue' to compensate for an excessive response to red light.

Spherical aberrations Lens fault which causes loss of definition. It is reduced by stopping the lens down. Many early 'portrait lenses' were intentionally not corrected for spherical aberrations to give a pleasing 'soft' image.

Split image See *Rangefinder*.

Spotlight A light source which produces a concentrated beam of light. Spotlights give hard-edged shadows and are used as a main light or to accentuate

a particular subject feature.

Spot meter An exposure meter which reads off a very small area of the subject. Spot meters have an acceptance angle of only one or two degrees. Their usefulness depends on careful interpretation by the photographer.

Standard lens See *Normal lens*.

Star filter When placed in front of the camera lens, a star filter gives a star-like appearance to strong highlights. They are usually available to produce 2, 4, 6 or 8 points to the star.

Stop Another term for aperture or exposure control. For example, to reduce exposure by two stops means to either reduce the aperture (for example, f8 to f16) or increase the shutter speed (1/60 sec to 1/250 sec) by two settings. To 'stop down' a lens is to reduce the aperture, that is, increase the f-number.

Stop-down metering TTL metering at the 'taking' aperture and not at maximum aperture.

Stopping down The act of reducing the lens aperture size ie. increasing the f-number. Stopping down increases the depth of field and is often used in landscape and advertising work, where sharp detail is needed over all the subject.

Straight line portion The centre portion of the characteristic curve where the film or paper responds proportionally to an increase or decrease of exposure. For example, each doubling of exposure results in the same density increase for the negative material being used.

Strobe light American slang for 'electronic flash'. More precisely, a strobe light is a pulsating electronic flash unit which repeats its flash at regular intervals. The rate of flashing can often be varied. They are used for cine work, multiple exposures, and in discotheques.

Subtractive colour synthesis The method of producing colours by subtracting the appropriate amounts of red, green and blue from white light. The subtractive colour filters usually employed in photography are yellow (subtracts blue), magenta (subtracts green), and cyan (subtracts red).

Supplementary lens See *Auxiliary lens*.

Swing movement Movement of the lens or film plane about a vertical axis to improve image shape and sharpness. Swing movements are found on most large format cameras and a few roll film cameras.

Synchronization The precise timing of flash light with the camera shutter. When using electronic flash the camera should be set on X sync and a shutter speed of 1/125 sec or longer (see camera instructions) for focal plane shutters and any speed with leaf shutters. With flashbulbs use M sync and 1/60 sec or longer (see camera instructions). If only X sync is available,

then use flashbulbs at 1/8 sec or longer.

Synchro-sunlight The combining of daylight and flash light. This technique is often used to fill-in harsh shadows on bright sunlit days. For colour work do not use clear flashbulbs.

T

Tacking iron A small electrical iron which is used to stick (tack) in place dry mounting tissue to the print and then to the board. The print and board are 'welded' together in the mounting press.

Taking lens The lens which projects the image on to the film, as opposed to the viewing lens which only views the subject. See *Twin lens reflex*.

Teleconverter An optical device which is placed between the camera body and lens, and increases the magnification of the image. For example, a x2 converter when combined with a 50mm lens, gives effectively a 100mm lens. These combinations are inferior to equivalent focal length lenses, but are much cheaper and easier to carry.

Telephoto lens A long focal-length lens of special design to minimize its physical length. Most narrow-angle lenses are of telephoto design.

Through-the-lens (TTL) metering Any exposure metering system built into a camera which reads the light after it has passed through the lens. TTL metering takes into account filters, extension tubes and any other lens attachments. These meters give only reflected light readings. See also *CdS, GPD* and *SPD* cells.

Tilt movement Lens and film plane movement which is made about a horizontal axis. See *Swing movement*.

Time exposure Any exposure which exceeds one second. See *B camera* and *T settings*.

TLR See *Twin lens reflex*.

Tonal range The comparison between intermediate tones of a print or scene and the difference between the whitest and blackest extremes.

Transparency A colour or black-and-white positive image on film designed for projection. Also known as a slide.

Tripod A three-legged camera support. Various tripod heads are available offering a variety of adjustments, and some tripods also have a centre column for easy height control.

T setting A shutter setting used for exposure times longer than one second. The shutter has to be operated twice, once to open the shutter and again to close it.

TTL metering See *Through-the-lens metering*.

Tungsten film Any film balanced for 3200K lighting. Most professional studio tungsten lighting is of 3200K colour quality.

Tungsten-halogen lamp A special design of tungsten lamp which burns very brightly and has a stable colour throughout its relatively long life. Its main disadvantages are the extreme heat generated and the difficulty of obtaining precise control of lighting quality.

Tungsten light A light source which produces light by passing electricity through a tungsten wire. Most domestic and much studio lighting uses tungsten lamps.

Twin lens reflex (TLR) A camera which has two lenses of the same focal length—one for viewing the subject and another lens for exposing the film. The viewing lens is mounted directly above the taking lens.

Type B colour film Former name for *tungsten film*.

U

Ultra-violet radiation Invisible energy which is present in many light sources, especially daylight at high altitudes. UV energy, if it is not filtered, causes excessive blueness with colour films.

Underexposure Insufficient exposure of film or paper which reduces the contrast and density of the image.

Uprating a film The technique of setting the film at a higher ASA setting so it acts as if it were a faster film but is consequently underexposed. This is usually followed by overdevelopment of the film to obtain satisfactory results.

V

Variable focus lens Slang term for a lens having a range of focal lengths. See *Zoom lens*.

View camera A camera whose taking lens produces an inverted image of the subject directly on to a ground glass screen. View cameras are normally of large format (10.2 x 12.7cm and larger).

Viewfinder A simple device, usually optical, which indicates the edges of the image being formed on the film.

Viewpoint The position from which the subject is viewed. Changing viewpoint alters the perspective of the image.

W

Wide-angle lens A short focal-length lens which records a wide angle of view. It is used for landscape studies and when working in confined spaces.

X

X-ray Electromagnetic radiation of short wavelength. An X-ray photograph is a 'shadowgraph' produced by passing X-ray radiation through the subject to be recorded by a special photographic emulsion.

X synchronization See *Synchronization*.

Zoom lens Alternative name for a lens having a range of focal lengths. One zoom lens can replace several fixed focal-length lenses, but results are likely to be inferior.

Index

Photographic credits

1 Bernard D'Abrera; 2 Malcolm Warrington/ Eaglemoss; 5 Michael Boys/Susan Griggs Agency; 7 Alasdair Ogilvie/Eaglemoss; 9 Jon Gardey

Chapter 1
13, 14 Con Putbrace/Eaglemoss; 15 Malcolm Aird/Eaglemoss; 17 (top) Clay Perry, (bottom) Bruce Coleman Ltd; 19 (top left) Anthea Sieveking, (top right) Jack Taylor, (bottom) E. Leitz; 20, 22, 23 Malcolm Warrington/Eaglemoss; 24, 25, 26, 27 Con Putbrace/Eaglemoss; 28, 29 Michael Taylor/ Eaglemoss; 30 Con Putbrace/Eaglemoss; 31 (top) Con Putbrace/Eaglemoss, (centre) Colin Barker, (bottom) Michael Busselle; 32, 33 Michael Taylor/Eaglemoss; 34, 35 Michael Busselle/Eaglemoss; 36, 37 Con Putbrace/Eaglemoss; 38 Barry Lewis/ Eaglemoss; 39 (left) Barry Lewis/ Eaglemoss, (right) Brian Brake; 40 (top) All-Sport, (bottom) Barry Lewis/ Eaglemoss; 41 Barry Lewis/Eaglemoss; 42 Con Putbrace/Eaglemoss; 43 Ron Chapman; 44 Steve Bicknell/Eaglemoss; 45 (top) John Meek, (centre) Suzanne Hill, (bottom) Peter Myers; 46 (top) John Bulmer, (bottom) Michael Busselle; 47 (top) John Garrett, (bottom) Tomas Sennett/John Hillelson; 48 Malkolm Warrington/Eaglemoss; 52 (top) Malkolm Warrington/Eaglemoss, (centre) Alfred Gregory, (bottom) Alan Hutchison; 53 (top) Eric Hayman, (centre and bottom) David Kilpatrick; 54 (top) Ed Buziak, (bottom) George Gerster/John Hillelson; 55 John Bulmer; 56 Ed Buziak; 57 (top left) Chris Kapolka, (top right) David Kilpatrick, (bottom) Ed Buziak; 58, 59, 60 Malkolm Warrington/Eaglemoss; 61 (top) John Sims, (bottom) Malkolm Warrington/ Eaglemoss; 62, 63 Malkolm Warrington/Eaglemoss; 64 (top) Malkolm Warrington/Eaglemoss, (centre and bottom) Gordon Ferguson/Eaglemoss; 65 (top and centre) Malkolm Warrington/Eaglemoss, (bottom) Gordon Ferguson/Eaglemoss; 66 (top) Robert Harding Library, (bottom) Malkolm Warrington/Eaglemoss; 67 Malkolm Warrington/Eaglemoss

Chapter 2
69 Con Putbrace/Eaglemoss; 70 Alasdair Ogilvie/Eaglemoss; 72 (top) England Scene, (centre) Eric Crichton, (bottom) Marc Riboud/John Hillelson; 73 (top) Con Putbrace/Eaglemoss, (bottom) Steve Bicknell/Eaglemoss; 74 Steve Bicknell/ Eaglemoss; 77 (top) Steve Bicknell/ Eaglemosss, (bottom) Jim Bamber; 78 (top) Malkolm Warrington/Eaglemoss, (bottom) Fujimex; 79 (left) Colour Library International, (right) Malkolm Warrington/ Eaglemoss; 80 Malkolm Warrington/ Eaglemoss, (bottom) Marc Riboud/John Hillelson; 81 (top) Malkolm Warrington/ Eaglemoss, (bottom) Alfred Gregory; 82 Malkolm Warrington/Eaglemoss; 84, 85 Steve Bicknell/Eaglemoss; 87 (top) Colour Library International, (bottom left) Martin Riedl/Eaglemoss, (bottom right) Michael Busselle; 88 Malkolm Warrington/ Eaglemoss; 89 (cameras) Malkolm Warrington/Eaglemoss, (chess pieces) Tina Rogers; 90, 91 Malkolm Warrington/ Eaglemoss; 92 (top) Mike Portelly, (bottom) Malkolm Warrington/Eaglemoss; 93 (top and bottom left) Malkolm Warrington/ Eaglemoss, (bottom right) Peter Scoones/ Seaphot; 94 Malkolm Warrington/ Eaglemoss; 95 Mike Portelly; 96, 97 Peter Scoones/Seaphot

Chapter 3
98 Steve Bicknell/Eaglemoss; 99 (top, centre bottom right and bottom right) Christopher Angeloglou, (centre top left and centre bottom left) Philippa Longley, (bottom left) Steve Bicknell/Eaglemoss; 100 (top left) Alfred Gregory, (top right) Eric Crichton, (bottom) Christopher Angeloglou; 101 (top) Con Putbrace/ Eaglemoss, (bottom) Hans Reinhard/Bruce Coleman Ltd; 102 (left) Steve Bicknell, (right) Keith Cunningham; 103 Keith Cunningham; 104, 105, 106, 107 John Sims/ Eaglemoss

Chapter 4
108 (top) Steve Bicknell/Eaglemoss, (bottom) David Kilpatrick/Eaglemoss; 109 David Kilpatrick/Eaglemoss; 110 (top) Tomas Sennett/John Hillelson, (bottom) David Kilpatrick; 111 Jon Gardey/Robert Harding Agency; 112 (top) Christopher Angeloglou, (bottom) Michael Boys/Susan Griggs Agency; 113 Tony Evans; 114 Steve Bicknell/Eaglemoss; 115 David Kilpatrick; 116 Michael Busselle; 117 (top) Michael Busselle, (centre) Malcolm Aird/Eaglemoss, (bottom left) Ernst Haas/John Hillelson, (bottom right) Aspect; 118 (top) John Kelly, (bottom) Roland Michaud/John Hillelson; 119 Suzanne Hill; 120 Con Putbrace/ Eaglemoss; 121 David Kilpatrick/ Eaglemoss; 122 (top) Aspect, (centre) Roland Michaud/John Hillelson, (bottom) Don Morley/All-Sport; 123 (top) Julian Calder/Susan Griggs Agency, (bottom) Bruce Coleman Ltd; 124 Gerry Cranham; 125 (top) John Garrett, (centre) John McGovren, (bottom) David Kilpatrick; 126 David Kilpatrick/Eaglemoss; 127 Steve Bicknell/Eaglemoss; 128 (top) Patrick Eagar, (bottom) John Sims; 129 Gerry Cranham; 130 Patrick Eagar; 131 (top) Tony Duffy/ All-Sport, (bottom) David Kilpatrick/ Eaglemoss; 132 (top) Suzanne Hill, (bottom) Raul Constancio; 133 John McGovren; 134 (top) Tony Duffy/All-Sport, (centre) David Kilpatrick/Eaglemoss, (bottom) David Kilpatrick; 135 Gerry Cranham; 136 Steve Bicknell/Eaglemoss; 137, 138 Lawrence Lawry; 139 (top left) Lawrence Lawry, (top right) Shirley Kilpatrick, (bottom) Patrick Eagar; 140 (top) Malkolm Warrington/ Eaglemoss, (bottom) Lisa le Guay/ Eaglemoss; 141 (top) Malkolm Warrington/ Eaglemoss, (bottom) Mike Newton/ Eaglemoss; 142 (top) Malkolm Warrington/ Eaglemoss, (centre) Gerry Cranham, (bottom) Colour Library International; 143 (right) Mike Newton/Eaglemoss; 144 (top) Mike Newton/Eaglemoss, (bottom) Malkolm Warrington/Eaglemoss; 145 (top left, top right and bottom right) Mike Newton/ Eaglemoss, (bottom left) Malkolm Warrington/Eaglemoss

Chapter 5
146, 147, 148, 149, 150, 151 Steve Bicknell/Eaglemoss

Chapter 6
152 Malkolm Warrington/Eaglemoss; 153 (top left) Eric Crichton, (top right) Malkolm Warrington/Eaglemoss, (bottom) Heather Angel; 154, 155 Eric Crichton/Eaglemoss; 156 Mike Newton; 157 (top) Paul Forrester, (bottom) Eric Crichton; 158 Malkolm Warrington/ Eaglemoss; 159 (top left and bottom left) Heather Angel, (top right) H. Gritscher/ Aspect, (bottom right) Suzanne Hill; 160 Eric Crichton/Eaglemoss; 161 Eric Crichton; 162 Malkolm Warrington/ Eaglemoss; 163 Eric Crichton; 164 Eric Crichton/Eaglemoss; 165 (top) Eric Crichton, (bottom) Eric Crichton/Eaglemoss; 166 Heather Angel; 167 Eric Crichton; 168 Malkolm Warrington/Eaglemoss; 169 (left) Eric Crichton, (right) Malkolm Warrington/Eaglemoss; 170 Eric Crichton/ Eaglemoss; 171 Ardea; 172 Heather Angel; 173 (top) Eric Crichton, (bottom) Eric Crichton/Eaglemoss; 174, 175 Steve Bicknell/Eaglemoss; 176 (left) Robert Glover, (right) H. Gritscher/Aspect; 177 (top left) Heather Angel, (top right) Chris Alan Wilton, (bottom left) Eric Crichton, (bottom right) Graeme Harris; 178 (left) Eric Crichton, (right) Heather Angel; 179 Graeme Harris

Chapter 7
180, 181, 182 Michael Busselle/Eaglemoss; 184 Michael Boys/Susan Griggs Agency; 185 (top) David Kilpatrick, (centre) Hoya Filters, (bottom) Tony Jones/Robert Harding Library; 186 (top left and bottom) David Kilpatrick, (top right) Hoya Filters; 187 Hoya Filters; 188 Steve Bicknell/Eaglemoss; 189 (top) Chris Smith, (centre top) Andre Louw, (centre bottom) John Sims, (bottom) Lawrence Lawry; 190 (left) Malkolm Warrington/Eaglemoss, (right) Raul Constancio; 191 Malkolm Warrington/ Eaglemoss; 192 (top) Jill Richards, (bottom) Hoya Filters; 193 (top) Peter Goodliffe, (bottom) Lisa le Guay; 194 (top) Lisa le Guay, (bottom) Hoya Filters; 195 (top) Hoya Filters, (bottom) Martin Riedl/Eaglemoss; 196 (top) Martin Riedl/Eaglemoss, (bottom) Malkolm Warrington/Eaglemoss; 197 (top) Martin Riedl/Eaglemoss, (bottom) David Morey; 198 (top left and bottom left) Malkolm Warrington/Eaglemoss, (top right and centre) Lisa le Guay, (bottom right) Colour Library International; 199 (top) Chris Alan Wilton, (bottom left) Eric Hayman, (bottom right) Colour Library International; 200 (top) Hoya Filters, (bottom) Derek Bayes/Aspect; 201 (top) Robert Glover, (centre) Alex Carpley/Aspect, (bottom) Julian Calder/ Susan Griggs Agency; 202 (top) Eric Hayman, (centre) Malkolm Warrington/ Eaglemoss, (bottom) Lisa le Guay/ Eaglemoss; 203 Malkolm Warrington/ Eaglemoss

Chapter 8
204 Malkolm Warrington/Eaglemoss; 205 (top) Vivitar, (centre) Braun, (bottom) Steve Bicknell/Eaglemoss; 206 (top) Braun, (centre right) Alasdair Ogilvie/Eaglemoss, (centre, centre left and bottom) Malkolm Warrington/Eaglemoss; 207 Steve Bicknell/ Eaglemoss; 208, 209 Michael Busselle/ Eaglemoss; 210 Steve Bicknell/Eaglemoss; 211 (top) Malkolm Aird/Eaglemoss, (bottom) Steve Bicknell/Eaglemoss; 212 Steve Bicknell/Eaglemoss; 213 Malkolm Aird/Eaglemoss; 214, 216 Malkolm Warrington/Eaglemoss; 217 (centre left and bottom left) Anthony Dawson, (top and centre right) Malkolm Warrington/ Eaglemoss; 218, 219, 220 Michael Busselle/ Eaglemoss; 221 (left) Michael Busselle/ Eaglemoss, (right) Bowans

Chapter 9
222, 223 (top and centre) Steve Bicknell/ Eaglemoss, (bottom) Eric Crichton; 224 (top) John Garrett, (centre and bottom) Steve Bicknell/Eaglemoss; 226 (top) Mike Newton/Eaglemoss, (bottom) Steve Powell/ All-Sport; 227 Mike Newton/Eaglemoss; 228 (top) Mike Newton/Eaglemoss, (bottom) Heather Angel; 229 Mike Newton/ Eaglemoss

Chapter 10
232 Steve Bicknell/Eaglemoss; 233 (top) John Garrett, (bottom) Malcolm Aird/ Eaglemoss; 234 (top) Tina Rogers, (bottom) Michael Busselle/Eaglemoss; 235 Malkolm Aird/Eaglemoss

Chapter 11
236, 237, 238, 239, 240 Steve Bicknell/ Eaglemoss; 242, 243, 245 Malkolm Warrington/Eaglemoss

Art work credits

Chapter 1
10, 11 John Wells; 16, 17, 18 Brian Mayor; 20, 21 Drury Lane Studios; 24, 25, 26, 27 Kevin Madison; 28, 29 Peter Sullivan; 30 Kevin Madison; 36, 37 Brian Mayor; 43, 49, 50, 51, 60 Drury Lane Studios

Chapter 2
68, 71 Drury Lane Studios; 77 Jim Bamber; 83, 85, 91, 93, 94, 95, 96 Drury Lane Studios

Chapter 3
103 Drury Lane Studios

Chapter 4
109, 115 Drury Lane Studios; 121 Eumig UK Ltd

Chapter 6
158 Jim Bamber; 163, 168, 176, 177, 178, 179 Drury Lane Studios

Chapter 7
191, 200, 201 Drury Lane Studios

Chapter 8
208, 209, 211, 212, 215, 216 Drury Lane Studios

Chapter 9
225 Drury Lane Studios

Chapter 10
230, 231, 234 Drury Lane Studios

Chapter 11
238, 239, 241, 243, 244 Drury Lane Studios